we won't have it again, possibly for many years. His forecasts should certainly be seriously considered by any advisor or investor. He is an invaluable resource to many of my best clients in financial services."

—Bill Good, Bill Good Marketing

"I first came across Harry Dent's books in a book warehouse that was selling dated books cheaply. The great thing about reading dated books that make predictions is that you can instantly verify for yourself whether the author's predictions turned out to be accurate. Well, his predictions speak for themselves, and I have been an ardent follower of Harry's work ever since. Except now I pay full price to read them hot off the press."

—Dolf de Roos, author of the *New York Times* bestseller *Real Estate Riches*

"If you want to understand a topic you should go to the best expert you can find. When I need to understand demographic trends and see how those trends will shape our economy in the years to come, I look to Harry Dent. Why? Because he has been right. For over a decade I have used his research and forecasts to help my clients plan for the years ahead. When I am training financial advisors, I always strongly suggest that they seek out Harry's research and incorporate it into their planning process."

—William J. Nelson, RFC, LUTCF, founder of the
Learning Institute for Financial Executives

"Harry Dent has one again provided a clear and compelling view into our economic future. It is almost as if he has a time machine that sends back economic briefings from the future. By utilizing a good set of investment disciplines and Dent's roadmap for the future of the world's economy, investors now have the tools they need to profit, while at the same time protecting their portfolio. Without question, an essential component for any investor's library."

—Andrew Horowitz, money manager and author of *The Disciplined Investor—*
Essential Strategies for Success; host of The Disciplined Investor podcast

"Harry Dent has been our chief strategist for over fifteen years. Without him my clients and I would have gone down the wrong path years ago. His advice and leadership has added millions to our bottom line."

—Michael Robertson, Robertson and Associates

"Eighteen months ago I began selling personal real estate before the bottom dropped in Florida and stopped building a corporate campus in Ohio because of what was learned from the Dent Newsletter and Demographics School. These decisions have been critical in saving me millions of dollars both personally and corporately. Additionally, my business has expanded dramatically into the senior and baby boomer health care market due to the demographic research provided by the Dent group."

—Jared Florian, newsletter subscriber, president of Universal Screen Arts, Inc.

"On a regular basis I have clients, friends, and family commenting on how the Dent research had been so accurate in so many ways. Demographics are not a day-to-day aspect of what moves the market. But there is nothing I know of that affects the economy more long term. Harry's insight and effort are much appreciated and needed by everyone who wants to understand where we really are headed."

—Joseph A. Clark CFP, RFC, managing partner, Financial Enhancement Group

"I have been an avid reader of Harry Dent's books and newsletter for many years and have attended his Demographics School. That investment has turned out to be worth millions. His predictions led me to sell some real estate holdings in 2006 for significant profit and be disciplined enough not to acquire any new properties for almost two years. As Harry says, all bubbles deflate. My investment partners and I are now in a position to take advantage of some significant distressed opportunities and not be saddled with losing positions. I can't wait to take advantage of Harry's updated predictions."

—Mike Rokoski, newsletter subscriber, managing partner,
Envoy Capital Management, LLC

"Being with the HS Dent organization for almost ten years has been one of the best decisions I made for the growth of my financial planning practice. Not only have I used HS Dent as a research arm for the investments of my clients, but the organization helped in the development of my company. I was now able to offer a more complete planning package for my clients that encompassed their total financial picture."

—Beth Blecker, Eastern Planning, Inc.

"Introduction to the HS Dent demographic research has been one of the most beneficial events in my professional career. Being able to explain the economic power of demographic groups has been the most powerful tool I have used to help clients understand the direction of the economy and look past the short term volatility of markets."

—Donald Creech, CFP, CLU, ChFC, CLTC, wealth
management advisor, Wealth Management Company

"Two days in Harry Dent's Demographics School opened my eyes to the storm we're in and practical means to weather it . . . and now a book that demystifies the headlines and hands families a compass through the uncertainties. Every family needs what's in this book."

—Kathy Peel, founder and CEO of Family Manager Coaching; author of many
books, including *The Busy Mom's Guide* and *Desperate Households*

"Working with affluent households in my financial planning practice, I found Harry Dent in 1995 and built an entire financial planning company around his macroeconomic predictions. The recent financial crisis came as no surprise to me or my clients; we were forewarned and therefore forearmed."

—Erin T. Botsford, CFP, CRPC, president, The Botsford Group

"Our association with Harry Dent has been both personally fulfilling and financially profitable for us and our clients. Harry's insights have become an integral part of our practice, both in the way we manage our client portfolios and how we communicate the complexities of the current market environment with them. The type of information Harry provides makes people really stop and think about their current situation, and whether or not they are doing the right things. We constantly get feedback from clients and radio listeners alike telling us they are truly grateful someone is out there saying the things he says, and that although it may not be what they want to hear, they need to hear it."

—Dean Barber, Barber Financial Group

"Harry Dent's diligence and research has provided insight and information allowing our clients to be significantly better prepared for long-term investing. Additionally, it has provided our practice with a base of knowledge that is constantly monitored, updated, and communicated to us. In turn, we are able to effectively inform clients about the projected changes that are primarily driven by demographic trends. Harry's philosophy has helped our business evolve from an economic 'at the moment' reactionary stance to a 'big picture' proactive outlook that keeps the economic moments in perspective with the client's overall long-term objective."

—Daryl J. LePage, CFP, Brook Wealth Management, LLC

"When it comes to economics I look toward pundits who are controversial. Too many people put Harry Dent in the day-to-day advisor category, which is not what Harry is or has ever been. Many critics incorrectly label Harry Dent's forecasts as inconceivable; nobody knows the future! Personally I never took Harry's predictions at face value—i.e., the Dow hitting 30,000—partly because I comprehended his words, unlike many critics. Harry's humble predictions are in the form of questions that keep you on your toes. To the prudent investor and saver Harry's questions are invaluable. I'm more prepared to take advantage of current market conditions because I believed in Harry's forecasts, which have a solid foundation based on demographics."

—Darrell Catmull, KTKK AM630, Salt Lake City, UT

"In my thirty-two years of interviewing the world's leading investment authorities, I have found that Harry Dent's practical application of demographic trends as a powerful tool for investment allocation is without peer."

—Joe Bradley, Bradley Enterprises, LLC, dba Investor's HOTLINE

"When Harry speaks, we all need to listen. He was right on the money when he predicted the real estate boom of the 1990s. Each time he's been on my radio show, *Real Estate Today*, he knows what's happening and he has an uncanny ability to predict the future."

—Louis Weil, The Star Team, Inc., Star Team Real Estate

"When Harry gave me a copy of *The Great Boom Ahead* in the early nineties, I thought it was voodoo economics. Then I saw just how much he got right by way of demographic research—the stock market boom, the tech boom, then the real estate boom. In all my years following market prognosticators, I've seen that no one gets it right all the time, but very few can anticipate the market with the prescience and accuracy of Harry. Careful readers of *The Great Crash Ahead* will find lots of hope. The book is loaded with ways to grow wealth during these turbulent times."

—Steve Cordasco, talk show host, WPHT
1210AM Philadelphia—*The Big Money Show*

"The economic and market analysis Harry Dent brings to my listening audience is of exceptional value. The absence of the usual Wall Street bias toward optimistic and self-serving predictions, along with fully supported historic trend research, is a gift to my listeners and fresh air for those willing to pay attention! Both short-term traders and long-term investors are well served by Harry Dent and his unique perspective."

—Bill Kearney, CFP, host /producer, *Financial $pectrum*, WKXL 1450

"I've known Harry Dent for many years as a regular guest on my radio show, SmartMoneyTalks.com. His work is incredibly thought provoking. It's helpful in giving his readers a broadened perspective on how they view their financial matters."

—David W. Cryden, CFP, host, SmartMoneyTalks.com radio show

"Three years ago, The Harvard Business School Club of San Diego hosted an evening with Harry Dent. We were all spellbound by his presentation. It's clear that Harry's insights can help you predict future trends with uncanny accuracy. Harry Dent's 'science of demographics' may be the most significant breakthrough in economic forecasting of our time. His work shows how a nation's economy is affected by the average age and size of its population. More important, Dent's insights can help you predict future trends with uncanny accuracy."

—Gabriel Wisdom, president, American Money Management, and
syndicated radio host for the Business Talk Radio Network

*f*P

The
Great Crash
Ahead

STRATEGIES FOR A WORLD
TURNED UPSIDE DOWN

HARRY S. DENT, JR.

with Rodney Johnson

FREE PRESS

New York   London   Toronto   Sydney   New Delhi

Free Press
A Division of Simon & Schuster, Inc.
1230 Avenue of the Americas
New York, NY 10020

First Free Press hardcover edition September 2011

FREE PRESS and colophon are trademarks of Simon & Schuster, Inc.

For information about special discounts for bulk purchases,
please contact Simon & Schuster Special Sales at
1-866-506-1949 or business@simonandschuster.com.

The Simon & Schuster Speakers Bureau can bring authors to your live event.
For more information or to book an event contact the Simon & Schuster Speakers Bureau at 1-866-248-3049 or visit our website at www.simonspeakers.com.

Manufactured in the United States of America

10   9   8   7   6   5   4   3   2   1

Library of Congress Cataloging-in-Publication Data

Dent, Harry S., 1950–
    The great crash ahead : strategies for a world turned upside down / by Harry S. Dent Jr.
    p.   cm.
    1. Economic forecasting—United States.   2. United States—Economic conditions—2009– .
3. Investments—United States.   4. Recessions—United States.   I. Title.
    HC106.84.D45   2011
    330.973—dc23   2011027675

ISBN 978-1-4516-4154-7
ISBN 978-1-4516-4156-1 (ebook)

Dedicated to:

My wife, Jean-ne
My mother, Betty
My sister, Dolly
My sister, Ginny
My brother, Jack
My stepson, Abel
My stepdaughter, Iomi
My stepson, Nile

And posthumously . . . my courageous father,
Harry S. Dent, Sr.

Acknowledgments

Thanks to our literary agent, Susan Golomb, and to our partner for business development at HS Dent, Harry Cornelius. For marketing: to Michael MacDougall and The Darwin Agency. To our key and most valued employees: Nicole Nonnemaker, Lance Gaitan, Bill Washinski, Stephanie Gerardot, Doug Davenport, Nancy Milne, and David Okenquist. And to our directors of the HS Dent Network: Mike Robertson, Joe Clark, Don Creech, Daryl LePage, and Jim Lunney.

Contents

The
Great Crash
Ahead

The Economy on "Crack": The End of Keynesian Economics

Imagine someone very close to you, someone who is part of your everyday life and upon whom you depend, is a drug addict. The person goes "cold turkey" one day and inevitably begins to suffer symptoms of withdrawal and detox. Along comes the drug dealer and he begins throwing not just more drugs, but harder, more addictive drugs at this person. Do you chase away the drug dealer and nurse your friend through detox, knowing that this is a difficult period but a necessary part of the process? Or do you welcome the drug dealer and actually cheer as more drugs are taken? This might sound a bit outrageous, but it is exactly what we are experiencing in our economy! The patient/friend is the economy in which we all live; the drugs are debt, interest rates, and printed money; and the drug dealers are central bankers and the federal government. In a strange, perverse world, our markets are cheering as the patient is given more of what caused the illness in the first place!

In *The Great Depression Ahead* (Free Press, 2008), we forecast a strong rebound in the American economy in response to government intervention quickly followed by a vicious downturn. In October 2010, we shifted our view that the markets would weaken largely as a result of declining economic trends; instead, the markets have been perverted by the massive buildup of government debt, previously unfathomable amounts of stimulus, and ultra-low interest rates. Out of desperation in the face of a total financial meltdown, in late 2008 the US Federal Reserve (the Fed), the central banking system of the United States, dropped short-term interest rates to zero. The Fed also created a program of "qualitative easing" (QE) that allowed banks to pledge potentially bad mortgage loans as security so that these lenders were able to borrow hard cash and thereby bolster reserves. The economy continued to fail. As this first stimulus program began to falter in 2010 (as we forecast in *The Great Depression Ahead*), the Fed brought out a rarely used and potent tool: quantitative easing (QE), basically the printing of money out of thin air. The two major devices that the Fed has to stimulate the economy (beyond fiscal stimulus from the Treasury) are: (1) lowering the Fed funds rate, and (2) printing to buy Treasuries or other bonds in the open market, which injects more money into the system.

In normal times, the Fed relies on lowering short-term rates to stimulate borrowing. Think of this as like giving the economy a cup of coffee or even a minor stimulating drug, such as speed. It revs up the system short term but probably won't do any long-term damage. However, in this latest downturn, the Fed thought it necessary to do even more. Only in exceptional instances will the Fed print a significant number of new dollars to buy, and for good reason. This powerful tool is very dangerous—akin to giving the economy a much more addictive drug, such as crack. The Fed has printed more than $2 trillion in new dollars, and this is in addition to its normal currency creation.

As part of the qualitative easing in late 2008, the Fed accepted mortgage bonds of questionable quality as collateral from banks in exchange for cash, which the banks used to replenish their reserves. But those pledges had to be paid back in short order. Realizing that banks with large loans from the Fed were in just as bad a shape as banks with mortgage bonds, the Fed changed its approach in spring 2009. Instead of holding the questionable mortgage bonds as collateral, the Fed began a program of simply buying these assets from the banks outright. Overall, the Fed bought from banks $1.4 trillion in mortgage securities, mostly Fannie Mae and Freddie Mac bonds, and bought as much as $0.5 trillion in Treasury bonds. This outright purchasing from banks gave the banks much-needed capital as their loan losses mounted. But that wasn't enough! After this program ended in April 2010 and the markets began to sputter, the Fed reemerged with another program, in which it bought an additional $600 billion in Treasury bonds in the open market from November 2010 through June 2011. These purchases increased the total assets and cumulative stimulus from the Fed to about $2.8 trillion! That does not count other stimulus programs, including bailouts, government tax rebates and credits, Cash for Clunkers, housing credits, the cut in Social Security tax for 2011, and many loan and debt guarantees, the costs of which were in the trillions on their own, although much of the bailout monies have been paid back.

These breathtaking moves may seem like a massive effort to "solve" our economic woes, but they are not; they are window dressing. As our work clearly has shown, the natural order is for booms to be followed by busts. What happens when the economy fails again as demographic trends continue to slow, especially after late 2011 when the largest numbers of baby boomers move past age 50 and begin making and spending less and less money?

It would be one thing if this injection of money went largely into lending and spending that bolstered the economy, eventually driving up tax revenues to help make up for the debt, but that has not happened. Bank reserves have risen by over $1.5 trillion, while business lending has barely moved off of its crisis lows. Consumer loans clearly have declined as well. Banks (and other investors) who sell their bonds to the Fed simply turn around and invest in riskier assets, like high-yield bonds, stocks, and commodities. Such investments lead only to greater speculation and greater bubbles! When does it ever end?

Lowering short-term rates merely makes borrowing and lending more attractive without expanding money supply directly. Lower rates also encourage banks to borrow short term and invest in longer-term Treasuries, which keeps rates lower than they would normally be. QE literally prints money out of nothing and currently is being used to buy Treasury bonds and mortgage securities. This activity puts money directly into the system; as a result, longer-term rates are pushed even further down by adding more demand (the Fed's buying of bonds) in an attempt to bolster borrowing and asset prices. And the Fed has used QE more than once: a second round, QE2, was implemented in late 2010. Using QE is like using the drug crack, whereas lowering short-term rates is more like using the drug speed.

The first side effect of these drugs is the sudden drop in the value of the dollar, which results in higher import, food, and gas costs for everyday consumers. The second is a return of bubblelike market activity in everything from stocks to junk bonds to commodities. Such bubbles will burst eventually, critically injuring aging investors and retirement funds. The third is lower returns on fixed income, which directly impacts retirement portfolios and affects the ability of the largest segment of aging consumers to spend, forcing them to chase riskier investments. The rise in Treasury bond rates toward 4.5% that we have been forecasting is finally happening. The Fed's own QE2 stimulus program has actually driven rates up due to rising growth and inflation expectations to the point that they threaten already weak home sales, home prices, and the recovery of the economy as a whole, much as has been happening in Europe since April 2010. Rates on Treasury bonds have been rising since QE2 began in late 2010! The stimulus was supposed to reduce such interest rates but has increased rates instead, which indicates the bond market's disapproval of the policy.

The Fed stimulus will continue to fail, Treasury bond rates will ultimately rise as in Europe, and the overarching trends of slowing demographics and debt deleveraging will set back in. The great economic crisis of 2008 will likely return in 2012, or 2013 at the latest, and will be even worse.

Purposefully devaluing the US dollar not only raises the costs of imports and commodities like oil and food to everyday consumers who are already struggling, but also tends to set off trade wars among our global trading partners from Europe to China, as a falling dollar gives us an edge in pricing. This devaluation comes after we lectured the Chinese on keeping their currency too low! In the early 1930s, the Smoot-Hawley Tariff Act raised tariffs and set off trade wars, worsening the global downturn. Trade wars today over currency devaluation could have a similar effect. Perhaps more dangerous is that foreign countries and investors that have been buying US Treasuries (despite rising and vocal concerns against our deficits and stimulus programs) may decide that a falling dollar makes owning US Treasuries too risky. The Chinese use their trade surplus to purchase securities. Traditionally they have bought US Treasuries, but recently they have shifted their purchases more toward commodities and the bonds of other countries rather than US bonds. If the Chinese stop buying our bonds, either the Fed must buy many more of these bonds (out of desperation), or bond yields will rise sharply. Thus far, US bond purchasing by the Fed has greatly outweighed the reduction in buying by the Chinese. But if the Fed keeps buying, you can bet that the global bond markets eventually will see this as a sign of weakness and will force rates up anyway as they perceive rising risks. Again, the biggest risks are in the bubbles in stocks, commodities, and bonds that began accelerating in early September 2010. Such bubbles set up investors and retirement plans for another crash and brutal loss in net worth between 2012 and 2014.

Although QE2 depressed the dollar at first, the dollar, like Treasury bond rates, has been rising since early 2011, which goes against what most investors expected. This shows that such investors don't understand the new environment, which will be deflationary. In contrast, we forecast that the dollar and Treasury bond rates would rise in early 2011.

The Keynesian Drug: Invented in the 1930s, Adopted in the 1970s

Our government and most governments around the world have been on the Keynesian plan ever since the early 1970s when the last long-term boom came to an end. John Maynard Keynes first came up with his theory of the government stimulating to offset private economic slowdowns in the 1930s. Every time the economy slows, the Fed lowers short-term rates and implements fiscal stimulus that it hopes will rekindle consumer and business spending. We have been living off economic "speed" for a long time, since the 1970s, about the same time that baby boomers discovered recreational drugs as well. While drugs failed to resolve the social issues of the 1970s, the parallel economic approach has always seemed to work, because it coincided with the growth of the massive baby boom generation's demand for spending and credit, especially on housing as baby boomers grew into adulthood and matured.

However, the Keynesian approach has three problems. First, the economy never gets to "exhale" and fully balance out the excesses in debt and expansion from each growth surge, so it gets less efficient and trim—like getting more obese. Second, lower interest rates feed bubbles in asset prices, as we saw first in tech stocks, then in housing, then in emerging markets and commodities. When these bubbles burst, the Fed stimulates again, and that only drives the next set of bubbles. When does it ever end? Our economy just gets more perverse and volatile and less functional— just like any drug addict.

Why the "Great Crash Ahead"? The Fed has now stimulated a third and even more perverse bubble, which is the first bear market bubble we have ever seen. At least during the previous bubbles productivity

was growing rapidly, fueled by new technologies and demographic growth. The current bubbles only have government stimulus as fuel because economic trends are slowing, which is why the stimulus has had such disappointing results this time. The current bubbles in stocks, gold, commodities, and junk bonds will burst and bring back the housing, mortgage, and banking crisis even stronger, greatly injuring investors, retirees, and pension/retirement plans again.

Chart I-1 initially came from the July 2010 issue of our newsletter, *The HS Dent Forecast*, and it is probably the most critical chart for illustrating the actual impact of the desperate Fed stimulus on stocks. It shows three major bubbles that also form a larger "head-and-shoulders" pattern, which indicates a massive fall in the coming years, most likely between late 2011 and late 2014. A "head-and-shoulders" pattern is a chart pattern that reflects a small rise and fall as the left shoulder, a larger rise and fall as the head, and then a final rise and fall as the right shoulder. The left shoulder and head fall back to what is called the "neckline," but the right shoulder

Chart I-1: The Three Bubbles, Dow Log Chart, 1995–2010

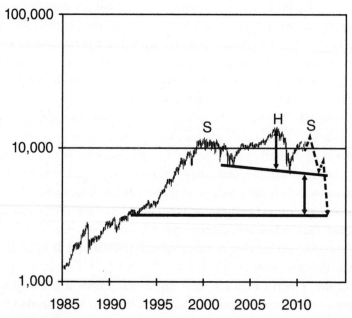

Data Source: Yahoo Finance

is usually followed by a dramatic drop. This is why recognizing such a pattern is important. The first bubble was around tech stocks and peaked in early 2000. A huge crash followed, especially in tech stocks, which bubbled the most. The NASDAQ was down 76%. The bubble formed the left shoulder of the head-and-shoulders pattern. Very low short-term rates after the 1990–1991 recession and the S&L crisis helped to fuel that bubble. The second, broader and higher bubble peaked in October 2007, with an early 2006 peak in real estate and a mid-2008 peak in commodities on each side. The greatest bubble here occurred in emerging markets and oil. That peak formed the head. That bubble was fueled by short-term rates, pushed down to 1% by the Fed. Now we are seeing a bear market bubble in stocks (US, Europe, China, and emerging markets), commodities, and bonds (especially junk bonds, which have rallied 83% since late 2008—the same as the S&P 500 since March 2009). The NASDAQ has rallied 110%, and emerging markets have rallied even more, 135%. Gold and silver have rallied 105% and 185%, respectively, since October 2008 and are reaching new highs, forming one last perverted bubble. The fear surrounding the desperate stimulus programs, reflected in the size of the programs themselves, is a sign of the coming end of all bubbles, as we warned in the paperback edition of *The Great Depression Ahead*! This bubble is forming the right shoulder that now looks as if it could peak between October 2011 and April 2012. The Fed helped fuel this bubble with 0% short-term rates and an unprecedented QE program.

With the Fed keeping short-term and long-term interest rates low, investors are chasing higher yields on corporate and junk bonds as well as stocks. The natural fall in the dollar at first lifted commodity prices. (Commodities trade in US dollars, so a falling dollar means such goods cost more to us, as do all imports.) This rise in commodities prices has been especially pronounced in the gold and silver markets. People fear the debasement of the US dollar and fear a potential domino effect, as other countries react and devalue their own currencies to remain competitive with the United States.

This third bear market bubble projects a fall in the Dow to approximately 3,300 sometime between late 2013 to late 2014, according to our cycles. This lines up with our observations that almost all bubbles either go back to where they started or fall even a little lower. The stock bubble started in late 1994 at 3,800 on the Dow, so we have been expecting 3,800 or lower for an ultimate bottom. The housing bubble started in early 2000. Home prices would have to fall 55% from the top to get back to those levels. The more a bubble grows, the more it attracts investors, but such a bubble also will fall farther, creating another wave of havoc.

It would be one thing if the government's plan actually worked, creating sustainable economic growth so that high debt and asset prices would not be such a burden. However, the demographic and debt deleveraging trends we face are massive and will make sustaining a recovery even more difficult than for Japan in the 1990s, where a demographically induced crash that started in the early 1990s is still in force. Today the GDP of Japan is little higher than it was in 1990, 21 years ago! The big picture is very simple: adding stimulus and debt always works at first, but never works long term. It takes more and more stimulus to create less and less effect, until the economy finally dies or nearly dies from the side effects— just like an addict on drugs!

Debt and Stimulus Is Like Any Drug: It Takes More to Create Less Effect

Chart I-2 tells the story about as well as anything could. For every additional dollar of debt we have added to the economy since 1958, we have generally gotten progressively less growth in GDP. This graph from the *Economist* goes only through early 2010. If the graph were updated, we would probably be right near zero effect presently. Hence, as potent as the newer quantitative easing policy is, it is not likely to revive the economy substantially at this late stage of debt abuse. Consumers have not been buying houses even though long-term mortgage rates have been at unprecedented lows, like 3.5% to 4.5% in late 2010! Why would another 0.5% lower make much difference? Lowering mortgage rates from 8% to 5% makes a big difference, but going from 4.0% to 3.5% doesn't make as much of a difference. What happens now that this bold and aggressive stimulus program is starting to backfire and long-term rates are rising, much as occurred in 2010 in Europe? Rising interest rates will be the final nail in the feeblest housing market since the 1930s, as we have been warning for years in our newsletter. The real impact of QE now is simply to encourage more speculation in asset prices. The money injected into the economy has to go somewhere, and lower long-term rates increase

Chart I-2: GDP per Dollar of Debt

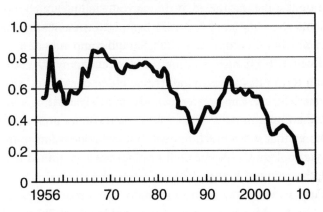

It's a drag
US GDP growth in $ per additional $ of debt*

Sources: Bureau of Economic
Analysis; Federal Reserve;
The Economist

*All domestic
nonfinancial debt
3-year moving average

Data Source: © The Economist Newspaper Limited, "Repent at Leisure," June 4, 2010

the value of all assets, including stocks, commodities, and real estate. The money clearly is not increasing lending.

There comes a point at which drug doses a person takes are so high that they could kill the user. Think of Michael Jackson in recent times. He wasn't partying night after night. He was just trying to get a peaceful night's rest. The cumulative toxicity from many years of increasing painkillers and drug use caused his body constantly to attempt to "detox," making it harder and harder for him to sleep. Such high internal activity must have made him feel like he had fire engines inside, always rushing to the next fire. After many years of such drug abuse only a very potent anesthesia was able to help Jackson sleep, but the high dosage finally killed him.

Corporations have hundreds of billions of dollars on their balance sheets that they don't invest in their businesses, as they are uncertain about future growth, taxes, health care costs, and everything else. But lower interest rates give corporations the incentive to borrow money, which they use to finance acquisitions, to buy back equity to create greater earnings per share, or simply to pay key shareholders, which also drives up stock prices. The junk bond trend, which started with Michael Milken in the 1980s, most likely experienced a final, sharp spike in prices (drop in yields) in 2011. The recent surge was fueled by dramatically falling junk bond yields due to QE and the temporary recovery from government stimulus after the spike in junk bond yields in late 2008. Should companies be leveraging up internally in such a dangerous time as today's economy? Of course not! But low long-term rates are proving irresistible to companies, who then take on more debt, creating greater leverage and risk at a time when they are already drowning in debt. Thus, lower interest rates are not the cure for an economy that is too much in debt. But everyone wants more crack once they are hooked! Corporate credit ratings have continued to decline since 1980, as a result of higher debt.

What happens when the economy finally slows more markedly and these junk bond yields spike again, as they did in late 2008? We already forecast that this will likely begin more seriously as early as late 2011, with stock markets starting to correct again. More stimulus . . . more debt . . . more bubbles . . . when will it ever end? Bubbles always end! The final bursting of this unprecedented world bubble should mean the end of Keynesian economics—finally!

This comes back to our most basic argument. A 25-year trend in rising baby boom spending that we cover in Chapter 2 (1983–2007 on a 46-year lag from rising births from 1937 to 1961) has peaked, and economic growth will slow overall into at least 2020 and perhaps until as late as 2023, especially after 2011. This declining wave of spending is not something you can fight with a few trillion dollars in stimulus here and there—and the US government has already gone further than we thought the bond markets would allow, after the European "debt call" in April 2010 by the "bond vigilantes." A similar rise in interest rates is finally about to come to the United States, as we forecast, albeit later than we originally would have expected. It would take tens of trillions of dollars to offset such natural downward trends and a necessary shift to saving for an aging generation that is the deepest in debt of any generation in history. More important for the near term, the greatest debt and credit bubble in history peaked in 2008, at $56 trillion in private and government debt plus a bare minimum (in the most rosy economic assumptions) of $46 trillion in unfunded liabilities for Social Security and Medicare/Medicaid ($66 trillion, according to private analysts like Mary Meeker). The United States faces a total indebtedness of at least $122 trillion, seven times GDP at the top in 2008 and as much as $122 trillion or almost 9 times GDP under more realistic assumptions! By way of comparison, our total indebtedness reached just two times GDP at the top of the Roaring '20s boom. Our total private credit reached $42 trillion in 2008. This number more than doubled from 2000 to 2008, which means $22 trillion in debt was added to our economy within 8 short years in the private sector alone. In 2008, private debt was more than four times the size of our government debt, excluding unfunded entitlement liabilities. This private debt will continue to deleverage for years to come, and at a faster pace than government debt rises . . . creating deflation, not inflation.

The seemingly most intelligent and awarded of Keynesian economists around the world, such as Paul Krugman, argue that the government has not stimulated enough. That would make sense in light of the US banking crisis of the 1930s, in which the economy melted down to extremes without help from the government. So why not be smarter this time and stimulate more and sooner? Because it wouldn't be smart to ignore the crack addiction analogy that occurs in real life. The more the stimulant is applied, the less it works, and it will kill you in the end. You end up worse, not better, before you are forced to go through detox!

Japan has stimulated the equivalent of just over 100% of its GDP since its bubble boom peaked in 1990; that would be the equivalent of about $15 trillion for the United States. Japan's stock market still fell over 80%, real estate fell over 60%, and the country is still in an on-and-off slow growth and recession economy 20 years later. Such stimulus eased the pain but caused government debt to skyrocket to the highest levels by far among the countries in the developed world. Japan has the fastest aging society, to boot. Private debt did not get written off as fully as it could have, so the Japanese system still has too much toxicity and needs to detox further. Therefore, we clearly don't think that this is the policy that the United States should follow. European governments are already moving in the right direction long term—toward austerity—despite the short-term pain and riots.

The Japanese are not public complainers, but they have become very frugal. Japanese lifestyles have been compromised substantially, with no light at the end of the tunnel. Government debt ratios are high, savings rates are plummeting, and government benefit payments are rising, due to the rapid aging of the Japanese population. The *New York Times* recently featured an article that showed a man who bought a condo 17 years ago for $500,000—after the real estate bubble had burst and was deflating, so not near the top of the real estate market! After paying down his mortgage for 17 years, he sold the unit—and still owed $110,000. The man now is likely to have to go into personal bankruptcy. That's why we don't advise you or your kids to buy a home now, despite the recent fall in prices. Why didn't the Japanese government allow and/or force the banks to write down these debts to sustainable levels? They simply didn't want to go into detox or admit their mistakes in letting the bubble happen in the first place, much as the US government is doing today, protecting the banking system over the interests of everyday citizens!

In contrast to the long, drawn-out approach used by the Japanese government, the United States responded to the recent economic crisis with a typical "shock and awe" policy, stimulating very strongly right at the beginning. Thus, most of the "ammunition" was used up early on, creating even greater bubbles and imbalances than those that caused the initial crisis—which only feeds the next, worse crisis. But now the United States has less ammunition with which to fight!

We have proposed that the government not use stimulus to try to revive an economy that is already mortally wounded and needs to deleverage and rebalance. Instead the US government should use government debt to help cover the losses that banks incur from actually writing down loans to their real values. Such a move would have the potential to save more than $1 trillion per year in interest and principal payments by consumers and businesses for decades to come. That is a real stimulus plan that is focused on the root cause of this economic crisis: an out-of-control debt bubble and the aging of the massive baby boom generation, which has led to a decrease in consumer spending.

Ultimately, whether through years of free-market debt deleveraging, as occurred from 1930 to 1933 (and as has been prevented thus far largely by the government's stimulus program in the current crisis), or through a government-driven program that actively encourages or forces banks to write loans down to their real sustainable value, the result ultimately will be reduction of around $20 trillion of private debt, mostly mortgages and financial sector debt. This amount will represent 90% of the $22 trillion of private debt created in the debt bubble from 2000 to 2008. At 5% average interest rates, that would save consumers and businesses $1 trillion annually in interest and will reduce principal payments as well. That kind of stimulus keeps on paying. If the government wants to encourage write-offs and keep the best banks from going under, it may have to offer to cover, say, 20% of the loan write-offs, which could create trillions more dollars in stimulus. Having $5 of private debt written off for every $1 in government debt incurred is a great trade-off, especially given that interest rates on government debt tend to be lower than for other kinds of debt.

We will discuss the total debt picture in more detail in Chapters 3 and 4. The largest and most toxic debt we incurred was in the financial sector, which is now deleveraging the fastest; about $2.5 trillion in debt has been written off since 2008. Most of the $17 trillion in this sector went into real estate, in which prices will fall to near where they started or lower, just as in every bubble in history. Thus, the most deleveraging or elimination of debt should happen here. The business and consumer sectors have deleveraged only a little thus far, which clearly demonstrates how far we have to go in mortgage and debt write-downs. Since 2008, the total decline in these two sectors has been close to $1 trillion, for a total of near $3.5 trillion in the private sector. In contrast, government debt has grown about $3.5 trillion since 2008. Thus far, the rise in government debt has been offset roughly by the fall in private debt, which is why the United States is sitting at a modest inflation rate, despite the greatest stimulus program in history. When the stimulus fails and the economy goes back into detox— which it really, really wants to do—then the private debt will deleverage much faster and more than the government debt will rise, leading to deflation.

Deflation is the only possible scenario in the decade ahead. This will be the Decade of Deflation, much like the 1930s. Why? Because deleveraging and deflation always follow debt and asset bubbles, such as happened in the 1820s, 1860s, and 1920s in the United States and in the 1980s in Japan; there are no exceptions in modern history! It is merely a matter of how long the US government and others can be allowed to keep stimulating to ease the pain and avoid the necessary detox—and that policy now, finally, looks likely to fail, as we forecast it would.

All the king's horses and all the king's men couldn't put Humpty together again.

—from an English nursery rhyme

Here is where we perhaps have the most shocking of our forecasts for the years ahead in this deflationary crisis: **The US Dollar will appreciate and be the safe haven—not gold, silver, the Euro or the Swiss Franc. Chart I-3,** which graphs the US dollar index from 1980 to 2011, shows that the US dollar was debased in the boom. It peaked in value in 1985 and has fallen nearly 60% in two major crashes. It was the massive creation of $42 trillion in private debt, which grew 2.65 times the growth of GDP from 1983 to 2008, which created massive amounts of new dollars and devalued the US dollar. Since the financial crisis in 2008 the dollar has only moved sideways to up. During the actual meltdown of the financial system in late 2008 and early 2009, the dollar went up 23%! Gold and silver went down. Oil crashed most extremely. Stocks here and around the world all crashed. Real estate crashed. The dollar was the safe haven in late 2008, and it will be the safe haven for likely many years to come in the period of debt deleveraging ahead.

During the periods where there is the perception of a financial crisis, gold and silver rise. But when the crisis actually hits, they fall and it is the dollar that rises. Why? During a financial meltdown, that massive

Chart I-3: US Dollar Index, 1980–2011

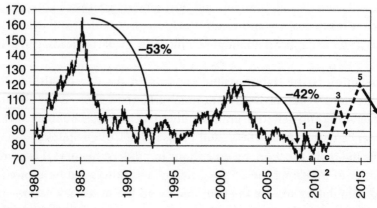

Data Source: **Bloomberg**

$42 trillion in private debt will see major write-offs and restructuring and that destroys dollars. By destroying dollars you make them scarce and valuable again—you actually reverse the debt and credit bubble—and fewer dollars means fewer dollars chasing consumer goods, or deflation in prices, not inflation! Understanding the difference between deflation and inflation is the key to prospering in a crisis unlike any you have seen in your lifetime.

Deflation could come slowly, as it did in Japan due to high and consistent stimulus over time, or it could come rapidly, as in the early 1930s when the government did little more than lower short-term rates to stave off the pain of detox. In this cycle, the United States has embraced a "shock and awe" policy that at first was more effective than the policies of Japan but proved more dangerous long term, due to the bubbles the US approach is creating. Now that such an unprecedented, desperate, and aggressive program is starting to fail, it is likely to fail miserably, as it has only made our debt levels worse and has put off the necessary crisis and detox. We have been advocating a policy wherein the government creates only enough additional debt to cushion the write-down of much larger debts in the private sector, which should generate more than $1 trillion in lower interest and principal payments for consumers and businesses for years and decades into the future.

However, that policy is too sensible; it treats the real cause of this debt crisis, not the symptoms. And human nature is all about reacting to and treating the symptoms. Hence, this crisis and shift toward deleveraging debt and deflation will not happen voluntarily, just as any crack addict would not go into painful detox voluntarily. Such a policy will manifest only when the crisis overwhelms the US government and other governments—when the stimulus ultimately fails fully and housing prices and the economy fail again, in all likelihood triggered by the coming long-term interest rate spike.

This crisis is likely to be at its worst by early 2014, or by early 2015 at the latest, and only after stocks crash to between 3,300 and 5,600 on the Dow by the end of 2013, or 2014 at the latest. Home prices will fall by 55% to 65% from the top before this crisis is over. Also, the crash will be worldwide, not just in the United States and Europe, as the dramatic China bubble comes to an end. This book is about telling you how to prepare and prosper now that our long-standing forecast for

the next deeper depression phase is beginning to occur. Hold onto your life jacket and climb into the lifeboat. The next few years and the next decade will be the most challenging you have ever seen or will see in your lifetime. The secret to prospering is to understand the very different nature of and rules for deflation, as opposed to the inflationary environment most of us have seen all of our lives. Even gold will not save you in this new deflationary era . . . in a world turned upside down!

You can get free access to Harry's very popular webinar "Understanding the Economy and What Lies Ahead" by registering at http://www.hsdent.com/webinar.

CHAPTER 1

Deflation Is the Trend— and It Changes Everything

It wasn't supposed to be like this. For over 30 years Patti, the godmother of my [Rodney Johnson's] children and wonderful friend, took the steps that were supposed to ensure not only her success, but also her financial security. She graduated from Tulane University and worked her way up in several organizations, in which she consistently beat client expectations. She earned six figures, of which she saved and invested quite a bit. She worked overtime and weekends and traveled exhaustively. She was a "hot property." Then she was fired in the summer of 2010.

Fired, laid off, downsized—whatever it was called, the latest company where she worked was acquired by another. During the process of integrating her unit into the succeeding firm, she and other executives were dismissed. It was typical. You get called into a meeting with higher-ups, at which you are told that the company is moving in a direction for which your services are no longer necessary. You are escorted to your office and a human resources representative watches you pack your things to ensure that you do not steal from or harm the company that you poured your life into for years—the company that you helped to make a success story and an acquisition target. Finally, you are marched off the premises like any other nondesirable who might have wandered in off the streets. Such is the way of corporate life.

If this had happened during the ordinary course of company evolutions in normal times, when mergers and acquisitions typically create gains and losses for investors and employees, perhaps it would not have been such a blow. But these are not what most of us would consider normal times. Patti walked out of that company in the summer of 2010 as a 50-year-old woman and into a job market that already held over 14 million unemployed people. She left with her savings and investments greatly diminished after the crash of 2008–2009, and she carries the burden of a home that continues to fall in value. It wasn't supposed to be like this, but it is. Patti is just one of millions of casualties in what is a continuing economic catastrophe. The economic meat grinder is taking its toll, reducing not only what we as consumers and workers have in terms of gainful employment and assets, but also taking away some of our ideas of what we can achieve. In short, for many, tomorrow looks grim.

As we sat around Patti's kitchen table discussing this state of affairs, she was downtrodden but defiant about her employment. This stint of work was over, for all intents and purposes, but she would live to work again. Like the mythical phoenix, she would rise up in perhaps a different form, developing a niche to service groups like her previous clients, writing a book about her area of expertise—on-boarding large corporate clients for complex services—or simply find a similar position in another company. This was not her first rodeo. She had successfully reinvented herself before. While the work situation definitely caused her concern, it was nothing compared to the financial loss in her portfolio and her sheer lack of clarity about her financial future, which caused something closer to despair.

"I should have spent it," she said. "Instead of socking it away, meeting with my financial advisor on a regular basis, and tweaking my investments, I should have blown it on all the vacations I wanted to take. Even though I was responsible, saving and paying my own bills, never spending beyond my means, I'm suffering for it. Other people blew up their own situations, and at the same time the government did absolutely nothing to stop financial institutions run amok. Here I am paying the price."

We just witnessed the greatest credit and real estate bubble in modern history. Just as debt, housing, stocks, commodity, and business values skyrocketed, they will now collapse and create the greatest deflationary environment since the 1930s. Do you know how to invest and navigate your business and career in an environment that you have never seen before?

Patti's points are well taken, and her sentiments are shared by many across the country and around the globe. While most people understand some of the events and trends that led us here, it is still hard to grasp why this situation has become so much bigger, so much more encompassing, than anything since the Great Depression.

Patti not only can survive, but she can thrive, as will a minority of Americans and citizens around the world. Even everyday citizens in China and India will feel this global deflationary crisis. Patti will continue to keep her financial house in order, working more and saving more than she would have otherwise. But the questions and doubts she raises deserve answers. We have just lived through the greatest economic bubble in the history of the world, and now we are dealing with the aftermath as that bubble deflates. The bones and debris are scattered everywhere—investments, jobs, education, retirement, politics—nothing is left untouched. Our net worth has been greatly reduced. The median family earns less income today than 10 years ago. We are going backward.

As we go through what will be a long and difficult period of adjustment, we have choices. We can choose to bury our heads in the sand, ignoring the changing world around us and hoping for the best but doing nothing. Or we can choose to recognize that the era we just left—that time of growth and seemingly easy prosperity that marked most of the past three decades—is over. What lies ahead will be difficult, but through education and proactive efforts, we not only can see what lies ahead but also can profit from it. As you might expect, this book is all about choosing education and prosperity!

The trends for the coming decade are crystal clear: we are going to experience a deeper downturn and deflation in prices, not inflation. We call this the Winter Season; it comes predictably once in a lifetime, currently every 80 years, which means that very few people will understand what is happening.

- **The largest generation in history will be spending less and saving more for retirement, which are trends that follow aging. The continued aging of our population as well as of the populations of developed countries around the world is deflationary—just ask Japan.**
- **The greatest credit and real estate bubble in history will continue to deleverage and deflate. The US government and most world governments have implemented extreme stimulus measures to prevent financial systems from melting down as they began to do in late 2008. These measures will fail, probably by late 2011 to early 2012**

and certainly by late 2013. We will undergo the first extreme deflationary crisis since 1930–1933, with all major investments crashing.
We will suffer business, bank, and job losses unlike anything we have
ever dealt with in our lifetimes. Crashes of this magnitude won't be
repeated for another 60 years or more.

- China is leading a global bubble by greatly overbuilding industrial
  capacity, real estate, and infrastructure. Most of the emerging world,
  along with Canada, Australia, and New Zealand, is feeding China's
  bubble with materials and energy. The bursting of China's bubble
  together with the peaking of a very reliable 29- to 30-year commodity cycle will make this a global downturn despite long-term rising
  demographic trends in the emerging world.

**We're here to wake you up to the greatest financial crisis of your life-
time and to get you onto our lifeboat to save your family and business
from financial ruin before it's too late!**

This book can be thought of as having four sections. The first part
(Chapters 1 and 2) discusses how we got here, including the driving forces
of demographics and consumption. Starting in the Roaring Twenties
boom, demographics quickly became the key driving force in the world
economy, as middle-class living standards spread. This force will continue
to accelerate among emerging countries as billions of people see their
income and consumption levels grow. Economists do not understand
the impacts of this most critical factor, which is why they did not predict
the magnitude of the global boom and why they now do not perceive the
magnitude of the inevitable global slowdown ahead.

The second section of the book (Chapters 3 through 5) describes where
we are now: in an economic Winter Season, with a massive debt overhang
that must be worked out. We are referring to the debt bubble that occurred
primarily in the private sector, not to the US federal debt, which is huge
on its own. From 2000 to 2008, private debt more than doubled, from
$20 trillion to $42 trillion, whereas government debt grew from $5 tril-
lion to $10 trillion over the same period. Unfortunately, government
debt, which has since grown to $15 trillion, continues to rise. The most
pressing problem in the government sector is $46 trillion to $66 trillion
in unfunded liabilities for Social Security and Medicare/Medicaid. Our
system cannot continue to function and certainly cannot make any real

attempt at a recovery with all of this debt! In the next decade, particularly between 2012 and 2015, we will undergo the greatest debt restructuring in history, and that destruction of debt will actually cause deflation, not inflation. This is what makes the coming economic Winter Season so different from the last extended downturn in our economy, from 1969 to 1982. That period represented an economic Summer Season, in which we experienced a wave of inflation and innovation. The investment and business strategies that work in a deflationary period are very different from and are often the exact opposite of what works during inflation.

The third part (Chapters 6 through 8) illustrates why we will not be coming out of this crisis anytime soon. We identify that the emerging world, led by China, has its own bursting bubble, which includes commodity prices. We also look at why the seemingly successful policies of the government have only "kicked the can down the road," making the debt crisis and mortgage crisis worse. These policies cannot work against the massive downward trends in demographics and debt deleveraging.

In the final section (Chapters 9 through 11), we discuss how we as a nation, as investors, as business owners, and as citizens can best position ourselves in order not just to survive the next several years, but to thrive! The adversity we face today is simply a different set of opportunities and challenges than those of yesterday. As the weather reflects the seasons, we see winter coming and prepare by stocking up on firewood, buying coats, et cetera. We store away the water skis and bring out the snow skis! Every season has its opportunities and challenges. You simply need to change your strategies for each season. We finish in Chapter 12 with a look at not just big changes, but sweeping, revolutionary-type changes that are occurring here and around the world. Just as the Industrial Revolution radically changed the world starting in the late 1700s, the Information Age is not even close to finishing what was started in the 1970s and 1980s.

Twenty years ago we forecast an economic Winter Season that would stretch from 2008 to 2023. The season has arrived, and it brings with it great challenges and great opportunities. Once we understand what is possible and let go of yesterday, we can begin rebuilding.

How We Got Here: 25 Years of Economic History in a Few Short Pages

Looking back, the trajectory of the "bubble economy" is obvious, but at its height, many people were describing it as unprecedented progress. The typical way of describing how we got here is usually done by chronicling business and policy developments of the last 25 years. It goes something like this:

In the mid-1990s our economy was doing well, as we had moderate interest rates, rising government revenue, and a well-functioning capital market. The United States had shaken off the problems of the 1970s and early 1980s and was riding the wave of productivity and earnings that came from the invention of desktop computing and the advent of the internet. The possibilities seemed limitless.

As the internet craze took off, there was a mad rush to take companies public, which was met with an equally mad rush on the part of investors to get in on the speculative investment boom. This was fueled not only by the obvious game-changing nature of the internet, but also by what the internet brought us: day trading and instant access to our investments. Suddenly, people were discussing stocks to buy just like they would discuss dinner choices at a restaurant ("I think I'll have some Cisco and Yahoo!, but I'm torn because the Intel and the JDS Uniphase sound so good!"). Yields on bonds were falling, so equities seemed to be the overwhelming choice for growing wealth.

After languishing through the 1970s virtually unchanged, the Dow Jones Industrial Average (Dow) shot higher over the next two decades. The index increased by 325% in the 1980s and then by over 400% in the 1990s. By 1998 and 1999, CNBC was a household name, Amazon no longer was just a river in South America, and a sock puppet (Pets.com) was quickly becoming the most reviled figure on television. The rush to capitalize on the internet and investment frenzy led to the dot.com bubble and eventually to the bust of 2000–2002, which ended with many portfolios in shambles and a recession to boot. Fortunes were lost, and retirement plans were wiped out. To help the economy recover, the Fed lowered interest rates in early 2001. It didn't help much. The economy did not fall much further, but it also did not make big gains. The year 2001 was spent eating through excess capacity and dealing with a short, shallow recession. Then tragedy struck: 9/11.

The markets were closed for four days. The world was in a panic. There were wild estimates as to what would happen when the markets did reopen. One thing was sure: interest rates would be dramatically lower. The Federal Reserve took swift, dramatic steps to flood the US economy with enough buying power to keep a questionable situation from turning into a cascade of bad events.* The Fed had already lowered short-term rates from 6% to 3.5% over the course of 2001 leading up to 9/11. After that fateful day, the Fed lowered short-term rates another 1.75% in a matter of months and yet another 0.75% during 2002 and 2003, finally allowing short-term rates to bottom at 1% in that cycle. In just over two short years, the Federal Reserve lowered interest rates from 6% to 1%. It was determined to make our economy move, and move it did—although perhaps not in the way that the Fed intended.

As the Fed was aggressively lowering interest rates, lenders were aggressively stepping up their efforts to shovel money out of the door. Cheap dollars meant that loans were easy to afford, so borrowers could take out bigger and bigger loans. What to do with all of those borrowed dollars? Buy the biggest leveraged asset possible, of course! Americans went on a home-buying, condo-buying, investment-property buying binge, especially after they had lost in tech stocks and were looking for what seemed to be more solid investments. Although a family might be able to afford a $1,500 mortgage payment, the total size of their loan would change depending on the interest rate. At a 7% mortgage, the family could afford to borrow $250,000. At 5%, the same family, for the same $1,500 monthly mortgage payment, could afford to borrow over $350,000! It seemed like magic! Suddenly Americans were flush to buy the highest priced, most leveraged asset they would ever own! The housing boom was on!

Lenders were competing with US government–backed lending institutions Federal National Mortgage Association (FNMA, or Fannie Mae) and Federal Home Loan Mortgage Corp. (FHLMC, or Freddie Mac), which could get really cheap dollars because of their implicit, and later explicit, government backing. FNMA and FHLMC got most of the prime loans, those loans taken out by borrowers with good credit who were purchas-

---

* Historical Changes of the Target Federal Funds and Discount Rates: 1971 to Present. Online chart, updated December 12, 2008. Federal Reserve Bank of New York. Accessed March 2, 2011. Available at http://www.newyorkfed.org/markets/statistics/dlyratesfedrate .html.

ing traditional homes to live in and who were putting down 20%. Other lenders charged a slightly higher interest rate but made loans to people who had lesser credit scores, who were buying investment properties, who were making a smaller down payment, or who had some other nontraditional aspect to their loan.

As time went on, the falling interest rate environment had a curious impact on the value of homes. As buyers could afford bigger sale prices, they bid up the price of homes. This caused the development and sale of real estate to become the hot industry and caused existing real estate to shoot up in value. Loans that were backed by real estate were seemingly bulletproof, as the default and foreclosure rate plummeted. Who would default on a mortgage when the property had increased in value? Just sell it! At one point Wells Fargo actually had a negative cost of foreclosure, meaning that the bank made money on homes they took back from borrowers.

Through the impact of lower interest rates and lenient standards, the traditional ratio of income to borrowing power for home mortgages was expanded dramatically, as we show in **Chart 1-1.**

Are you aware that the average household's borrowing capacity for a mortgage went from 3.3 times household income to 9.2 times income in just the 6 years between 2000 and 2006? We have never seen anything remotely like that in modern history!

At the same time, the lending industry took the opportunity to greatly expand the cash-out refinance business so that current homeowners could unlock the value of their homes and use the funds for anything they wanted. Homes no longer were just long-term investments or places to live, but also were really big ATMs.

The beauty was that anyone could play the game. As values continued to climb, lenders fought over borrowers. Lending standards went out the window; ever more exotic loans were developed to allow more borrowers to qualify for bigger and bigger loans. Of course, banks no longer really financed loans. They simply originated loans and then sold them to other institutions. Because the banks did not hold the loans, there was no limit on how many loans could be made. Also, the motivation for making loans was not to ensure repayment but to get as many loans out of the door as possible.

The Federal Reserve began raising rates in 2004, but the snowball was

Chart 1-1: Borrowing Power of a Typical Home Purchaser, 1995–2008

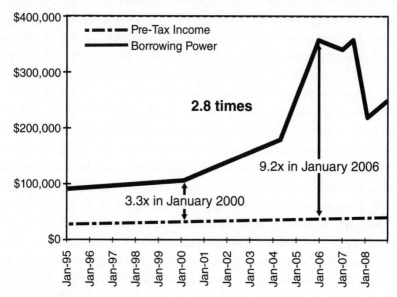

Data Source: Amherst Securities

already rolling downhill, gaining in speed and size. The housing market juggernaut, with all of its baggage, was moving at light speed. Then, in late 2005, it started to slow down. The pool of borrowers was not growing as rapidly, and the building industry had ramped up its efforts to the point that inventory was coming online very quickly at higher and higher prices. By 2007 there were questions about many of the subprime mortgages and about the ability of the borrowers to pay.

In early 2008, when the music stopped, large financial companies began to shudder: first Bear Stearns, which was followed by FNMA and FHLMC, Lehman Brothers, and too many banks to mention. The US government got in on the act in May 2008 with a $168 billion stimulus plan and then took over FNMA and FHLMC that summer. At the height of the credit crisis the government implemented the Troubled Asset Recovery Program, or TARP. The White House changed hands, Congress passed an $800 billion stimulus program, and in March 2009 the United States became the largest shareholder of General Motors and AIG.

So far, this narrative posits credit—the creation of it, the access to it, and the misuse of it—as the genesis of our current crisis. If that were true, then a simple correction to our credit markets would be able to put the United States back on a sustainable economic path. This is exactly the type of policy that the United States has pursued, seeking to make dollars even easier to get through interest rates that are now at zero, creating tremendous reserves at banks ($1.5 trillion on hand), and trying to force lenders to make loans. But it's not working. Instead of taking on more debt in order to buy more things, consumers have turned away. Those who are creditworthy have chosen a more frugal path and are no longer swayed by the idea of a bigger home, a fancier car, or simply more stuff. What happened? To hear typical economists describe it, consumers are fearful. Their current lack of trust in the future is causing them to hold back on purchases, which slows down the business cycle and causes the economy to drag.

There is a reason that consumers are fearful: their gut tells them that something is very wrong. The entire debt of the United States has more than doubled in the last decade to well over $100 trillion, as Chart 1-2 shows. Our total debt as a percentage of GDP is roughly 5 times as great as it was in 1929 before we entered the Great Depression!

We will cover the topic of debt in great depth in Chapter 3, but to summarize, the greatest problem is not the Fed's stimulus of $2 trillion plus

Chart 1-2: US Debt Creation, 1980–2009

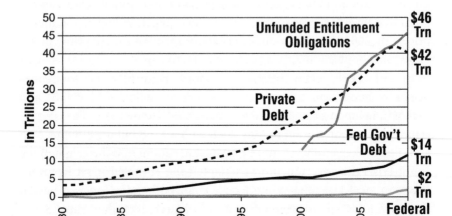

Data Source: The Chart Store, St. Louis Fed, Treasury Direct, US Treasury

or even our federal debt, which is approaching $15 trillion and forecast to reach $20 trillion to $25 trillion even in a rosy economy in the next decade (which won't happen). The greatest problem is a double whammy of the private debt of $42 trillion in our economy (more than double the level of debt we had in 2000) and the unfunded entitlement programs of Social Security and Medicare/Medicaid, which have increased more than three times since 2000.

There Is More to the Story: What You Will Not Hear from the Mainstream Media

Is this really what happened, and is it an accurate picture of where we are? Did we simply get pulled into a debt-fueled spending spree and then get scared? If only it were so simple. Like so many things, the reasons are more complex, and the time frame is much longer. This was indeed a bubble—in fact, the greatest bubble in history; however, the bubble did not start with stocks in the 1990s or home prices in the 2000s; it started with people. In particular, it started with little people, babies, over 60 years ago.

The incredible surge in births from about 1937 to 1961 was called a baby boom, and those children came to be called baby boomers, particularly those born from 1946 through 1964. They also became known for their behaviors and views on society. This huge group of people came of age in the 1960s and 1970s and then went about the rest of their lives. At every single stage of life, this outsized group has turned markets and institutions on their heads. When this group was going to elementary school in the 1950s and 1960s, we could not build schools fast enough. When they entered the workforce in the late 1960s and 1970s, there were not enough jobs. We saw the greatest inflation in modern history because it is expensive to raise kids and then integrate new workers into the workforce (a severe, prolonged lack of productivity growth). In the 1980s, they started families, bringing about the term "soccer moms" and driving demand for SUVs to carry all of those people and all of that stuff. As this bubble of people, the boomers, went about living their lives, they drove demand for goods and services in very predictable ways at very predictable ages and stages of life. This generational explosion eventually fueled demand and consumption approximately 46 years later, when the typical household is at the height of its family spending.

The reason the spending patterns of this group of consumers, or any group of consumers for that matter, are so important is that personal consumption makes up 70% of gross domestic product (GDP) in the US and a similar percentage in most developed countries. Over two-thirds of our economic activity in any given year is directly related to the choices made by consumers. When consumers spend more, businesses make investments to expand their capacity to satisfy the increasing demand. This also leads to rising tax revenues for governments (sales tax, income tax, property tax, fees, etc.), which allows for greater government spending. So when the largest group of people (boomers) inside the largest spending group (consumers) makes a change, everyone pays attention. The remainder of GDP is split among businesses (15%), government (20%), and the net of imports/exports (-5%). (Currently we bring more into the country than we sell to other people, so this last number is negative.) Recently, businesses have been spending much less and the government has been spending much more. Even so, it is changes to personal consumption that are the most important, as consumers drive the entire train over time.

We will explain this in greater depth in Chapter 2. Our economy rises and falls on an approximately 46-year lag to the birth index, as greater numbers of people in a new generation such as the baby boom generation reach their average predictable peak in spending, which we show in Chart 1-3.

As the largest group of consumers in our society reached the peak of their personal demand for consumption around late 2007 (as we forecast 20 years ago that they would), they were desperate for the "fuel" needed to spend, which was credit. The industry responsible for creating credit was working overtime to meet the incredible demand. When the credit bubble—which was an outcome rather than the cause of the rise in demand—fell in on itself, the consumption demand of the boomers was already starting to flatten out. This trend line of demand will naturally decline for many years. The credit crisis just accelerated the slowdown in baby boom spending that was already in the cards, because it was put in place almost 50 years ago. The first phase of the slowdown demographically was a flattening in spending that has already begun, similar to what occurred from 1966 to 1970 in the last generational peaking process 40 years ago. Back then we saw more serious recessions in 1970 and

Chart 1-3: The Spending Wave, Births Lagged for Peak in Spending

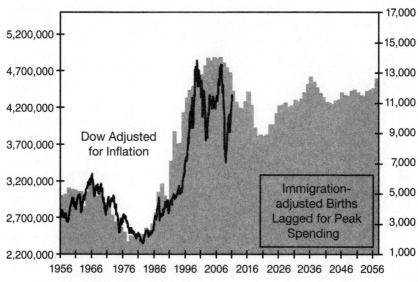

Data Source: Census Bureau, Bloomberg, HS Dent

1973–1974. The last of the baby boomers' kids are likely to leave the nest by late 2011, creating the next serious economic downturn between 2012 and 2014.

This is an important point. Although spending peaks at age 46 on average, there is a plateau into age 50 while the kids are leaving the nest. The average kid is born to the average parent around age 28. The kids who enter the workforce after high school will leave the nest when their parents are about age 46. The kids who go to college won't leave until their parents are age 50. It is this 4-year plateau in baby boom spending that we have seen from late 2007 through late 2011. From 2012 forward, we should see a more serious decline in income and spending by baby boomers.

Chart 1-4 shows what happened the last time a generation peaked in spending and the Fed tried to stimulate at first to stave off the inevitable downturn. The last generation peaked in 1968 on a 44-year lag as people got married and had kids earlier back then. There was a first strong crash into 1970, then a Fed-stimulated rebound into 1972, and then a deeper crash in 1973–1974. The Fed stimulus worked better in the plateau stage

Chart 1-4: Dow Adjusted for Inflation, Comparison of 1968–1974 with 2007–2013

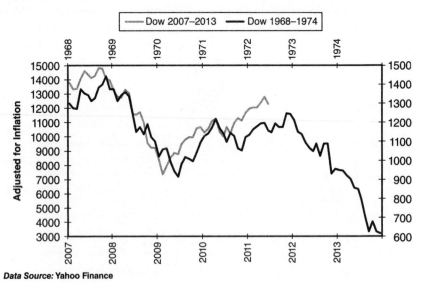

Data Source: Yahoo Finance

from 1969–1972, but finally failed in the decline stage that began on a 4-year lag. Our current scenario is proceeding similarly with the crash into early 2009, followed by a rebound in stocks into late 2011. This 4-year lag for more serious demographic downtrends would suggest that the Fed stimulus plan that has continued to fail from one program to the next is likely to take the economy beyond the Fed's ability to stimulate without setting off risk alarms for the bond markets as has been occurring in Greece and southern Europe since April of 2010. If we continue to follow a similar scenario, we should see a deeper stock crash into late 2013 or so, and as low as our 3,300 target for the Dow. We have cycles that suggest we could see a more extreme crash that bottoms as early as late 2012, or a more drawn-out decline that lasts well into 2014.

Now we are in a completely different type of environment. No longer are we working in an economy with an ever-growing appetite for consumption. Things have changed. The boomers are now focused on saving and paying down debt, although they splurged a bit in late 2010 and early 2011 after cutting back so much from late 2008 into the summer of 2010. They have taken their credit cards and gone home. The boomers have followed a very predictable path, spending more incrementally as their children got older and peaking in their spending just as their children were getting old enough to leave home. From that point forward, the game becomes all about preparing for retirement. The boomers may take the occasional vacation, refurbish the bathroom or kitchen, or throw a big party, but by and large the focus of those in their 50s is to save enough to retire comfortably. Achieving that savings is possible because as their kids leave the nest, they do not have to spend as much on daily living; fewer people are in the house to support. So what happens when the largest group in your economy changes from being spenders to being savers? Suddenly, your economy goes slack. Just ask the Japanese, who went through this transition in the early to mid-1990s. As that large generation moves on to the saving phase, what's left behind is a marketplace with too much capacity and too few consumers. There are not enough people in the next generation, Generation X, to fill the shoes of the boomers—especially in housing, the largest and most debt-intensive purchase.

This type of economic analysis, based on demographics, is exactly what we do at HS Dent. For over 20 years we've been explaining to audiences and readers how our economy changes based on people. As much as we would like for people to do what *we* want, it is much more likely that they will do what *they* want. This is critical to understanding our economy, and yet economists pay little attention to demographics!

Much of the economic theory used by the US government to try to grow our economy is based on consumers behaving rationally. Unfortunately, the government's idea of rational behavior is reacting to interest rates and price movements in a vacuum, with no regard for the current situation of the individual consumer! What person decides to spend more or less without thinking about things like raising their kids, saving for retirement, or job security? This makes no sense! When creating incentives, government should try to assess where consumers are in their lives, but it doesn't. This is the biggest failure of economic theory and government intervention today!

Most people are going to make a decision based on what's happening in their household, not on what's going on in the larger economy. This is why we can go through so many difficult things in our economy, like wars or terrorist attacks, and yet people will continue to spend. No one likes these types of events, of course, but if we still want guitar lessons or new clothes for our children, or if the tuition for after-school care is due, we are going to pay for it. As the children leave home and we're no longer burdened with these responsibilities, we begin to focus on the next change in our future, which is retirement. Let the savings begin!

But China and the Emerging World Will Save Us, Right? Think Again!

Many claim that the rising demographic trends of younger populations in the emerging world and the spectacular growth of China will keep world-wide growth more robust, offsetting the slowdown from demographics and debt deleveraging in the developed world. First, note that over 65% of world GDP is still generated in the developed world, despite the remarkable growth in the emerging world. Our standard of living in the United States is more than six times the standard of living in China, even adjusted for purchasing power. As we will cover in more depth in Chapter 8, China's government has been creating the last great bubble in this unprecedented global bubble boom. To keep its populace happy with an unelected government, it has been building roads, railways, and real estate developments, including cities like Ordos, a complex that can house up to one million people but is completely empty! China's capacity for major industries, from cement to aluminum to steel, has expanded to 20% to 40% more than its current production and world demand. China's economy is not driven largely by growing consumer demand like it is in the United States. Instead, in China 35% of GDP is driven by exports and 50% or more is driven by fixed-capital investment, largely by the government.

In short, China is building at a hurried pace for a future that will not materialize as a result of a slowing world economy and the rapid aging of its own population. China will be the last bubble to burst. That bursting will slow down the emerging countries in Asia, Latin America, the Middle East, and Africa that are supplying China's unprecedented infrastructure boom with materials and energy. Excess capacity and an eventual slowdown in China's purchase of commodities will bring the next commodity price collapse between 2011 and 2015, which will hurt the economies of most emerging countries. This will be a bust and deflation crisis worldwide, not just in the developed world.

You can get free access to Harry's very popular webinar
"Understanding the Economy and What Lies Ahead" by visiting
and registering at http://www.hsdent.com/webinar.

Demographic cycles peak around every 39 to 40 years, as we show in
Chapter 2. However, commodity cycles, which are more likely to drive
economies and exports in most emerging countries, occur every 29 to 30
years on average. Our reliable 29- to 30-Year Commodity Cycle, shown in
Chart 1-5, is set to peak between mid-2008 and mid- to late 2011 or so.
This cycle is not likely to turn upward again until the early 2020s, which
indicates a slowdown in most emerging countries in the decade ahead,
despite continued growth in demographic trends. We will cover this topic,
along with the very different factors that drive emerging country economies and growth, in Chapter 8.

**Emerging countries from Asia and Latin America to the Middle
East and Africa will be the clear growth areas of the world for decades
to come after the developed countries age and slow demographically.**

Chart 1-5: The 29- to 30-Year Commodity Price Cycle

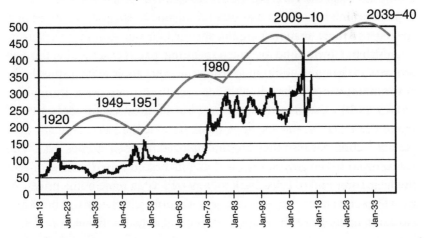

CRB Index (PPI before 1947) 1913–2040

Data Source: **Bloomberg**

However, the next concerted growth surge for the world and emerging countries is not likely to reemerge until 2020–2023. India is more likely than China to be the rising star of the next global boom as time moves forward.

The Government's Response: Anything But Pain

For consumers in the United States and most developed economies, the change from an economy based on consumption to one based on savings might sound reasonable (especially given the aging of the baby boomers). However, such change is not what governments want, especially not the US government. Why? Because it's economically painful to the nation as a whole in the short term—just look at what happened in the United States from 1930 to 1933! As we shrink our economy or deleverage the credit outstanding, there will be a dramatic slowdown and even a temporary decline in the standard of living. This shows up in many ways—such as higher unemployment, failing banks, falling business activity, and falling asset prices—that impact household net worth. While everyone supports more financial responsibility, they support it more in theory than in reality. When these undesirable side effects arise, there is an outcry for the government to fix the situation. When unemployment runs high, people always ask what the government will do to fix it.

While it might strike you as odd for anyone to suggest that more borrowing and more spending are the answer to a situation that arose from too much borrowing and too much spending, that is exactly what the government is doing, in addition to using the other tools at its disposal. The government can and has directly intervened in many ways throughout history and in the present downturn, but its most useful tools are still interest rates, taxes, and spending plans. To ease the pain that many people are feeling because they are unemployed, as their homes decline in value, or both, the government is doing its best to raise the level of economic activity and to bring back jobs as well as increase home prices. As we will explain later, these governmental actions ultimately will not work. No government has ever been able to prevent a major bubble from deflating or to stop an aging generation from saving, but it can slow the process and ease the pain temporarily—however, only at great expense, as Japan has proven over two decades of economic malaise.

The government is taking on more debt through its own borrowing and its own activities in an effort to stimulate lending and spending. In short, the US government wants us to do a lot more of what got us into trouble in the first place. This does not mean that our representatives do not understand the situation. Instead, what we have been told is that we should work toward an economic recovery quickly and then work on our fiscal responsibility later. What if "later" never comes, as has been the case for the Japanese economy for the last two decades?

The hope is that you and I as consumers and business owners will suddenly feel more confident and will spend more of our money as well as grow our businesses. However, that assumes that the reason we're not spending today is because of a lack of confidence, which isn't true. The reason we are not spending is because our kids are leaving the nest and we as consumers are now more interested in saving for the next stage of our lives: retirement. This trend of kids leaving the nest will accelerate from 2012 forward, making the demographic downtrend more obvious and the government's efforts to fight it more difficult. Businesses, having recognized that our spending patterns have changed, have lowered their output to match the new level of demand. Stimulus programs were begun back in May 2008 and have taken several forms over the past two years. None of the stimulus programs so far has had lasting effects. While some have had a dramatic immediate impact (think of the Car Allowance Rebate System, aka "cash for clunkers," or the First-Time Home Buyer Credit), none has done the job that it was intended to do, which was to stimulate greater demand that would last well beyond the program.

Regarding the larger stimulus plan, which was passed in spring 2009, $800 billion has flowed to many different corners of the country and the world. Unfortunately, much of that money has gone to entities such as cities and states that were poorly run to begin with. Cities and states not only are facing annual budget deficits, but also are under contract to fund tremendous obligations, such as pensions and health care for retired workers. Local governments simply do not have the money to fund such obligations fully. Many states borrow money just to balance their books on an annual basis. Sending even more funds to entities that were running deficits to begin with does not solve the issue; it simply pushes it down the road to be dealt with another day.

To handle our current economic situation more effectively, the US government should instead look toward reducing the amount of debt outstanding in the private sector. While economic activity has slowed of its own accord due to the changing situation and goals of the boomers, the depth and breadth of the downturn has been made dramatically worse because of the explosion in debt that occurred in the 2000s.

In order to erase the unprecedented bubble of the Roaring 2000s, we anticipate devastating losses in housing and business values. Bringing down debt to match this decline would require a write-off of up to $20 trillion in private debt (roughly the amount incurred in the United States from 2000 to 2008). Such a write-off would create savings of well over $1 trillion in interest and principal payments a year for consumers and businesses; now that's a stimulus program that keeps paying off year after year for decades! That level of debt deleveraging is greater than the entire federal debt, which is now approaching $15 trillion.

This overhang of debt and its eventual deleveraging will make the next economic downturn even more painful, just like a detox program is for a drug addict. However, it is the only long-term solution. If the government does not deal with the problem and allow these debts to be written off, as occurred in the early 1930s, we will experience a very-long-term economic malaise, just as the Japanese have experienced for 22 years. Japan still has a weak economy and ever-rising government debt and debt ratios. History will not look kindly on Japan for its unwillingness to make hard decisions about major debt restructuring after its massive real estate and debt bubble of the 1980s!

The US economy and stock market are on "crack." Government stimulus has been a major factor in fueling the greatest credit and real estate bubble in history, and now the government is desperately trying to keep the bubble going at all costs. Funds from the even more desperate second quantitative easing stimulus program (QE2), which the federal government put in place from late 2010 into 2011, have not been going to consumers or into bank lending, but have been flowing directly into higher yielding bonds, commodities, and stocks. This misdirection of funds has led to a third and final bubble that will burst

between late 2011 and late 2014 but is likely to burst the most between early 2012 and late 2013.

On the employment side, we should pursue activities that would help to rebuild America. That rebuilding is not just about building roads and bridges and shoring up physical infrastructure, although that is important to do. It is also about rebuilding our electronic data infrastructure, including health records and educational reform. The idea is to help those who are currently unemployed through this difficult economic Winter Season while at the same time providing tangible results that improve the nation over time and generate revenues that can pay off the debts required for the investment. This is infinitely more attractive than temporary stimulus programs that create debt for only short-term results at best.

Businesses and Consumers: What We Can Do Right Now

The government has a lot on its plate, but so do business owners. Is now the time to expand? Should you be taking out a loan? What about that office building that suddenly got cheaper? All of these are questions that business owners are asking themselves. Our advice is to remain very conservative through at least 2013 and possibly through 2014 if the government drags out the artificial recovery a bit longer. This is a time to conserve your assets, meaning cash and credit lines. Create a business plan as to which competitors you would like to buy or which clients you would like to have. In the months and years ahead, you should be able to expand your business using your cash and credit to buy those competitors that overextended or that were inefficient to begin with. Expanding in good times is easy; there is plenty of growth for you and your competitors to share. Living and managing a business during a downturn with a shrinking economic pie is very difficult and comes with hard decisions, such as firing long-term employees and shedding lower-performing businesses and assets. Business owners who make it through such bad times should be well prepared when the next season of growth begins and are likely to gain market share, dominating their markets for decades to come.

The personal side is not much different—each of us is running a business: our personal household. During the current economic Winter Season you should not be looking for as much growth in your portfolio and assets, because this season is marked by deflation and low returns, especially on the typical fixed-income investments that are best for retirement. Instead, you should be using the time to generate and cultivate streams of income. The idea is first to preserve the capital and assets you have, and then to receive or create as much income as possible, thereby growing your capital base as prices fall. This will set you up to buy assets at even lower prices in the years to come, which will prepare you for the next economic season.

Now is a crucial time for those who are close to college age. Unfortunately, much of the advice that you will receive will be based on the recent past. Many vocations or career paths that will be suggested will follow the assumption that our economy is going to bounce back quickly. You should call into question even the basic determination of whether to go to college. Is it worth it for what you want to do? Is an Ivy League education worth pursuing if it means accruing hundreds of thousands of dollars of debt? These questions become more important when the possibility of high-income growth in your working years is less certain.

As we contemplate the previous two decades, we should recognize them for what they were: a period of high growth that was driven by the concerted earning and spending patterns of the baby boom generation, exaggerated by an unprecedented debt bubble. We have since moved to a period that is marked by greater savings, less spending, and the deleveraging of debt and that could last well into the next decade. This change in economic season will have profound effects in many areas of life, including employment, income, personal portfolios, business valuations, health care, and education. If we understand what led us to this point, we may be able to manage the situation not only to protect what we have, but also to assist those who are in need. If we do not recognize the factors at work, which are mostly driven by individual demands and desires, then we risk throwing the wealth of the nation into programs and efforts that are doomed to fail. Just as "China will save us" is not the answer, neither is hoarding gold or Swiss francs. Investors who have done well in these investments are simply projecting out recent returns and could end up meeting the same fate as those who thought real estate couldn't go down in the 2000s. We are likely to see gold start to decline, as we warned in

March 2011. It may rise once more as 2012 approaches before collapsing for years ahead, much as oil did from 2008 onward.

The aging of massive baby boom generations among nations across the wealthy developed world and the deleveraging of the greatest credit bubble in history will lead to deflation in prices. The 1970s was what we call the economic Summer Season, characterized by rising inflation (like rising temperatures) because of the sluggish productivity that accompanies the integration of large numbers of young adults into our economy. We are entering an economic Winter Season, similar to that of the 1930s, in which deflation (or falling temperatures) is the trend, as populations age rapidly in the still-dominant developed countries from Europe to North America to East Asia.

While some analysts and forecasters see this debt crisis for what it really is, most still think that the massive stimulus from the government is going to create inflation due to the unprecedented printing of money and low interest rates. They are wrong, and their strategies for the future likewise will be wrong. Deflation requires personal and business strategies that are entirely different from strategies used during other economic trends—and that is what we will be talking to you about in this book.

In Chapter 2 we look at the primary argument that we have been making for over 20 years: that the main trend that drives economic growth, inflation, home buying, and almost everything else is demographics. We will show how people do predictable things as they age, affecting every facet of our economy, and why the largest generation in history will be saving more, spending less, and causing deflationary trends as they increasingly retire.

Demographic Trends Are the Key Driver of Our Economy: Why Consumers Matter More Than Government

On Tuesday morning, September 11, 2001, I, Rodney Johnson, was sitting at my desk at work in Dallas, Texas. At a few minutes after 8:00 a.m. CDT, a bond salesman friend of mine called and asked if I'd seen that a plane just hit one of the World Trade Center towers. I turned to the television to watch. My friend and I discussed how strange it was that a plane should hit the tower given that flight patterns don't go anywhere close to that part of Manhattan. We gabbed about what type of plane it might have been. Then the news helicopters began streaming live video and all hell broke loose.

Within an hour the next plane hit. A plane crashed into the Pentagon. There was a rumor of another plane in trouble somewhere on the East Coast; that plane later went down in a Pennsylvania field. The president of the United States was on a plane. My wife received a call that our children were being released from school immediately. I closed the office of HS Dent. By 11:30 a.m. I was at home.

The phone rang and a familiar voice said, "Hello, Rodney, this is your uncle David. My plane was forced to land at DFW and now I'm being kicked out of the airport. Come and get me." I had not seen or spoken to Uncle David in two years. My life was very busy with small children, and he lived far away in Alabama. When I arrived, Uncle David told me that his flight was originally bound for Colorado, but when the towers were struck all air traffic was required to land at the first available airport. To emphasize the point, military jets were escorting planes and circling the airports. Once on the ground, planes sat on the tarmac for over an hour before the passengers were allowed to deplane. Everyone's cell phones were buzzing, so the passengers were filled in quickly on the events of the day.

In the terminal, announcements were made that the airport would be closing completely. Everyone was required to leave immediately, to get off the premises now. With thousands of passengers diverted, there were no rental cars to be had. There were no hotel rooms. There was only mass confusion. My uncle and I did the only logical thing. We went to lunch. We drove to the original Chili's restaurant in Dallas on Greenville Avenue and found the place jam-packed. Apparently we were not alone in our impulse to go out to eat. That evening my uncle borrowed one of our cars and drove back home to Alabama.

The days after 9/11 were chaotic, to say the least. Were more attacks imminent? Who was responsible? What would happen to the US economy? Would anyone venture to a public place in the future, given fear of an attack? At HS Dent, even though the markets were closed, our phones were ringing off the hook. For over a decade we had forecast that the US economy would continue its growth trajectory until 2007–2010, largely based on consumer spending. Considering the events of that fateful day and the presumed shift in people's behavior (stay indoors, away from malls, etc.), were we going to change our forecast? We told people the truth: "We will wait and see how individuals react." Even before 2001 we had often been asked what could derail our forecast for strong consumption through the end of the 2000s. We usually pointed to a war on our soil, which had not happened since the mid-1800s. Well, here it was: the terrorists brought the fight to us.

Then an odd, unexpected thing happened; Americans went shopping. In fact, October 2001 clocked the highest auto sales in US history up to that point. US consumers quickly regained their economic footing. We were beginning to emerge from a recession (albeit the lightest recession ever recorded) after the dot.com bust, we had just experienced a terrorist attack, and the US was soon to enter two wars, but the economy continued its mending and moved on to sustained growth, just as we had forecast. We did not see 9/11, of course, but what we saw was the power of an incredible force, that of personal consumer spending.

Why did consumers bounce right back after 9/11? There is no question that the nation felt badly and that consumers were dramatically impacted in a very negative way, so it was not a matter of our sentiment driving us higher (so much for consumer confidence being the driver of consumer spending as economists are arguing for today!). The sheer enormity of the situation was clear to everyone; we would soon be committing soldiers to combat operations in which young men would die. Terrorists bent on the destruction of the US or at least of our way of life had proven in dramatic fashion that they could cause mayhem. Still, we not only continued our trend of consumption, but took it to new heights, growing our spending, our economy, and especially our debt. How could this be? Why would frightened people spend more and borrow more? The answer is that consumers are not just units of potential or actual economic activity; consumers are people, too—with predictable needs and spending habits as they age.

The Third Dimension of Economics: Want

The field of economics tends to treat consumers as faceless masses, herding together and reacting to whatever stimulus is placed before them. Or even worse, the field of economics treats consumers as if they can be summed up in the notion of one "model consumer" whose actions are reactions that can be estimated, measured, and even manipulated with great accuracy. Whether it be higher interest rates, cheaper dollars, lower prices, or greater choice, economic theory uses a couple of lines on a supply/demand graph to explain what people will do and why, all on the basis of external forces (price, quantity, etc.). All points are connected on these demand curves, which lead to a nice, two-dimensional representation of all potential outcomes. This is bunk! Just on the face of it, we know that these assumptions and assertions are not true!

Most economic theory begins with the premise that consumers *must* demand things, and that all forces are external and quantifiable. If prices go down, we buy more; if prices go up, we buy less—and that's true up to a point, affecting only marginal demand. When the economic disasters of the 1930s proved this basic premise wrong (prices fell dramatically, but spending did not increase) and pointed out that there might be more to the economy than previously thought, John Maynard Keynes described a lack of spending as a lack of confidence in the future. While this has some merit at the extreme, it is woefully short of explaining the whole picture. What Keynes was trying to explain is why people save money; however, he was creating an explanation inside of the same old economic theories. His view that people were scared or lacked confidence implied that the desire to consume existed at the same level as it had before the crisis. Why does this have to be the case?

Keynes should have been asking a bigger question. Is it possible that people could change their spending habits, and what might make this happen? In the short run, such a change could reflect a lack of confidence when something dramatic happens (such as the odd financial meltdown, a market collapse, etc.). In the long run, our view is that the spending habits of consumers change because their situations change as people; in effect, we have a natural "life cycle." As we go through our lives, we have different needs, wants, and abilities. Sometimes saving is a great idea. Sometimes spending is what serves us best. Sometimes spending our parents' money makes sense. It is the recognition of this change in our circumstances as consumers that most economists miss entirely. This recognition is what we believe is missing from mainstream economics, and certainly it is what we believe is missing from the analysis of Keynes.

Keynes identified continued savings as a "disease" that was caused by a lack of confidence. His theory was that people were fearful that prices would continue to fall, which of course they will in a deflationary era, so people were holding back on their spending. Keynes then developed a prescription for curing the disease—extensive government spending to restore the business cycle to growth. Unfortunately, because he had misdiagnosed the disease, his prescription made no sense and has never worked to create renewed prosperity, as we will address later. To put it another way, this may have been the worst economic innovation in history! But that has not stopped governments and political pundits from pursuing such strategies, as it is a great way to offer an "instant cure" for people's economic ailments. Of course, it is also government controlled, which is always a plus if you are a politician. They believe that failure to achieve results is no reason to abandon their efforts; instead, they choose to redouble them. If only we spend even more, we will get the desired effects!

None of this is meant to be a disparagement of economists or of economic theory over the past hundred years; we have to remember their circumstances. At the end of the nineteenth century our economy was changing. We were on the verge of moving through the Industrial Revolution and into a time of plenty after being in a period of scarcity since the beginning of time. Think about that for a minute. In 1900, there were almost no cars and therefore no tractors (not to mention hot showers and flush toilets). Farming was still a very labor intensive and inefficient occupation that operated along much the same principles as it had for 10,000 years. In 1900, almost 40% of the population worked on farms. By the year 2000, less than 2% of the population worked on farms (see box, page 319). The amount of discretionary income spent on food dropped from 25% in 1900 to about 10% by 2000.* Henry Ford brought us the production line, which vastly improved our ability to manufacture, and with that productivity wages soared. Through innovation, technology, and new management techniques, we were able to provide mass quantities of standardized products, hence lowering costs and making such goods available to the broader public. These changes dramatically increased the standard of living for the everyday citizen through both lower costs of goods and higher wages. That is the history of economics, which took a quantum leap in the early 1900s.

At the same time the storehouse of value for the individual was changing from real estate or land holdings, given that it was an agrarian society, to that of currency or coin, which was more reasonable for an urban society. The US was becoming city-based; most citizens did not grow or raise their own food, did not make their own clothes, and did not build their own shelters any longer. The country was quickly changing into a society of much more specialized workers who used their income to purchase all of the diverse things needed for everyday life. The history of economics, going back to Adam Smith, is all about the greater specialization of labor in order to raise the standard of living for all. As this transformation occurred, the ability of consumers to choose *less* consumption never seemed to enter the minds of economists. The idea that a consumer would hoard cash—not spending it, not investing it, just simply having that stored-up consumptive energy ready for whenever the consumer wanted it—was not considered. This break in the continuum of spending along the price quantity line created by savings is what sent most of the field of

* Paarlberg & Paarlberg.

economics into a tailspin. Consumers were too cautious. They were too pessimistic. They were greedy, just waiting for even lower prices. They were dumbstruck by the events of the day. There is another possibility.

Retirement for the masses. Social Security–style government payments for all only began as a concept in the 1930s, coinciding with the emergence of middle-class living standards and longer life spans. As the consumers got older, their needs and desires changed. They no longer wanted to buy everything possible. With their kids out of the nest, consumers were now more interested in saving for tomorrow. As the economic situation deteriorated even further in the 1930s, the need and desire to save grew only stronger. This is where we have been able to bring greater understanding to the field of economics, by recognizing and documenting the predictable consumer spending patterns that exist over a consumer's lifetime.

For over 20 years we have been explaining to audiences and readers (via *The Great Boom Ahead*, 1992; *The Roaring 2000s*, 1998; *The Great Depression Ahead*, 2008, among others) that there is more to consumers than a couple of lines on a price/quantity graph or an interest rate spending/saving graph. There is also the internal motivation of the consumer, which changes over time and is based not only on the consumer's forecast or confidence in tomorrow or their price quantity preference, but also on the consumer's personal situation, which can change dramatically as a person ages.

Who among us had the same priorities and preferences at 25 years old vs. at 55 years old? How absurd is it to believe that what will influence or persuade a young college graduate is the same as what will sway a new mother or an empty-nester couple or even a retiree? As we move through our lives, we change. Target Marketing 101 tells you to determine your best client or most likely buyer and then focus on that person or group. Who is going to market minivans or reading glasses to a person right out of college? What financial advisor is going to spend all of his time trying to find twentysomethings with money to invest? Or what dirt bike manufacturer is going to spend its ad budget in *AARP* magazine? These are obvious, outrageous examples, but they serve as illustrations of the fact that in clear, measurable ways, we change our consumption habits as we age.

Consider McDonald's, the purveyor of fast food. For over 60 years the company has brought us its basic offering of a small number of menu items prepared in a systematic way meant to keep quality consistent and time to a minimum. On the face of it (burgers, fries, etc.), their offerings seem appropriate for the young, but McDonald's keeps pushing the envelope, adding things like salads to its menu. These items clearly are not aimed at teenagers. They are aimed at the largest segment of our economy, the boomers, who are getting older and do not spend as much time in fast-food restaurants, and when they do find themselves in these establishments, they tend to want healthier food. In short, businesses adapt or die, but old, broken economic theories live on!

What Motivates Us: We Are All in It for Ourselves

I, Harry Dent, did not just happen upon the relationship between age and spending. I was researching demand patterns for my consulting clients from the largest Fortune 100 to the smallest new ventures—why people buy stuff—and had gathered a tremendous amount of data. Two of the many charts I developed were births in the US and the S&P 500 adjusted for inflation. I discovered the correlation by accident in 1988 when I saw the two graphs on my desk at the same time. The similarity between the shapes of the two graphs was astounding. However, the dates of the curves were just over 45 years apart, and I already knew from demographic research that the peak spending age for the average family was in the mid- to late 40s. So I didn't consider this a random correlation, as many economists would; I knew the reason right away. Many charts can correlate without good reasons, being completely unrelated but having similar patterns. A common example is a chart that plots the production of butter in Bangladesh, which happens to match a chart of the S&P 500 very closely. This does not mean that the two charts have anything in common whatsoever. The two charts are a coincidence; they do not have a causal relationship. This is where I began searching out the data in more depth. What was the connection between births and the growth of the economy and equity markets, inflation, borrowing, investing, purchasing homes, camping equipment, and so on? This is the genesis of HS Dent, and what has driven our research for over two decades.

One of the most comprehensive surveys out there is the US Consumer Expenditure Survey, which has been conducted by the US government every year since 1984 (previous surveys were conducted in 1975 and 1982). The survey is comprised of a diary portion and an interview portion. The main purpose is to determine what people buy. There are well over a thousand different categories for spending (alcohol for home consumption, alcohol away from home, etc.). The survey also asks many descriptive questions about the consumer, concerning age, sex, marital status, income, education, employment, family size, etc. In essence, this one survey provides a cross-sectional look at consumers, detailing not only who they are, but also what they buy. This allows researchers to look at the data in several ways, including using the data to determine what type of person buys a specific good or service. In this way I was able to connect the dots between spending and people.

In addition to providing a tremendously detailed look at what type of person bought a product or paid for a service, the survey also showed information in the aggregate. So we were able to verify quickly from a US government survey that consumers, on average, spend the most money between ages 45 and 49. This dovetailed exactly with the discovery of the similarity between the birth chart and the S&P 500. What we understood from the Consumer Expenditure Survey was that consumers grow their spending through their adult life, peaking in spending at approximately age 46 just as their kids tend to leave the nest for the average person (it is later for higher-income households with kids who go to school longer). The linchpin is that this spending drives the economy higher. As the economy rises, corporate profits rise as well. It is this follow-through, from predictable consumer spending habits to economic activity to corporate profits to the equity markets, that was such a breakthrough. Because this study is conducted every year, we could narrow down over time that the peak in average household spending did indeed occur around age 46, indicating that there is a consistent pattern, rather than the peak in spending changing from year to year.

To make this knowledge useful, we had to find out how many people are in our economy at each age. Is the number of people reaching age 46 rising or falling? Will the trend be toward a growing or a shrinking economy? Finding the answer as to the spread of the population by age was not as simple as it sounds, as the Census Bureau does not reconcile from year to year; instead, it tries to get only an accurate estimate of people in each singular year. To arrive at a reasonable estimate of the number of people in the US at each age, we took data from the National Center for Health Statistics (NCHS) to determine how many live births there are in the US every year, which gave us the Birth Index. To enhance this information in 1996, we adjusted the Birth Index to include immigrants. Using information from the US Immigration and Naturalization Service, we then were able to put immigrants in their proper birth year. If a person immigrates to the United States in 1990 and that person is 20 years old, then on the Birth Index that person would be put in the year 1970. Using this approach, we get an accurate picture of the true age of people in the United States. This adjustment is crucial given that we have experienced massive immigration in the past decades.

We then take this Immigration-Adjusted Birth Index and move it forward 46 years to estimate the ebb and flow of economic activity (**Chart 2-1**). This gives us a remarkably accurate forecast of economic activity based on when the population will reach its peak spending years, shown in **Chart 2-2.**

This insight—the ability to forecast whether the economy would grow or contract based simply on demographics—was a giant leap forward in

Chart 2-1: Immigration-Adjusted Birth Index

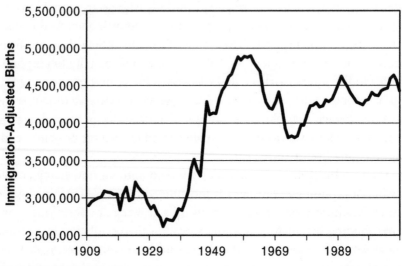

Data Source: **Census Bureau**

Chart 2-2: Spending Wave, Births Lagged for Peak in Spending

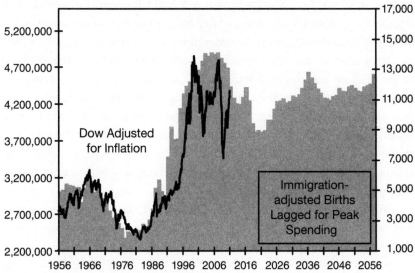

Births Lagged for Peak Spending

Data Source: Census Bureau, Bloomberg, HS Dent

economics, as it speaks directly to the internal motivations of consumers. Think about the story at the beginning of this chapter: 9/11. We each have a story about this fateful day. What is so amazing is that we did not as a nation simply snap our wallets shut. And it was not just 9/11. What about Black Monday in 1987? The first Gulf War in 1990? The meltdown of Long-Term Capital Management and the Russian bond default in 1998? The dot.com bust? The wars in Afghanistan and Iraq? Oil at over $140 per barrel? In response to each of these, we as American consumers continued to shop. There's no question that we felt badly and that our confidence was shaken, but still we spent. Looking back at **Chart 2-2,** you can see that even though these bad things happened, we were in a fundamentally growing economy based on demographic forces. What looked like resilience or even sometimes irrational behavior was simply 92 million Americans raising their families.

In addition to seeing aggregate demand, we at HS Dent were able to see an entire economic life plan laid out before us. This life plan wasn't based just on what a consumer might buy; instead it was based on where consumers are in their personal lives. Where a person is in his or her personal life is what drives him or her to purchase specific things. You can think about your consumer life cycle mirroring your personal life cycle. Generally speaking, a young person will enter the workforce at around age 20, depending on education. After that a very typical pattern evolves, which includes living in multifamily units, or apartments, and spending on items such as camping, gyms, and beer. In our mid-twenties we tend to get married and combine households. Americans typically get married at age 26 and have their first child around age 28, thereby starting the long process of family spending. This family spending involves buying a first home around age 31, buying a trade-up home between ages 37 to 42, and finally peaking in expenditures around age 46, with a plateau of spending into age 50, as the children are leaving the nest, depending on whether they go to college or not.

The ages and stages of life as illustrated in **Chart 2-3** are well documented. Now think about the things we buy at each age and stage of life. Better yet, consider what we buy and what we do not buy. Common sense

Chart 2-3: Change in Spending at Each Age and Stage of Life

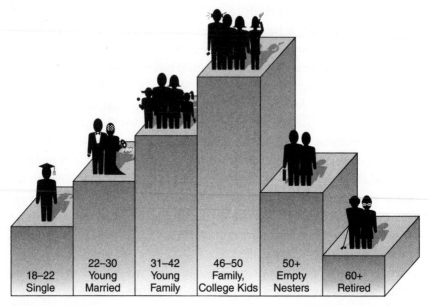

| 18–22 Single | 22–30 Young Married | 31–42 Young Family | 46–50 Family, College Kids | 50+ Empty Nesters | 60+ Retired |

Data Source: **HS Dent**

will show you that what we want and therefore purchase changes over time. Minivans typically are not purchased by 23-year-old single men, but instead are bought by families with young children. Designer clothes for teens are bought by parents in their 40s, not parents in their 20s or early 30s with toddlers. The greatest quantity of breakfast cereal is bought when the head of household is in his or her late 30s, which corresponds exactly to this person having had his or her children around the age of 28 to 32 years and to these children being 6 to 10 years old and eating cereal by the bucketful!

After our children leave home, our goals change. No longer do we need the newest gadgets, bigger cars, or ever more designer clothes. We start looking further down the road. What we see in front of us is scary—we're talking about retirement, and it's not that far away. By the time that we reach 50 years old, retirement is only 15 short years away. Unfortunately, most of us have not prepared very well. According to the US Federal Reserve's Survey of Consumer Finance from 2007 (the latest available survey), of Americans 45 to 54 years old, the median value of financial assets held (meaning the value right in the middle) was $42,400. This means that if you lined up everyone in America between those ages and sorted them by the amount of financial assets they have, such as stocks, bonds, cash-value life insurance, IRAs, etc., the person with $42,400 would be exactly in the middle. If you are 50 years old and have saved only $40,000 for retirement, you have a lot of catching up to do!

If we look at the next group, those 55 to 64 years old, the numbers are better; their median amount of financial assets is $85,700. That's an improvement, to be sure, but is it great that the median person around 60 years old has only roughly $90,000 socked away for retirement? Of course not! You can see how someone's goals and priorities would change dramatically! It's no wonder that spending habits change dramatically after the children leave home (typically between ages 46 and 50), when consumers are still working and earning, because consumers, who are people, too, are clearly focused on preparing for the next big stage of life—retirement—as they should be!

So what steps do consumers take to prepare for retirement? We pay down debt, save, and invest. However, it doesn't mean that we live badly; far from it. It simply means that the days of large, leveraged purchases are usually behind us—those types of purchases that are based on credit. We might still buy new cars or go on trips, but we tend to pay more in cash rather than relying as much on credit or loans as we would have in the past. In general, people in their 50s and 60s don't drive cars nearly as much as soccer moms, who cart the kids to school and soccer practice.

Understanding just these few concepts should you give you enough insight to see how our urbanized, modern economy is based on demographics and on the resulting personal needs and wants of consumers. Everything that we discuss happens inside of the family or has to do with a person's age and stage of life. This does not mean that outside factors don't count, simply that they are not the only drivers of how people decide what to buy and when to buy.

Looking at the Economy Over Generations: The Pattern Repeats

Looking at **Chart 2-1,** the Immigration-Adjusted Birth Index, you can see the tremendous rise in births from about the late 1930s through the early 1960s, which, of course, represents the baby boomers. Think about this group as they have gone through the different ages and stages of life so far. As they started elementary school in the 1950s and 1960s, there was not enough space; we were building a school every 6 feet, or so it seemed. Moving on, in the late 1960s and 1970s, there were not enough jobs for all of those young people entering the economy. Once they were working and starting families in the 1980s and 1990s, consumer spending and therefore economic activity exploded.

You can see that the number of people born each year changes dramatically over time, going up and down in waves. These waves represent generations, which we discussed in great detail in previous books. It is important to focus on the size of the waves, or generations, because the size of the group is what gives it power, as the number of people all doing the same thing at the same time creates a "thundering herd." Just as the boomers have stretched and changed every part of the economy they have touched as they have gone through their economic lives, they have also left something behind: excess capacity. The reason is because the generation after them is smaller.

After the boomers finished the preteen stage of life, we had too many elementary schools because there simply were not enough people behind the boomers to fill the gap. The good news is that there is another large generation already in the economy, the young group that was born from 1977 through around 2007, which will walk up its own Spending Wave as those consumers go through the very predictable ages and stages of their lives.

Generations tend to come in approximate 40-year waves, with a wave comprising the full rise and fall of births. With regard to the baby boom generation, the wave actually includes a falling number of births in the years 1962 through 1976. For marketing purposes, we call this group generation X (Gen-X), but it is really part of the full late 1930s to mid-70s generation. If we look at the Birth Index and keep in mind the very predictable nature of consumption, we can see how long, 40-year waves emerge. **Chart 2-4** shows how our stock market has peaked every 39 years in the last century. After the stock peak in 1929, it took until 1953—24 years later—for stocks to get back to the level reached in 1929. After the peak in 1968, it took 25 years. What if you had been retiring around those tops? How would your portfolio have performed in your retirement years that followed?

Chart 2-4: 39- to 40-Year Generation Cycle of S&P 500 Adjusted for Inflation

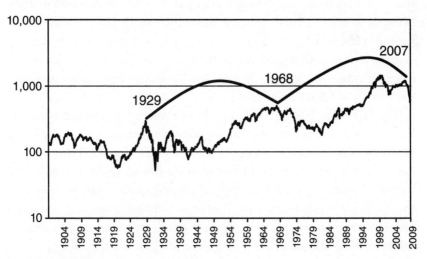

Data Source: **Bloomberg**

Generational waves regularly occur as a sequence of large waves of similar duration and magnitude. A large generation of people well beyond anything previously seen is followed by a generation that is of similar size. This pattern brings with it interesting social and economic dynamics.

Inflation/Productivity

When a new generation that is much larger than previous generations first enters the economy, it is very expensive. Think about who provides for all those children. The US Department of Agriculture estimates that it takes $222,000 for a middle-income family to raise a child born today. This does not include college. That is just to feed and clothe the child and get him or her out of the door at 18. This tremendous burden is borne by the parents. However, who provides the public education? Who provides the roads and other infrastructure necessary to accommodate all of the extra people? It is the greater society through the government. So while this new group of very young people is finding its way, the rest of the country is paying for it! When this group leaves home and enters the workforce, the burden becomes even greater. Because this is the largest generation so far in a society, there are not immediately enough job openings to employ them. Even if there were enough job openings, the workers themselves, being fresh out of school, are very unproductive. This is the driving force behind traditional inflation. When you track workforce growth on a 2.5-year lag to account for gains in productivity and compare it with the government's main measure of inflation, the Consumer Price Index (CPI), the correlation in **Chart 2-5** is very high.

The last huge bout of inflation in our society happened when the baby boomers were entering the workforce en masse. This huge influx of young people who were unproductive caused massive dislocations in our economy. Once the flow of new workers slowed down and the bulk of the baby boomers became more productive, inflation started to fall and the economy began to pick up. This huge inflationary/innovation boom occurs when a large generation enters the economy. Because generational waves arrive in the pattern of a very large wave followed by one of similar size, huge inflationary pressures tend to come every 80 years, or every other generation. We have written at length about this subject, including

Chart 2-5: Inflation Indicator, Workforce Growth vs. CPI

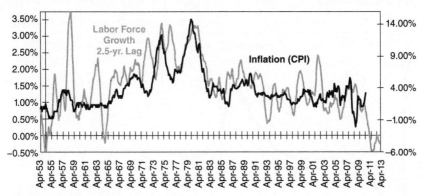

Data Source: Bureau of Labor Statistics, HS Dent

the interplay of S-curves and productivity gains. If you would like to read a greater explanation of this, please refer to *The Great Depression Ahead,* pp. 51–70.

But it's not all bad! This incredible influx of young people is also the great driver of innovation. As the boomers entered the workforce in the late 1960s and 1970s, the seeds of the next generation of technological advances were being sown. From personal computers to the internet, the roots of our digital society can be traced back to this period. Looking back a full 80 years, we can see the automobile, the airplane, and the harnessing of electricity all coming about at the turn of the twentieth century. So while the explosion of people into the economy every 80 years causes a surge of inflation, it is also a time of great innovation.

Since the second wave of the two-wave, 80-year generational pattern tends to be the same size as the first, the same inflationary pressures are not brought to bear on the economy as the system has already stretched enough to serve a group of that size. It also seems to be the case that the same innovative spirit does not exist either. As to why this is, perhaps it is a reaction to innovative parents, or perhaps it is the overbearing nature of the preceding generation. This is up for debate and has been well covered by authors such as William Strauss and Neil Howe (*The Fourth Turning*).

If we track the force of spending as well as the combined force of inflation/innovation, we can develop what becomes an approximate 80-year economic cycle that allows us to graphically illustrate major trends in our

Chart 2-6: Simple Four-Season Economic Cycle, 80-Year Cycle
in Modern Times

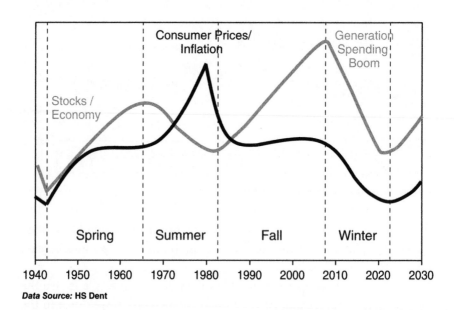

Data Source: **HS Dent**

economy decades in advance—**Chart 2-6.** We break this chart down into
four main sections, or seasons, just like the weather. These four sections
are comprised of roughly 26- and 14-year breaks, which when combined
make 40-year generational waves, with the two combined waves making
the 80-year cycle.

Spring Season: Cautious Growth

After a dramatic crash in our economy that is brought on by strong consumption and a credit bubble, the next generation of spenders will emerge
and begin pushing our economy higher as they spend on their own children. This period is marked by more conservative social attitudes and is
one in which people are generally more risk averse, ever wary of what
happened before. There is not as much innovation during this Season as
people and companies are more focused on making existing technology
more efficient and mass affordable. The 1942–1968 time frame in the US
is a great example of the Spring Season, when the Bob Hope generation

brought autos and air travel into the mainstream. This is a long, 26-year Season.

Summer Season: Innovation/Inflation

The Spring Season is the result of a generation having a large number of children and providing for them. Just as this huge generation of children leaves the nest, the parents spend less and save more, causing an economic malaise because the as yet unproductive generation is entering the workforce just as the old, smaller generation slows its spending, causing a lack of employment opportunities. This is like summer, when the weather is hot and growth is a struggle. The economic Summer Season is shorter, lasting approximately 14 years, and is what occurred in the US from 1969 to 1982. This period was described by Alexander Haig as plagued by "stagflation," a combination of high inflation with a lack of growth. This is interesting because traditional economics will tell you that the combination of no or low growth and inflation is not possible. Inflation is supposed to be caused by too many dollars chasing too few goods because of strong demand. The paradoxical period of the 1970s led economists to question some of their assumptions and to create the new term *stagflation*.

However, with so many young people in the economy, there is a huge positive to the Summer Season—innovation. This is the time when young people, with nothing to lose and a feeling of superiority, try many different things to see what sticks. While it causes social and cultural unrest (think hippies on the White House lawn), it also brings about radical disruptions in technological innovation and business, which sets up the next economic season.

Fall Season: Glorious Growth!

As the large generation of kids finally gets fully into the workforce, becomes productive, starts families, and begins marching up its own Spending Wave, the economy takes off in what we call the economic Fall Season. This would be the long, 26-year-period between 1983 and 2007. Just like fall, the weather is not to hot, not too cold, and there is a lot of harvesting to be done! With all of the technological innovations from the Summer Season in hand, this large, productive, free-spending generation makes great strides in productivity and living standards. This is a Goldilocks period for the economy. Not only is demand marching higher, but productivity is also on the rise, causing inflation to fall. Again, as this happened from the 1980s through the mid-2000s, mainstream economists were flummoxed! How could demand be so incredibly strong and yet inflation was falling? For more than two decades traditional economic theory once again had no answer.

Winter Season: Good Things Don't Last Forever

As the large generation passes its peak in spending and begins to slow, the economy starts to fall. The lack of demand causes falling prices. This situation leads to falling output and rising unemployment, which only exacerbates the lack of demand. Just as fall gives way to winter in weather, our economic Fall Season gives way to our economic Winter Season. This is no longer a period of growth. This vicious cycle causes deflation. While Keynes and others described it as the outcome of fear or uncertainty, when it is actually the very natural outcome of the largest generation changing from a focus on spending to a focus on saving, which shrinks demand and leaves behind excess capacity and a hangover of debt. These conditions typically last around 14 years (1929–1942, and expected from the late 2000s through the early 2020s), before the cycle begins anew and the Spring Season reemerges.

So the 80-year cycle follows a very predictable four-season cycle. When spring arrives after winter it is like an awakening. Things seem new and growth returns. But then summer shows up and it's a little too hot for getting much done; everyone seems to be on vacation. The fall comes along and the weather is perfect much of the time, the harvest is the best of the year, and cupboards and cellars are overflowing. It is during this time that everyone should be thinking about the coming change in the season and salting away as much of the bounty as they can. No matter how good things are, winter will come—sometimes early, sometimes late, but it always shows up. If you have not properly prepared, it could be devastating. If you have prepared, you actually can enjoy some aspects of it.

Mostly, you wait. Finally, when it seems like it will never get warm again, the winter starts to slowly thaw, the days get a little longer, and spring reemerges.

So where are we today? Obviously we are a couple of years into the Winter Season. It will be cold. Many things will perish, and most will go dormant. This does not mean that the economy dies off or that everything must stop! Indeed, just as in nature, a number of areas thrive in winter, but they are not as easy to spot. We must be more diligent in our planning and more flexible in the alternatives that we consider. But the most important insight is simple: you harvest in late fall and look to replant for the next spring season.

If that was all there was to it—a slowdown or decline in spending—perhaps things would not be so bad. Unfortunately, there is more. A lot more! As the boomers spent more, there were many consequences besides just a growing economy. We must deal with the painful process of shrinking the excess capacity that exists because of falling demand. What makes this process such an enormous drag on the economy and the nation is the fact that our demand was not driven just by what we could buy through our own earnings, but also by our ability to borrow. As our nation went further into debt, consumers, businesses, and government entities pushed spending to dizzying heights. We spent OPM (Other People's Money) on cars, houses, TVs, eating out, trips, clothes—you name it, we bought it.

Using debt to purchase items is basically the creation of a claim on future earnings. If we borrow to spend, we are making a pledge to use some of the money we make tomorrow to pay back the debt we are incurring today. This means that we expect our situation to improve in the future or that we are willing to sacrifice some of our future standard of living to make our lives more comfortable today. This is a philosophical way of looking at debt. It is much more likely that consumers, bombarded with offers to take on more debt at every turn, thought, "Why not?"

The rising consumption of our society even got its own name, "conspicuous consumption." The cashier at Target asked, "Would you like to charge this to your Target credit card today?" Every company had its own VISA or MasterCard deal, and home equity loans were all the rage. The world was a giant ATM. All you had to do was promise to pay—and we did. Now the music has stopped.

The huge number of people in the baby boom generation caused a very predictable surge in spending that we have consistently forecast would be followed by a period of economic contraction. Unfortunately, our nation's love affair with debt, which apparently knew no boundaries, caused this surge in spending to go parabolic and create what has become a one-two punch to the economy. We will spend less as boomers prepare for retirement, but at the same time we must pay back the debt we incurred along the way. The overhang of debt in the US and around the world acts like an economic anchor. Each of us understands our own debt; we can simply look at our mortgages, credit cards, auto loans, and whatever else we might carry and add it up. But what about the government debt we carry? Are you aware of how much debt is piled onto taxpayers and constituents at every level? The voter revolt of 2010 is shedding much-needed light on a problem that has been festering for too long unattended. At every level of government we have been growing our debt and liabilities, sometimes for generations, without highlighting how this will affect us in the years ahead. Now that the Winter Season is here, people are finally realizing the enormity of the problems we have with public and private debt. As we will show in Chapter 3, we have entered the economic Winter Season carrying a massive burden on our backs!

The Greatest Real Estate and Credit Bubble in Modern History: Bubbles Almost Always Go Back to Where They Started

From a McMansion to a Shoebox

In the early 2000s, Mark (not his real name) was doing quite well. He was educated, working for an international communications company, and married with children. He bought a house that was befitting his income, a 7,000-square-foot McMansion, and had over $200,000 in his retirement account. Life was good. Mark's wife started a small business in retail. It took quite a bit of start-up capital to get it going. With the house and the cost of education, Mark ended up spending some of their savings outside of retirement accounts to start the business, but he also used credit cards. His debt had grown, but the business seemed to be reaching breakeven.

Mark was getting the urge to start his own business as well. He worked in an area that involved international trade. With his contacts around the world, starting a consulting practice would be simple; he was the product. In 2007, after months of preparation and positioning including the development of several contracts, Mark left his job and ventured out on his own. The contracts were signed. Life was still good, but the storm clouds were gathering.

As the economic crisis developed at the end of 2007 and early 2008, Mark's wife's business faltered. Foot traffic simply vanished. The store closed. In addition, even though Mark had signed contracts from potential clients, they were not calling him for services. In some cases, clients did not pay for services already rendered. The walls began to close in. The debt incurred to finance his wife's business was substantial. Mark's family had no income stream for living expenses. They began living out of their retirement accounts.

Mark and his family moved to another city, rented an apartment, and attempted to sell the "big house." There were no buyers. There were no offers. There was nothing. Mark and his wife rented out the house, but the rent wasn't enough to cover the costs of the mortgage and upkeep. The retirement accounts were dwindling. The consulting service was going nowhere. Near the end of 2008, Mark was looking for a job. Unfortunately, none was available.

By early 2009, Mark and his family were going to food pantries, charities, outreach programs—doing anything and going anywhere to save money. The house was lost to foreclosure. The retirement accounts were tapped out. Mark applied for family assistance at a local charity. Days before his family was to be evicted from their apartment, Mark received a call from that charity. They had found space for Mark, his wife, and his daughters: a dorm-style living arrangement with 260 square feet of living space of their own. They had fallen far.

Mark's story is neither happy nor unique. While not many went through the extremes Mark did, millions of Americans ended up borrowing money, often against ever-rising real estate equity. These Americans were fully confident that they could pay the money back, until their circumstances and the economy changed for the worse. In Mark's case, he spent an entire year living in the cramped space with his family while he looked for a job. He eventually found one and is rebuilding his life. It will take time. This cautionary tale speaks to all of America, as we work through a period of rebuilding after a credit binge. It won't be easy. Most of us will not end up moving from a mansion to a shoebox, but there will be adjustments.

We stressed in Chapter 1 how the greatest debt bubble in history occurred in the last boom, from 1983 to 2007, and especially between 2000 and 2008. The greatest part of that direct debt was in the private sector, not in the federal government. The US government has taken on ballooning debt since the financial crisis began in 2008 as a means to combat the crisis that occurred in the private and financial sectors. An even greater debt exists from the unfunded liabilities for Social Security and Medicare/Medicaid. We will discuss these unfunded liabilities in Chapter 4, along with the $15-trillion-and-rising federal debt, the unsustainability of the federal debt and deficits, and the municipal crisis, which is much smaller but is more immediate. Cities and states will feel the impact on employment (they will have to fire hundreds of thousands of workers) and worker benefits (they will have to slash paychecks and require higher employee contributions into benefit plans) much earlier than will government workers at the federal level. The debt crisis is likely to hit the federal government last, between 2013 and 2015, but will affect us all much more deeply.

Private debt stood at a whopping $42 trillion by 2008, and $22 trillion of that was created in 2000 or later. The amount of private debt we accumulated from the inception of the nation through the year 2000, over 224 years, was more than doubled in just 8 short years! Much of that debt was driven by the most liberal lending standards in American history for homes and commercial real estate combined with a financial innovation in securitization and derivatives that has been unprecedented in modern history.

The real estate and private credit bubbles have only begun to shrink; the process has been stalled somewhat because the US federal government used every tool known to modern economics to prevent the natural deleveraging and meltdown that began in late 2008. We have said from the beginning that the government would not be able to stimulate its way out of the greatest demographic downturn and the greatest credit bubble in modern history. We stand by that forecast and expect to see the consequences between late 2011 and early 2015, which is later than we originally expected, between late 2010 and 2012. We were surprised at the level of stimulus that the US government and the Federal Reserve were willing to extend, and we were even more surprised that the global markets were willing to accept this plan. The global markets reacted very differently to Southern Europe's stimulus plans, which began in April 2010.

In a sense, our current economic woes were baked into the cake as soon as the boomer generation was born. This demographic group, the largest in our nation's history, followed the typical path of consumers over the course of their economic life—working, raising a family, preparing for retirement, and then retiring. Because this normal set of events hap-

pened in an abnormally large generational group, it led to a huge spending
bubble in the US economy about 46 years after the peak in births, right
on cue. It also led to an outsized inflation and innovation wave in new
technologies when these baby boomers were young, and then a greater
productivity wave and new boom in information technologies into the
Roaring 2000s, as we forecast many years ago. This is a replay of the auto,
phone, and electricity boom that first occurred in the Roaring '20s, which
was the last Fall Season of the long-term economic cycle.

The consumer demand that drove our economy so incredibly high during the 1980s, 1990s, and 2000s was very predictable. Even without the
present debt crisis, that cycle was expected to slow down a bit naturally
as the plateau began of the baby boom birth cycle, on a 46-year lag from
2003 to 2007. The economy was expected to diminish further from 2008
to 2011 and to slow dramatically from 2012 onward, as the "baby bust"
really took hold. By then the members of the baby boom generation were
expected to be fading fast. Their kids would be moving almost totally out
of the nest, which would reduce spending demands for the future and
allow for even greater savings for retirement.

What was *not* fully part of the natural ebb and flow of economic forces
based on generational cycles was the amount of money this generation
borrowed to satisfy the desire to spend—especially from 2000 to 2008.
We naturally take on more debt as we age, especially from age 26, as we
get married, to age 37 to 42, as we buy our largest homes. At the same
time, inflation and interest rates naturally fall; it is the Fall Season, as
we described in Chapter 2. As consumers, we took on more than the
normal amount of debt; we took on enough debt to choke an elephant!
The Fall Season always includes bubbles in asset prices like stocks and/or
real estate, because consumption goes on for so long, people believe it is
going to go on forever. This has happened in most every Fall generation
or long-term boom in history. The generation that drives the boom of the
Fall Season has never seen a Winter Season or depression (they are too
young) in which such credit bubbles burst, so they are more likely to borrow to extremes than the previous generation (the Bob Hope generation,
in this case). Unfortunately for us, the Roaring '20s (the last Fall Season)
had nowhere near the credit bubble of recent times, which was driven
by the availability of credit, the mass affordability of homes, and creative
banking.

The sheer magnitude of the debt that we took on is astounding. The debt bubble that accompanied the growth boom of the last economic season required a number of willing participants: consumers to spend, bankers to lend, shadow bankers to lend even more, investors to buy the debt in the form of bonds, lawmakers to deregulate, credit ratings agencies to turn a blind eye, and policy makers to make borrowing cheap through low interest rates and easy monetary policy. Over time, the debt spending machine became a great intertwined mess of motivations that fed on itself. We racked up debt at a rapid pace, and almost everyone benefited—so no one wanted to stop the train of debt and apparent progress. Consumers borrowed too much and creditors lent too much. For whatever reason, we simply did not believe or want to believe that the party would ever end. This always happens toward the end of a Fall Season.

We still don't. The aging baby boomers are still spending (on things other than housing), even though their spending cycle has come to an end. The younger echo boomers are much more cautious across the board, including in their approach to housing, according to our best economic and leading indicators. Inside of the boomer generation, it is the top 20% of households by income, those who got most of the financial gains of the recent decades and also drove the spending and asset bubble, who have not learned anything from the crash of 2008 to early 2009. These boomers are spending freely again, because the Fed has pumped up the stock markets with its quantitative easing, or "crack" injections, and this group gets most of the benefit from those types of wealth gains.

Along the way, a small minority of economists, pundits, and ordinary folks, including ourselves, claimed that our debt binge would end badly—"out there," sometime in the future. Well, the future has arrived. Late 2011 to early 2015 is the period that we will see the great reckoning in debt, and we are even more likely to see this between 2012 and 2013.

The last three years have been painful. People from all walks of life and at all levels of income have had to make many adjustments (and more are to come), but the everyday consumer and household have been hit the hardest. The easy flow of credit has not just been interrupted, it has been cut off—except for government-backed lending for housing, which caused a lot of the problem in the first place. The demand for credit has slowed dramatically, because consumers and businesses are totally saturated with debt after such an unprecedented binge, slower economic growth, very few jobs being created, and home and real estate prices that are still near or below their bottom in May 2009. Our time of reckoning has just begun.

The long process of reducing our debt is underway, but we are not anywhere near the finish line. By understanding how we got to this point and quantifying the amount of debt that we owe, we can begin to see the enormity of the problems we face and to understand exactly what lies ahead—and it's not pretty!

Personal Spending and Debt

As the boomers entered the economy and began progressing through the stages of life, they wanted to spend more—a lot more. There were kids to raise, children's sports and educations to finance, cars and more cars to buy, bigger houses to purchase and furnish, lots of food to be eaten, and most important, our kids had to get into the best schools and colleges. Ninety-two million people (counting immigrants), 65% more than the previous generation, were unleashed on the economy, first as workers, then as the building blocks of families, and finally as spenders. The boomers were marching up their Spending Wave, bursting at the seams to provide for their children and to grow their standard of living. The US economy came out of the malaise of the 1970s and then weathered the harsh, double-dip recessions of 1981 and 1982. After that, interest rates fell, unemployment dropped, and things improved. Life was looking up, but problems were slowly building right below the surface—like a frog sitting in slowly warming water and then realizing as the water finally begins to boil that it's too late to jump out! He's cooked!

"Live within your means" is a good general piece of advice. We all take it to mean that a person should spend only as much money as he or she earns or at best can foresee reliably earning in the future. Most people strive to live this way, using their own income to provide for their family and resorting to outside help only occasionally. External assistance is used once in a while to help with finances, and that assistance is debt or borrowing. Only in modern times, since the end of World War II, has it been natural to borrow money for housing over decades, not just over a few years. Only since the 1950s has it become common to borrow money for everyday spending by using credit cards. And it has been only recently that the ability to purchase items such as fast food from places like McDonald's using plastic became widespread. In American families the idea of using debt only sparingly began to fade over the past six decades, especially in the last two decades. Although we definitely were using our income and modest debt to spend as we advanced in our family spending cycles, which is natural, those sources of funding failed to meet our rising expectations.

So what was a family to do? Stop spending, don't buy that bigger house, forgo the family vacation, tell the kids that Christmas will be light this year, tell the kids you can't afford to have them go to the best schools? Not in America! We instead made the decision to change the mixture of internal and external funding. In short, we loaded on the debt. In this case everyday households took on much more debt than upper-income households, which had experienced significant gains in income and wealth! **Chart 3-1** shows the incredible rise in the debt carried by households over the past 20 years, which peaked in 2008.

This rise in debt corresponds exactly to the years that the largest gener-

Chart 3-1: Household Debt

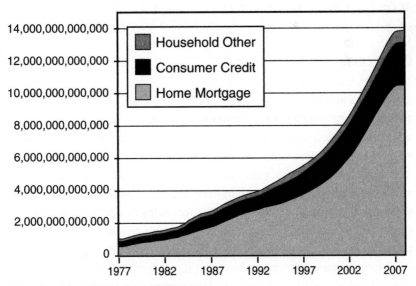

Data Source: Federal Reserve Flow of Funds Report

ation in our economy was raising children. We easily could have foreseen the desire or demand for debt. What we did not expect was the complicit nature of the providers of capital, the US government, and the other players in the debt or credit markets in our demands.

Before we go into just how extreme the credit and debt bubble was in consumer, mortgage, and financial markets for the first time in modern history, let us give a caveat. Before the late 1930s, a home mortgage was a 3- to 5-year note, typically interest only with a balloon payment at the end. The ability to finance a home over 15 or 30 years instead of 3 to 5 years is a sign of progress in higher-middle-class and more creditworthy households that adds a clear and enduring benefit to our financial evolution.

Who would want to wait until the kids had nearly left the nest to be able to afford a home, unless we built the home with our own two hands or were very affluent? This was the case until the late 1930s. Even then, the mass affordability from longer mortgages did not make significant inroads until after World War II and the GI Bill. Likewise, credit cards and revolving credit at stores make transactions easier and a lower credit risk overall, to a degree. The point is that, much as in any exponential growth trend in history, we as consumers and lenders eventually get complacent and abuse such new opportunities to the point that we fail and have to sort of "unlearn" and correct past excesses.

Enablers All Around

There are a number of ways to borrow money. You can go to the bank and ask for a loan, you can use a credit card, or you can borrow directly from a retailer through a store-specific credit card or charge account. Typically each of these lenders will want to figure out if you are a good credit risk. The lender might check your credit score, ask about your income, and check on your employment. All of these things are natural questions when you want to figure out whether somebody will pay you back. If you as an individual were going to lend money to a friend or a neighbor, you might ask the exact same questions. Let's face it: when you make a loan, you want to get your money back. But what if you were lending someone else's money? What if you earned money simply by processing the loan and were not on the hook if the loan went bad? Or what if you were a government-sponsored entity with a backstop behind you if you failed? Would you be as diligent in verifying that the borrower could make the payments? Putting aside for the moment the possibilities of fraud and simple lying, wouldn't it be compelling to make the largest number of loans in the highest loan amounts that you could? This is more or less what happened in the private financial system, as the tether between the original lender of money—say, your local bank—and the borrower was cut.

Securitization: A Financial Invention Run Amok

The process of securitizing a loan is relatively simple. In the old way of doing business, a bank takes in deposits and pays interest on those deposits. The bank then lends out most of the deposits to borrowers, such as home buyers and businesses, and charges a higher rate of interest than it pays the depositors. This is called "borrowing short" (on deposits; it doesn't cost much in terms of interest paid) and "lending long." You can charge a higher rate of interest on the lending. The bank then earns the difference between the rate that the bank pays the depositor vs. what it charges the borrower. This difference is called the spread.

In **Diagram 3-1,** the bank is limited in the amount of loans it can

Diagram 3-1: Traditional Money and Lending Flow

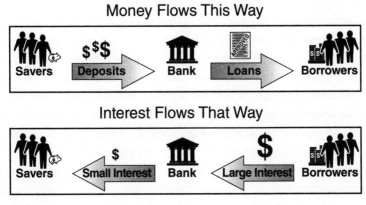

Data Source: HS Dent

make by the amount of deposits it has received. But what if the bank takes a different approach? If a bank can sell the loans it has made, then it can replenish its capital and reserves and make new loans. This is what we mentioned in the first chapter: banks often do not hold mortgages like they used to; they simply sell them. The trick for the bank is to generate fees on the loans that it originates and then sell the loans to someone else at a slightly lower interest rate than the original loan was made in order to earn profit both ways: from fees and a slight spread in interest margins. When the bank sells the loan, it then has fresh funds available to make yet another loan; eventually the bank will sell that second loan as well. The relationship between the bank and the borrowers is severed. If the borrower reneges in 3, 5, or 10 years, who cares? The investor, pension fund, etc., that bought the loan will certainly care, but the bank won't! (Banks now are starting to care, as pension plans and other investors are suing the bank for not properly evaluating the loan or for knowingly packaging toxic loans!) This idea of selling loans gets even more convoluted.

Instead of simply selling a loan, the bank can bundle a loan with other loans and then sell pieces of the bundle. This last part—bundling loans together and then selling pieces of the bundle, or pool—is the essence of securitization. It can be done by the bank that makes the loans in the first place, or it can be done by a firm that buys loans from banks and then bundles them together into pools. Once a pool is created, pieces of that pool are sold to investors in the form of bonds. These bonds are backed by the loans in the pool, which are backed by the assets that were purchased with the loans, such as the homes or commercial real estate holdings pledged against the mortgages (**Diagram 3-2**).

This process allows investors (the ones who buy the loans or pieces of the pools) to diversify their exposure to the risk of borrower default. If an investor buys one loan of $100,000, then the investor has complete exposure to the person who took out that one loan. If that one borrower loses his job, has medical issues, or simply walks away from the loan, then the investor who now owns the loan is going to suffer a loss. However, if the same investor buys $100,000 worth of a pool of mortgages that have been bundled together (securitized), then the risk of nonpayment has been spread among many borrowers. The pool of mortgages could represent hundreds or thousands of loans. If one of the borrowers in the pool stops paying his

Diagram 3-2: Securitization

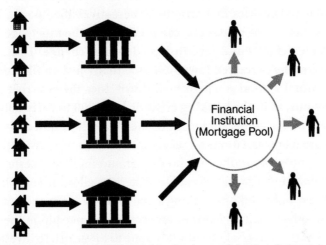

Individual home buyers get loans from banks, each bank sells loans to one financial institution that puts all loans in one pool, and then the institution sells the pieces of the pool to investors.

Data Source: HS Dent Foundation

mortgage, then the investors in that pool could see less than a tenth of 1% of their investment impaired. That's the beauty of diversification.

That is also what makes securitization valuable. When a financial firm issues bonds and then uses the money to buy individual loans that are combined in a pool that is sold in pieces, the individual pieces of the pool are less risky than the individual loans. This allows the financial institution to sell the pieces of the pool at a lower interest rate than the borrowers are paying on their mortgages, which is how the financial institution earns the *spread*, or the difference between the rate of interest at which the financial institution bought the loans from the banks and the rate of interest the buyers of the pieces of the pool of loans receive. If the mortgages in a pool have an average interest rate of 7%, then the institution that buys those mortgages is receiving 7%. However, once the mortgages are bundled together in a pool, then the pieces of the pool are sold at a lower interest rate, say 5%, because the pieces of the pool are considered less risky than each individual mortgage on its own. The difference between the 7% and the 5% is the spread—and that is enormous.

The diversification in pools of securitized loans appears less risky to

individual investors who buy into such pools. The pools generate lower interest rate payments and returns, which, conversely, add more profits to the financial entities that structure these diversified pools. The big insight is this: in the aggregate, the total risk of the mortgage market for ultimate defaults and foreclosures does not change. Thus, for the total system, the perceived lower risk is actually just an illusion! Only when the total system starts to melt down does the real risk become more obvious, as in the banking crisis of late 2008 to early 2009—and in the next one to come, sometime between late 2011 and early 2015.

There are many variations on securitization. Financial institutions will stratify the investors in the new pool, guaranteeing that a certain group gets paid first (and also will be paid less interest), allowing some investors to be interest only, and often taking some pools of loans and combining them with other pools of loans in order to sell ownership in the pool of pools. All of this financial invention is done to lower risk to investors in a way that allows the financial institutions to pay less interest to the buyers of the pools, which creates more spread.

This approach was, and continues to be, used on many different types of loans—mortgages on houses, second mortgages, car loans, credit card loans, boat loans, unsecured loans, etc. This type of security obviously is more difficult to analyze than, say, bonds issued by IBM or Coca-Cola. To figure out the risk on a securitized pool of housing bonds, you have to determine the creditworthiness of the borrowers, the risk of the loans being paid off early, and the likelihood of whether the underlying assets (the houses) will decline in value. Diversification across many borrowers is what gives investors a level of comfort. As the debt appetite of consumers grew, more and more securitized pools on different loan types were being offered for sale. The demand from investors was being fed by several forces, including rising values on the underlying assets (which implied that the rate of default was falling or nonexistent), the demand by pension funds and other large institutions for interest-bearing securities in a time when most companies were simply issuing stock, and falling interest rates. Lower interest rates made these securities more attractive and allowed borrowers to take on even more debt, which drove asset prices even higher and led to even more loans. The circle was complete, if unsustainable.

Whistling in Wyoming to Keep the Elephants Away

The role of the Federal Reserve (the Fed) is defined by the Federal Reserve Act of 1913, as amended. There are three goals of Fed policy: to moderate prices (create mild inflation), to create steady long-term interest rates, and to ensure full employment. The tools used by the Fed to accomplish these goals generally include setting short-term interest rates (Fed funds, or overnight rates for lending between banks) and determining the amount of money in the US system, or liquidity, as defined by credit availability. If the Fed believes that prices are rising too fast, generally it will raise interest rates to induce people to save instead of spend and also to make it more expensive for borrowers to access capital. This is expected to have a cooling effect on the economy, which theoretically will bring down prices. Liquidity, or availability of credit, works much the same way.

If our economy appears to be generating high prices and rising long-term interest rates, the Fed will reduce the amount of credit in our banking system, which curbs the ability of people to borrow and spend. If the Fed believes the economy to be moving too slowly or possibly if it wants to respond to an economic dip such as a recession, the Fed will lower interest rates, which should make loans cheaper through lower payments and should "punish" savers by paying them low rates of interest. At the same time, the Fed will make credit more widely available through the banking system, to aid the ability of borrowers to access capital and to boost the economy. While the theory is nice and neat, the reality is messy, especially when applied to an economy the size of the United States. With the use of such broad tools, Fed policy often will lead to unintended consequences, and sometimes those consequences can be devastating.

The Fed's policies of stimulating the economy in weak times and curbing it in stronger times also give an illusion of greater stability and lower risk. In practice, the Fed typically reacts too late and with too much stimulus that lasts too long in most downturns—and vice versa in upturns. When things are growing too quickly, the Fed tends to tighten too late and at too great of a rate, keeping monetary policy tight for too long. The Fed is just a group of people, like the rest of the participants in the financial markets: we are all generally too late and too dramatic in our reactions to stock and economic volatility, both up and down.

The Federal Reserve was created in 1913 to counteract extreme swings in interest rates that were impacting the economy from natural business cycles in the mid- to late 1800s. These cycles created an inordinate amount of financial panics and crises. The reason for such volatility was twofold. First, the United States was an emerging country back then and relied more on commodity price cycles, much like most "banana republics" today and much like the European economies to which it exported. Second, the world was in a longer-term Winter Season on a 500-year cycle back then, with greater depressions between the 1780s and the 1930s (depressions or panics happened in 1780–1784, 1835–1843, 1873–1877, 1883–1886, 1893–1896, and 1930–1942). The Fed was successful in countering the short-term swings in the interest rates cycles after 1913, despite the extremes of World War I. However, the Fed then actually created the most exaggerated bubble to that date in stocks and farm lending from 1915 into 1929, which led to the greatest depression on record from 1930 to 1933 through 1942.

After its creation in 1913, the Fed tamed short-term interest rate and economic cycles only to create a greater bubble and greater depression than ever seen before from 1915 to 1942. This cycle is like feeding a drug habit, which makes you feel better today but only weakens you longer term, leading to a collapse or breakdown before you get sober again. Tampering with the economy only shifted risk to higher levels and from short term to longer term—it did not eliminate it! That is the same thing that has occurred since the 1970s, when Keynesian economics, invented in the 1930s out of that Great Depression, finally became more mainstream, as we explained in the Introduction. The Fed and the US government have perhaps countered the depths of recessions a bit since the 1970s. However, their actions created an ever-escalating bubble that is now beyond compare with regard to the debt-to-GDP ratio vs. that of the last great US and world bubble in 1929. The present bubble is something like five times greater . . . and the government calls that reducing risk?

The last economic bubble of this degree was the South Seas (in England) and the Mississippi Land bubble (in France), which peaked in 1720 and caused stock markets in Europe to peak and decline for about 64 years. The bubble ended in 1784 and did not recover to new heights until the 1920s (see **Chart 3-2**). If the coming economic crisis that we have been

Chart 3-2: Stock Prices, 1700 to Present

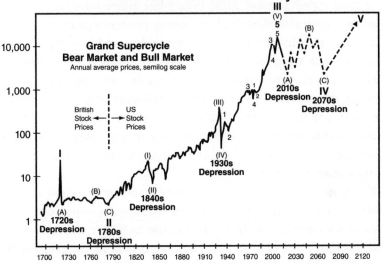

Data Source: Robert Prechter, *Conquer the Crash*, pg. 33, with projections forward by Harry Dent

warning about does not bring an end to Keynesian economics, then we deserve to be wiped out as a human race. Bubbles are natural in life, as we have commented in our past books; they bring innovations and great experimentation to create the maximum number of new products, solutions, and business models, which are quickly whittled down to the few good ideas and firms that get it right. We learn from our experiments and innovations what we did right (often by accident) and we also learn not to make the same mistakes in the future—we **unlearn** to progress!

The innovations that moved mainstream in the bubble of the 1920s drove rising work, technological, and organizational structures that advanced our standard of living immeasurably for decades to follow. To overstate the impact of the assembly line perfected by Henry Ford is not possible. However, Ford then made the mistake of running his company in the same top-down, autocratic manner of the railroads of the past—and thus General Motors passed him. Likewise, in the 1930s the US government could have provided some liquidity and could have been a lender of last resort to aid the banks during the credit crunch. Such actions could have made the transition to massive debt restructuring and demographic slowing less costly and more civilized.

Nonetheless, trying to prevent the present crisis at all costs still makes no sense. In the current crisis central banks and national governments have used monetary and fiscal policy like powerful drugs to attempt to deter the natural "detoxing" or healing process that must come after excesses or bubbles of any kind, in the body, environment, cultures, or economies. **This approach violates every natural law that drives our universe, our natural world, and our economy. By pretending to eliminate risk shorter term, we only increase it longer term.** The overstimulation approach does not represent a real understanding of risk and should be the greatest lesson of the great expansion and bubble that has been occurring since the early 1780s and that has accelerated from the 1980s through the early 2000s.

The best way to reduce risk is to have better information about how natural evolution, human learning, business, and innovation processes work and to learn from that information to better structure the specialization of work, organization, and relationships. This restructuring ultimately will yield better ways to predict and to react to the future. This type of learning and adapting is how we have evolved over millennia. Our greatest ancient insights revolved around first understanding the movements and migrations of animals. After that, we turned our attention to the seasons of our weather to assist with agriculture—and so we have continued to learn throughout the centuries. We continue to learn and evolve, taking our understanding from the most basic (weather) to the very complex ideas of human interaction.

From the 1920s forward, General Motors and its leadership focused on structuring its corporation, decentralizing decision making for the first time in history, and adapting to the upcoming generation of consumers as it progressed in income and its family cycle. Conversely, Ford did not adapt, but instead continued to produce more entry-level Model Ts. Like GM, we must learn to adapt to changing demographics. We now have the tools of demographic research, understanding of the long-term seasons of our economy, technology, and consumer adoption S-curves, which further our knowledge of how human beings and nature create bubbles of innovation, success, and learning, followed by failure, breakdown, and unlearning, which leads once again to progress and evolution.

Unlearning is the key to times of change and transition. What worked in a boom does not work in a downturn. What works in an inflationary period does not work in a deflationary period. What works when you are falling in love does not work when you are trying to live with that person over time. What works when your kids are little does not work when they are teenagers. What works when you are 30 does not work when you are 70, and so on. We are asking you to listen to us in this world turned upside down by debt deleveraging and deflation and unlearn what you think will happen to the economy and your finances; unlearn natural assumptions, like "gold prices will continue to go up and the US dollar will continue to crash." Deflation trends strongly suggest the opposite: that bonds will outperform stocks in the next decade, that cash and not owning (being content to rent) will outperform owning and investing, and so on.

From the 1980s through the 2000s, the United States enjoyed its best and longest period of growth and falling inflation in history. As students of demographics and predictable consumer spending trends, we can point to reasons why this occurred and even note that we forecast these trends back in the late 1980s (*Our Power to Predict,* 1989), and with even more powerful research in *The Great Boom Ahead* (1992). However, most analysts and financial market participants were not watching people and demographics and certainly were not content to allow economic nature to take its course. Instead, they insisted on tinkering with economic levers. This is exactly what happened at the Federal Reserve. Those at the Fed believed that their policies and actions were major contributors to the economic peace and tranquility of the times. The Fed viewed the economic growth and low inflation as signs that they had, for the most part, beaten the economic cycle.

This conceit eventually was proven wrong in the ensuing financial crisis, which is still with us today. The Fed had not, and has not, beaten the cyclical nature of the economy, but it remains undeterred by reality. Most important, the Fed did not create the great boom from 1983 to 2007; this happened because of the life cycle of the baby boomers—because of the new, innovative technologies the boomers began to create in the 1960s and 1970s when they were young and then began to adopt in the 1980s as they matured! The problem is that the government's actions have ramifications that all of us have to live with. US federal government actions from the late 1980s through the 2000s were particularly damaging, and the responsibility can be laid substantially, but clearly not fully, at the feet of the man at the helm.

In the past he has been called a maestro and a genius. Today, he is often regarded at best as a man caught in a hard situation or at worst as the choreographer of the worst financial crisis since the Great Depression. He is, of course, Alan Greenspan, the chairman of the Federal Reserve Board of Governors from mid-1987 through 2005. During his tenure, Greenspan seemed to take great pride in being not just difficult to understand, but almost unresponsive to questioning by Congress, the media, or anyone who asked what the Fed was doing in response to current economic conditions. As Greenspan famously said in a 1988 speech quoted in the October 28, 2005, edition of the *New York Times,* "I guess I should warn you, if I turn out to be particularly clear, you've probably misunderstood what I said." *

Greenspan took the role of the Fed very seriously. He adjusted his economic controls constantly, moving the Fed funds rate dozens of times during the 1990s, even though the Fed meets only every 6 to 8 weeks. **Chart 3-3** shows the movement in the Fed Funds rate, the overnight rate at which banks lend to each other, which is set by the Fed. You can see that the Fed was overly active in the 1990s and left rates very low for much of the 2000s. Greenspan's goal was to engineer a "Goldilocks" economy: one that was not too hot, but not too cold. What happened was that he engineered an economy that was too hot. The low rates in the early 1990s (after a recession) only helped to drive stock prices higher than normal, which resulted in greater speculation. The good news was that due to demographic forces, Greenspan was presiding over a period that would be marked by almost constant growth, with lower inflation and interest rates. This growth happened just as we forecast it would back in the late 1980s and early 1990s, and it would have happened regardless of who was Fed chairman or president.

Except for brief periods in 1990–1991 and 2001–2002, the US economy generally was moving higher, buoyed by the working, earning, and spending of millions of baby boomers. The bad news was that members of the Federal Reserve, the mainstream media, and the financial markets came

* Wikiquotes, http://en.wikiquote.org/wiki/Alan_Greenspan, accessed December 14, 2010.

Chart 3-3: Federal Funds Rate, 1988–2010

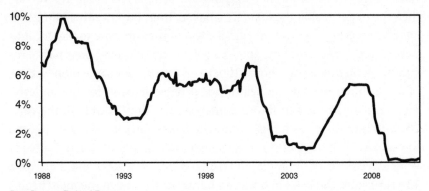

Data Source: **Federal Reserve**

to believe that Fed policy, not spending decisions by hundreds of millions of Americans, was what was keeping the United States on a path of growth. So when the terrorist attacks of 9/11 struck and America shut down for several days, the Fed decided to take drastic action, as it saw itself as the main engineer of economic change. Instead of holding back to see what would occur naturally, the Fed jumped in and cut interest rates dramatically, eventually lowering rates to 1%. This move added more fuel to an existing, somewhat naturally occurring speculation boom in housing and real estate that was fed by low margin rates from regulators. The boom coincided with the S-curve in PCs and cell phones that we predicted back in the early 1990s on technology cycles, even though we didn't know back in 1992 that the internet would be the key trigger.

Chart 3-3 shows that Greenspan & Company were bound and determined to make sure that our economy did not suffer any longer than necessary after the tech crash that they helped to fuel and after 9/11. They again used the heavy hammer of interest rates to get the United States back on track for growth as quickly as possible. The low interest rates were credited (largely incorrectly) as a major reason why the 2001–2002 recession was the shortest and shallowest recession in US history. This misguided policy of pushing interest rates down dramatically to 1% while making credit easy to get is what gave the debt bubble of the 2000s the fuel it needed to explode to new heights, creating the greatest mass housing and real estate bubble in modern history. Purchases made on credit (housing, cars, furniture, etc.) are obviously the most sensitive to interest rate changes, especially in housing and commercial real estate. If rates fall, then the payments on the loan are smaller. Thus, buyers either can better afford a mortgage because it will take less of their income to pay for it or buyers can increase the amount they will borrow, keeping their payments steady but buying "more" house (boat, car, etc.) for the same money. Both of these things usually are helpful for driving demand for the underlying asset. When the Fed lowered interest rates dramatically in the early 2000s to extremely low levels (without a depression), it essentially poured fuel on an existing fire of consumption, particularly home buying, already in its sweet spot of demographic demand between 1999 and 2003 on a 42-year lag for the peak in trade-up home buying and at the mere beginning of the vacation-home-buying cycle demographically.

Home Buying on Steroids

As Americans came through the bursting of the tech bubble in 2000 and then the terrorist attacks of September 11, 2001, the largest generational group (baby boomers) also was going through the consumer stage of buying its biggest homes. (Between the ages of 37 and 42, a consumer typically will buy his or her largest, or trade-up, home, which would coincide with 1999–2003.) This group also was moving toward its top in overall spending (at around age 46, which occurred in late 2007). Such spending tends to plateau around age 50, so spending trends would be expected to remain somewhat buoyant into around late 2011. In the extreme stock crash of 2000 to 2002, although their investment accounts were hemorrhaging, consumers were buying ever-larger homes in ever-larger numbers to satisfy the demands of their families. This created an interesting dynamic in which stocks were falling but home prices were rising.

With technology and stocks crashing, people naturally thought, "Why not invest in real estate, as it is the only asset that has gone up for our entire lifetimes and they aren't creating any more of it!" The Japanese thought the same thing in the 1980s, but we forget the lessons of bubbles every other generation. In this case we forgot within a decade; we saw Japan and somehow thought that the same thing could not happen to us.

Consumers were not stupid; they noticed that the prices of their homes were moving up dramatically, despite a stock market rout (2000), a terrorist attack (2001), a recession (2001/2002), a more dramatic stock crash, and even the beginnings of a couple of wars (2002 and 2003). Real estate was on fire, and people were clamoring for more of it! The Federal Reserve was doing its best to stave off any downturn in the economy, so it had brought interest rates down dramatically, to 1% short term, which allowed consumers to buy a bigger house and maybe even a few properties for investment. The double-whammy effect of greater innate demand due to predictable consumer spending patterns (buyers driving the market) and lower interest rates (the Fed enabling the market) laid the groundwork for a bubble in housing. The fuel of lower interest rates was poured on an existing fire of consumer-driven home buying. But that wasn't all; even more forces were at work.

The near-record-low short-term interest rates of the early 2000s allowed banks to create new adjustable-rate mortgages (ARM), short-term interest rates, and "teaser" loans for longer-term mortgages, and even more derivations, to the point that many marginal credit borrowers were getting option ARM loans with no interest and no principal paid for the first 5 years! Was that nuts, or what? As in Japan in the 1980s, banks and consumers assumed that real estate could not go down in price, except maybe for the very short term; hence, there was virtually no risk! Of course, the US government in these "good times" wanted to make everyone a homeowner, so through use of government-sponsored entities, the government promoted and financed increasing numbers of home loans to households with levels of credit quality and income that formerly would not have been considered good enough or high enough to secure a loan. This created the greatest leverage in the financial and banking system ever, and Wall Street was already on the bandwagon and adding to the party!

Investors Hunt for Yield

The 1980s were good to bond buyers. The early years were marked by high interest rates, which meant that bonds issued in the 1979–1983 time frame carried very high coupons, or interest rates. Investors who bought then saw only longer-term yields fall, which made their bonds more valuable if sold before maturity, as investors had locked in the higher interest rates. The rule in bonds is that you want to hold long-term bonds when interest rates are falling. The greatest bond bull market, even greater than that of the 1930s, occurred from 1981 to late 2008, and especially from 1981 to 1986. As those bonds matured in the 1990s and early 2000s, fixed-income investors were not able to generate as much income on their investments as they had become accustomed to receiving. Investors were constantly searching for high-quality, safe investments with higher interest payments than government securities. As interest rates remained low during the 1990s and then fell even lower in the 2000s, those who depended on fixed income to meet some or all of their investment goals were stymied. The growth in the asset-backed, securitized market gave these investors a way of capturing at least some yield, even though the Fed was holding interest rates down. It was here that the problems erupted. Driven by rising asset prices, demand for credit in general and home loans in particular, low interest rates, and investors' hunger for yield, our financial innovation got ahead of our common sense.

The Path of Securitization and Leverage

In the 1930s, the US government recognized that real estate was an essential part of the economy. If you want to get things going quickly, you should get consumers to make a large, leveraged purchase. But banks were wary. Real estate did not have a good track record in the 1930s, so lending was tight. In order to loosen the strings of lending, the US government came up with a plan to buy home mortgages from banks; this would allow the banks to lend more than their deposit base, because every time the bank sold a loan, the bank's capital would be replenished. It also took the risk of loss on the loan off of the banks. The US government created a secondary buyer of mortgages that we know today as the Federal National Mortgage Association, or Fannie Mae (FNMA). Thenceforth, a bank could make a loan for a home and then sell the loan to FNMA.

Where does FNMA get the money to buy loans? It securitizes the loans into pools, but with a twist. Because FNMA was set up by the US government, people assumed that the US government would stand behind the bonds of the organization even if something happened to the underlying mortgages. This implicit guarantee was debated for years, especially after FNMA was spun off from the US government in 1968 and made into a private company that eventually went public. Could it be that a private company carried a government guarantee? We found out that the answer was "yes" in the summer of 2008, when the US government took control of FNMA and affirmed its backing of all FNMA bonds. Equity shareholders were wiped out, but bondholders were guaranteed 100% of their investment. In essence, FNMA issued quasi-US government bonds in order to buy mortgages from banks. The FNMA bonds carried a low interest rate, because they were effectively government backed, so the money raised by FNMA was very cheap. This allowed FNMA to buy mortgages from banks at low interest rates, because FNMA did not have to earn a high yield from borrowers to pay the holders of FNMA bonds.

Now FNMA (and its sibling, the Federal Home Loan Mortgage Corporation, or Freddie Mac) was picky about the loans it would buy and would consider a mortgage only if that mortgage conformed to certain guidelines. Those guidelines called for borrowers to make a down payment of 20% of the cost of the home and to meet specific criteria in terms of credit score or credit history, income, job history, etc. The guidelines also called for the mortgage not to exceed a certain dollar amount. Mortgages that met these criteria were called "conforming loans." Instantly, funds were available for residential real estate.

Loans that were nonconforming—those that fell outside of FNMA's underwriting guidelines—could not be sold to FNMA, so lenders were at greater risk when they made nonconforming loans. This category (nonconforming) included jumbo loans for bigger houses, subprime loans, Alt-A loans, and eventually ARMs (adjustable-rate mortgages) and option ARMs (adjustable-rate mortgages, where borrowers can choose to pay less, adding the balance to their mortgage). To get a loan in this category, a borrower had to pay a higher interest rate on his mortgage than a borrower who took out a conforming loan. It makes sense—there is more risk to the lender, so the bank charges more interest.

Again, the illusion was that such a government guarantee reduces the risk of default and losses over time. It doesn't . . . it just passes them on to taxpayers!

The nonconforming loans were still securitized but were not handled by FNMA. Instead, large banks and eventually investment banks were the main drivers of securitized pools of nonconforming loans. The separation along these lines—FNMA handling conforming loans and other institutions handling nonconforming loans—fell out this way because of the cost of capital. The implicit government guarantee behind FNMA allowed it to borrow cheaper than anyone else, so this entity was able to more or less own the conventional, conforming market by offering very low interest rates to borrowers. Banks, investment banks, and other financial entities had higher costs of capital and were therefore relegated to the more exotic nonconforming loans.

Fast-forward to the 1990s and the early 2000s. As the boomers aged, the demand for housing grew dramatically. First, they bought starter homes, a surge that peaked in the late 1980s to early 1990s. Then they sold that starter home and bought a trade-up home, a bigger house for their growing children. This trend peaked in 2005 or 2006, although in the normal demographic cycle it was expected to peak around 2003. The peak was later due to easy credit, refinancing, and a continued strong economy. The biggest incentive for refinancing was to gain access to funds that were then spent on education. For the first time, average-income families had the chance to do something that very few affluent families could do throughout history: finance their kids' private school or college education during a time when such costs were growing faster than those for health care.

Along the way, the price of real estate escalated based on growing demand, falling interest rates, and readily available credit for borrowers. The collateral behind mortgages, the homes themselves, was steadily rising in value in tandem with higher demand and lower interest rates. Lenders seemed to be printing money, because there was no perceived risk. If a borrower paid, then lenders earned the interest. If borrowers failed to pay, then the house itself was worth enough to pay off the mortgage. Voilà! A riskless business that exploded! Staid, conforming loans were a big market, but as home prices rose and the real estate market went into overdrive, jumbo loans, subprime loans, Alt-a loans, ARMs, and option ARMs started to take over the world. This was a transformation unlike anything we had seen before in our economy—ever! In the Roaring Twenties bubble boom, more-affluent households could only get mortgages with as much as 50% down and with payment terms of often no more than 5 years. That is the case even today in strong emerging countries like China!

Home ownership in America hovered around 60% of all households through the 1960s and 1970s after the unprecedented GI Bill that followed World War II and the low interest rates and very expansive boom of the 1950s into the late 1960s. **Chart 3-4** shows that in the 1980s this began to change, as more people began making the move from being renters to being buyers. This makes sense, as the boomers were in their mid- to late 20s; they were starting families and putting down roots, especially from 1986 forward, as they got married in rising numbers.

The percentage of households that own homes in America continued to grow through the 1990s and became a self-reinforcing cycle. Those who bought homes not only were putting down roots, but also were making an investment. In recent memory (the 1990s) and in even in longer-term memory (World War II forward) these investments had only gone up in value. Home buying was not just any investment, it was a leveraged investment. Consider what might have happened if you had made a $20,000 down payment on a $100,000 home and had taken out an $80,000 mortgage. If you sold that home two years later for $110,000, the value of the home would have increased by $10,000, or 10%, but your investment would have seen a 50% gain on that $20,000 down payment—that is the beauty of leverage. Unfortunately, the lure of a leveraged investment

Chart 3-4: Percentage of Households That Own Homes, 1965–2010

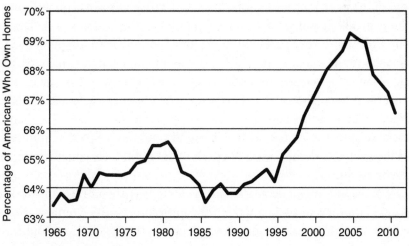

Data Source: **US Census Bureau**

that seemed only to go up in value was running up against a diminishing pool of qualified borrowers. As homeownership grew, by necessity fewer people qualified for conforming loans. Thus, financial institutions began taking on a bigger role in providing what the public wanted—more ways to access debt in order to buy homes.

Of course, it wasn't just homes. It was condos. It was ownership of a second home (not just buying a trade-up home, but truly owning two homes at one time), a trend that was accelerating in the demographic cycle from around 2000 forward. It was vacation property, rental property, outright speculative property, in which a buyer would purchase several condos at one time to sell them quickly (flip them) for a tidy, leveraged profit. It seemed that anyone and everyone in real estate was printing money, and it was happening at a time when other areas of the economy were particularly frustrating. Wages were flat, and while the equity markets had rebounded from their 2002 lows, the growth in those markets was unremarkable. Real estate seemed to have it all: fast returns, easy access, and a loan to fit any situation.

While conforming loans didn't change much, some license was being taken to qualify people for those loans. Don't have the money for a down payment? Don't worry! Just take out a second loan, or a "piggyback," in the amount of the down payment. Can't qualify for your monthly payment? Get a teaser rate, which carries a low rate of interest and therefore lower payments for the first several years, but adds the negative cost or interest you didn't pay to the back of the loan. Don't have any assets or, well, anything at all, but still want to borrow hundreds of thousands of dollars to buy real estate? Not a problem! Apply for a "no-doc" loan: simply state the answers to the underwriting questions about employment, salary, assets, etc.—those answers will never be documented or verified. This last type of loan came to be known as a "liar's loan." Then there is the famous NINJA loan, which loosely stands for "no income, no job, no assets." Who would make such loans? Who in their right mind would lend a person hundreds of thousands of dollars and not check their credit, their employment, or anything else?

It turns out, many people would, as there was a mad race for market share in this new financial market with apparently no risk from any major falls in real estate values, just like in Japan in the 1980s. How could we have not learned from the largest real estate bust in modern history in the largest city by far in the world, Tokyo, with the scarcest land for development? How can real estate go down in an environment of rising demand and extreme scarcity of developable land? Easy! Because it becomes unaffordable to everyone but the most affluent, especially after everyone has bought in!

Through securitization at firms like Lehman Brothers and Countrywide, investors bought trillions of dollars worth of nonconforming loans, of which hundreds of billions of dollars were funneled to people who took out loans that they could never dream of repaying in normal terms, meaning by paying the mortgage monthly using their income. Instead, these borrowers and the lenders and bond investors were betting that the homes, condos, etc., purchased would rise in value fast enough that the lender could either flip or simply refinance the property down the road.

The Road to Hell Is Paved with Good Intentions

From the late 1990s through the mid-2000s, we were in a race to lend ever-greater sums of money with ever-smaller guarantees of repayment. Consider what we were offering to anyone with a pulse:

- Home loans for no money down (take out two loans, a first mortgage for 80% and a second for 20%)
- Interest-only loans (and pay no principal for up to seven years)
- Loans that go backward (pay less than the interest cost, with the balance being added to the end of the loan)
- No-documentation loans (none of the information is verified)

These steps created a tremendous velocity of lending, because now literally everyone was qualified to borrow for a home or for a home equity loan! How could anyone get turned down if information was not verified? Is it any wonder that our financial sector debt increased by almost $15 trillion in just a few short years? Is it any wonder that consumer debt levels were more than twice that compared to income levels at the top of the Roaring Twenties bubble! Why? Mortgages were hard to get back then, as we have already described.

Chart 3-5: Japan Residential Land Values, 1953–2003

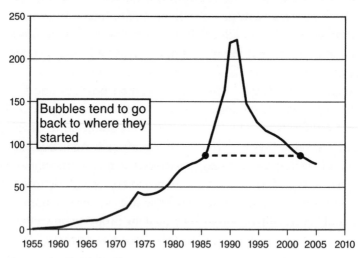

Data Source: Japan Statistics Bureau

The Japan real estate bubble, depicted in **Chart 3-5,** was a clear precursor to the US and world bubble in real estate. Japan's baby boom generation peaked fifteen years ahead of the baby boom in the rest of the developed world (as we warned in the late 1980s). Japan's experience illustrates an important principle that we have learned from studying all documented bubbles in the last 300 years of modern history:

Almost All Bubbles Return to Where They Started or Go a Bit Lower

Let us repeat that again a little more clearly:

Almost all bubbles return to where they started growing exponentially against natural boom or economic trends. The drop can go to at least where the bubbles started or can go a bit lower—sometimes, a good bit lower, like in the late-1929-to-mid-1932 crash for stocks. Such bubbles tend to occur only when interest rates are falling due to economic progress as new technologies move mainstream. This progress occurs during the Fall Season of our long-term economic cycle, as during this time the new (young) generation feels as if it is in a new era of progress that will last or plateau forever. This new generation has no memory of the last great bubble or depression that their parents and grandparents always warned them about.

Note in **Chart 3-5** that the collapse after 1991 in Japan's real estate market did not wipe out all of the natural gains made after the country's reconstruction from World War II in the early 1950s. It simply wiped out the exponential bubble from 1986 to 1991, in which prices had risen 2.6 times in just 5 to 6 years, and then fell a little more. US home prices took the same amount of time to bubble and peak 14 years later, between early 2000 and late 2005 early 2006, as shown in **Chart 3-6** from Case-Shiller. Stocks in the United States took the same approximate amount of time to bubble from late 1924 into late 1929, from late 1982 into late 1987, and from late 1994 into early 2000, and in Japan between late 1984 and late 1989.

For the US bubble in housing to return to where it started, we would have to see a 55% decline from the top, not the 34% decline we saw to mid-2009. It is likely that such prices will fall as much as 65%, back to the lows of 1996–1997. Do you think that the bank stress tests allowed for that? Do you now understand why the government is trying so hard to keep the economy going and interest rates, short term and long term, as low as possible? If housing doesn't recover most of its crash in values from early 2006, then the banking system will be largely bankrupt. All of the policies—from the Fed to Fannie Mae and Freddie Mac, all of the lack of regulation, all of the blindness of the mortgage and bond ratings agencies, all of the crazy securitization of mortgages, and all of the

Chart 3-6: Average US Home Prices, January 1994 to November 2010

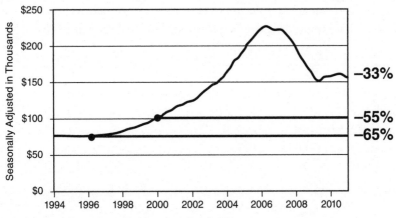

Data Source: Standard & Poor's Case-Shiller US 10-City Index

$67 trillion plus in derivatives by investment banks that were supposed to diversify and reduce risk—will look like either the greatest act of greed or the greatest act of stupidity and oversight in history, or both! "Both" is the likely answer! Why? Because everyone involved in this process—bankers, regulators, consumers, voters, buyers, sellers, investors, etc.—is human. We always tend to go with the herd to extremes, especially when our friends and neighbors do too.

Together we created this great bubble, and now together we all have to face this bubble bust and detox of debt, as well as the dimming expectations of ever-growing prosperity. We will address how to do this at all levels, from individual and family to businesses to government, in Chapters 9 through 11. Paradoxically, deleveraging now is the best thing we can do to guarantee our prosperity in a slowing demographic world ahead, where perhaps our economic growth is slower, but we still lead in technological innovation and military prowess.

In Chapter 4 we will look at how much debt we have in government, including federal debt and unfunded liabilities for Social Security, Medicare/Medicaid, and state and local debt. The most massive area for liabilities and restructuring obviously comes in our long-cherished entitlements. By 2013 to 2015, it will be increasingly obvious that we simply cannot afford these entitlements, much as corporations have increasingly realized for decades and as states and municipalities began to realize in 2010.

You can get free access to Harry's very popular webinar
"Understanding the Economy and What Lies Ahead" by
registering at http://www.hsdent.com/webinar.

CHAPTER 4

Unprecedented Government Debt: Especially Unfunded Entitlements

Other People's Money, and Promises That Cannot Be Kept

In 1996, the City of San Diego had a problem. It was short of cash. The city had many projects it wanted to tackle, but there was simply no room in the budget. In addition to the city's existing wish list, it was about to host the Republican National Convention in August, bringing to town thousands of conventioneers and gawkers, putting even more strain on city finances. The city manager went looking for a source of money and found one in the San Diego City Employees' Retirement System (SDCERS), or more specifically, in the city's responsibility to the SDCERS.

Like almost all other cities and states, San Diego was required to make annual contributions to pension funds (in this case, SDCERS) to fund current and future pensions for city workers, a reflection of benefits that had been negotiated over the years. However, given recent stock market gains in the early 1990s, the account was overfunded, according to estimates of how the fund's assets might grow and its obligations or liabilities might grow over time. The city had used some of the excess funds, or surplus, in the past to pay for other things, but what San Diego really wanted was to lower its required contribution. If the city could get the board of the SDCERS to allow it to contribute less, then the city could use that savings to fund other projects. To do that, the city would have to gain the approval of the board of trustees that oversaw the SDCERS, which had a fiduciary responsibility to the workers covered by the retirement plan. In the end, the city and the board struck an agreement in the summer of 1996 that came to be called Manager's Proposal 1, or MP1. Under this accord, the city would be able to reduce its contributions to SDCERS, but in return the board of SDCERS demanded increased retirement benefits to the workers it covered. Yes, you read that correctly. The city of San Diego agreed to put *less* into the retirement system on the basis that it would actually be responsible for funding *more* benefits in the future. There was either tremendous faith that the equity markets would continue their bull run or incredible irresponsibility on behalf of the city and the board of SDCERS to make such an agreement. Of course, there could have been a little of both.

The City of San Diego enjoyed its newfound revenue, funding not only the convention but also things like Petco Park. Meanwhile, the equity markets marched higher in the late 1990s. Even though the city was making lower contributions than what its pension specialists had called for (actuarially required contributions, or ARC), the fund had roughly 90% of what it needed to meet its obligations, which is well within an acceptable range. So far, so good. Then the markets turned bearish in 2000. The value of the SDCERS dropped dramatically. Because the city had not been making its ARC, there was no surplus to fall back on during down years. In 2002, the fund fell below a predetermined threshold of approximately 82% of what would be required to make good on all current and future pension payments. This threshold was supposed to trigger a balloon payment from the City of San Diego to the SDCERS, but the payment did not happen. Instead, the board of the SDCERS and the city came up with yet another plan, this one was called Manager's Proposal 2, or MP2. In a case of déjà vu, the new plan called for the city to get a break on the amount it was required to contribute to the pension fund and in return more retirement benefits were promised for the city workers covered under SDCERS. As a show of how concerned the SDCERS board of trustees was about this agreement, they asked the city and the board of SDCERS for indemnification for trustees concerning any decisions and actions taken by the board. The indemnification, like the MP2 proposal, was approved.* Needless to say, this all turned out badly.

Currently San Diego has an unfunded pension liability (to all pension systems it owes) of about $45 billion, or just over $15,000 for every man,

* Luftman, Reish, Reicher & Cohen, *Investigation for the Board of Administration of the San Diego City Employees' Retirement System,* Navigant Consulting, Jan. 20, 2006.

woman, and child in the city. The city owes $1.3 billion in health benefits and has funded about $40 million of that liability, or 3%.* The new board of the SDCERS is requiring all covered members who are still working to either make greatly increased pension contributions or settle for lower benefits when they retire. Current retirees, especially those who retired from 1996 through 2003, continue to receive their full benefits. The losers in this story are the taxpayers of San Diego, as they do not receive any of the benefits—unless they happen to be city workers—but they are on the hook for the unfunded liabilities. In addition, the citizens of San Diego have seen their services cut and taxes go higher in efforts to divert funds to pay for these liabilities.

The city council of San Diego played fast and loose with "other people's money"—taxpayer money—exchanging promises of large payments down the road in exchange for work and employee contributions received today. In essence, the elected officials avoided making difficult decisions about taxes and revenue and allowed the city to fall down on its part of the pension plan bargain, which was employer, or city, contributions. The result was inevitable. The downturn of 2000–2002 brought down the house of cards. This situation of government employers (cities, counties, and states) failing to make required contributions to retirement plans has been echoed around the country for over a decade as government bodies chose the easy route when budgets got tight—find a category of spending that you can put off until tomorrow without much political fallout. Retirement plan contributions fit the bill perfectly. Who would notice a missed contribution? Who would complain? Current retirees are still (mostly) receiving their checks. This problem is far in the future, right? Not anymore.

The current financial crisis has exposed the ugly side of government finances, where neglected long-term liabilities—pension and retirement health care benefits—have been growing steadily while government entities failed to make their required contributions. The cost of this neglect? A cool $1 trillion across state-level retirement plans, and that is a conservative estimate! This is not the total amount that must be paid, this is just the unfunded amount, or what state plans would

* Stuart, Buck. "Trouble Brewing in San Diego," the Foundation for Educational Choice Policy Brief, October 2010.

have to come up with today in order to make their retirement plans whole.

Of course, this number pales in comparison to the national deficit, debt, and unfunded liabilities we owe. Right now the annual US government deficit ($1.5 trillion) is larger than the entire unfunded status of state pension and health care obligations. This means that we are adding trillions to our national debt every year. Unfortunately, even these large numbers are miniscule compared to what we owe nationally in unfunded liabilities (think *tens of trillions!*). As we will describe in this chapter, from cities and states up to the federal government, we have created a colossal debt and promise machine that has run amok!

Government workers—firemen, policemen, teachers, sanitation workers, state inspectors, etc.—traditionally received lower pay than private-sector workers, but they had great benefits, including pensions and health care, to which they also contributed part of their paychecks. The employers—cities, states, counties, etc.—were required to put money aside as well. But the employers didn't keep up their end of the bargain. The liabilities kept growing, and continue to grow right this minute, yet in many instances the pension contributions by the states and cities that were supposed to be made have not happened. Sometimes, the employer got creative about avoiding the contribution.

In 2005, the State of New Jersey reported that it had made a $551 million contribution to its teachers' pension fund. This was true, technically. What the state failed to mention—but was later reported by its actuary—is that the state had also withdrawn or used the entire $551 million contribution from the fund for other items, such as health care. By contributing but then diverting the funds, the state had made no contribution whatsoever.* The State of New Jersey has not made its full required pension contribution in 14 of the last 17 years.†

In 2010, the State of New York determined that it did not have the funds necessary to make a several-billion-dollar required pension contribution. As other states have done, New York went looking for a place from which it could borrow the monies to make the contribution. How-

* Mary Williams Walsh, "N.J. Pension Fund Endangered by Diverted Billions," *New York Times*, April 4, 2007.

† Steve Kroft, "State Budgets: The Day of Reckoning," *60 Minutes* segment interview with New Jersey Governor Christie, December 19, 2010.

ever, unlike other states, New York decided to borrow the money from the pension fund itself!* In an economic sleight of hand, New York borrowed money from the exact fund to which it was making a contribution simply to be able to claim it had made the contribution. The net effect was nothing. The fund has no more money than it did before the gimmick, but it does have an IOU from the State of New York, for whatever that is worth.

One of the worst offenders is the State of Illinois. In 2003, Illinois issued $10 billion in pension bonds, which is essentially robbing Peter to pay Paul. The state issued a bond to raise money that it then contributed to its pension fund, which did nothing but transfer the state's indebtedness from the pension fund to bondholders. Then it got worse. The state failed to make its required contributions in the years after, and then the pension funds fared badly in the financial crisis, which means the state is on the hook for even more at the pension fund while still being liable for interest and principal payments to the bondholders. So what did Illinois do? It borrowed even more money—$3.5 billion in 2009 and $3.7 billion in 2010.† The situation is so bad in the State of Illinois that a trustee of the Illinois State Board of Investment (ISBI), Thomas E. Hoffman, has claimed that the state is not running a pension fund but instead is running nothing more than a failed Ponzi scheme.‡ His point is underscored by the fact that several state-level pension funds in Illinois are using all of their current contributions from employees plus some of the body of the funds to make required payments to retirees, essentially drawing down the assets. The funds are going broke and taking cities and states with them. But going broke for a city or state is different from going broke for a person or private company.

When we think of any entity—a person, a company, etc.—that gets overrun with debt, we often consider the end game, which is bankruptcy. The idea of bankruptcy is to restructure what is owed (what creditors will get) in line with the assets on hand and income of the borrower. In this scenario, the people who are owed money—a bank, a vendor, a credit card

---

* Danny Hakim, "State Plan Makes Fund Both Borrower and Lender," *New York Times,* June 11, 2010.

† Peter Whorisky, "Illinois Seeks to Borrow $3.7 Billion to Shore Up Pension Shortfall," *Washington Post,* February 22, 2011.

‡ Barry Burr. "Are Illinois Plans Just Ponzi Schemes?" *Pensions & Investments,* November 29, 2010, p. 10.

company, and employees perhaps—will get some of what they are entitled to but not all. Even when it comes to pensions, there is a method for dealing with companies that go broke but owe contributions to their pension funds that cover current and future retirees. The benefits of these retirees are somewhat guaranteed under a government entity, the Pension Benefit Guaranty Corporation. Retirees would still get some of what they are entitled to, but usually not close to their previous benefit levels. This is not how it works for governments and government workers.

Cities can go bankrupt, but the laws that govern municipal bankruptcy are murky. There is no bankruptcy code for states, which are required to use their taxing authority to make good on all general obligation debts. When it comes to the retirement benefits owed to public employees, there is no safety net at all. The pensions of private employees are regulated under ERISA (Employee Retirement Security Act of 1974), and the more recent Pension Protection Act of 2006. These laws spell out how companies are to fund their pensions and what actions will be taken if funding for pensions does not occur or falls below certain levels (benefits cease to accrue, stepped-up payments are required, etc.). ERISA and the Pension Protection Act do not apply to public employee retirement plans; there are no federal regulations that do. Public employees are at the mercy of city, county, and state administrators to actually make good on their contributions. As time wears on, these plans are falling further behind—some are at the point of no return. These issues are already starting to turn up in court, where retirees who are getting nothing are suing their public pensions for what they are owed.

The size of this problem—unfunded liabilities owed by cities and states—ranges between $1 trillion and $3.5 trillion, depending on whom you ask and how it is calculated. The fact that this is a massive problem facing many cities and states around the country is not in question. The magnitude of the debt owed by cities and states will severely limit the ability of these government entities to take on projects in the future or even to pay their other bills.

Simply put, retirement benefit costs are painting these cities and states into a corner. Taxes go up, services get cut. Residents see their standard of living go down. Current municipal workers are required to pay more into the system and accept lower benefits than they were promised decades ago, simply because elected officials failed to do

their job. It has become a game of hot potato, with each player trying to hand off the responsibility for putting more money into these funds. Unfortunately, the final responsibility will most likely fall on taxpayers, and it will fall hard!

How Pension Funds Are Supposed to Work

Pension funds and retirement health care funds are established to receive contributions (usually from both employers and workers). These funds are then overseen by their trustees, who work to grow the funds through investments over time in order to meet the obligations of the funds as workers retire and claim their benefits. This is a simple description of a very complex arrangement. The benefits that a pension fund must pay are known years in advance. The amount of money the fund will have is usually in question because funds rely on three sources of income—employer contributions, employee contributions, and earnings on the existing fund assets. Employee contributions are usually very consistent. However, employer contributions and the earnings of the funds themselves can vary dramatically, and usually at exactly the wrong time.

If a pension fund is earning a high rate of return because the equity markets are going up, then the fund will require lower contributions from the employer to stay fully funded. But think about when the markets would do well—when companies are making a lot of money. The opposite is also true. If a pension fund is falling in value because the equity markets are falling, then the fund will require greater contributions from the company in order to make up the shortfall. However, it is most likely that the equity markets are falling when companies are losing money, which is exactly when companies cannot afford to put more into their pension funds!

Just as with private companies, this same pro-cyclical relationship between funding levels and general economic health exists with city and state pension funds. In good economic times, these entities are usually experiencing an increase in tax revenue, just as their pension funds are rising in value. When the economy falters, not only do the pension funds fall in value, but also tax revenue declines and these government entities are not in a position to make up for shortfalls.

This is why the best course of action is to continue contributing to pension and other retirement benefit accounts even when they appear to be fully funded, more or less saving for a rainy day, preparing for the time when the economy goes south. While this is what employers should do, it is not necessarily what they have done. During the go-go years of the 1990s, many cities and states worked out deals to lower what they had to contribute to retirement funds. Then, during the 2000s, many of these same entities simply skipped their required payments. Without a federal watchdog of any sort, who was going to make them cough up the money? So here they sit, in the midst of the greatest economic crisis in a decade, facing not just underfunded retirement funds, but also ever-increasing liabilities as their ranks of retirees continues to grow. In response to this situation, states have some hard choices to make. They can:

1. Tell retired teachers or firefighters or policemen that they will receive less, effectively trying to reduce benefits (which is illegal in many states).
2. Have politicians take on their employees (both unionized and not), telling the employees that they must contribute more to their own pensions or receive less in benefits when they retire because the government mismanaged the funds.
3. Tell taxpayers that, in the midst of the greatest economic downturn in a generation, they must pay more in taxes so that a certain class of workers can receive its guaranteed benefits even though private workers have no guarantees and are struggling to retain their jobs and pay.

Somehow that just doesn't sound like a good list of options. Right now reports of exhausted pension funds leading to the bankruptcy of cities are infrequent, and it has not happened to a state. Not many people pay attention to Prichard, Alabama, or Vallejo, California, two cities that are currently dealing with the exact situation of pension funds bankrupting the towns. However, there are bigger storms brewing. The State of Illinois is the frontrunner in the race to the bottom, as outlined at the beginning of the chapter, and others are not far behind. The Pew Center researchers and reports on the funding status of state pensions as well as Other Post-Employment Benefits (OPEB), which is simply code for health care benefits while in retirement. States are shamefully late in reporting their funding status, so the latest numbers available are for 2008, before the crash. Even so, the numbers are mostly terrible! Here are the numbers for pension funds from ten large states:

STATE PENSION FUNDING STATUS			
	Total Pension Liability (in millions)	Amount Underfunded	% Underfunded
Arizona	$ 39,831	$ 7,871	20%
California	453,956	59,492	13%
Florida	129,196	(1,798)	−1%
Illinois	119,084	54,383	46%
New Jersey	125,807	34,434	27%
New York	141,255	(10,428)	−7%
Ohio	148,061	19,502	13%
Pennsylvania	105,282	13,724	13%
Texas	148,594	13,781	9%
Virginia	65,164	10,723	16%

Obviously Arizona, Illinois, and New Jersey are struggling. You see that New York is showing a negative unfunded balance, meaning that the state has more in its pension fund than is required, as does Florida. That's a good thing! However, once you see their OPEB, or health care fund, the picture darkens for these states as well.

STATE RETIREMENT BENEFIT FUNDING STATUS			
	OPEB Liability (in millions)	Amount Underfunded	% Underfunded
Arizona	$ 2,322	$ 808	35%
California	62,466	62,463	100%
Florida	3,081	3,081	100%
Illinois	40,022	39,946	100%
New Jersey	68,900	68,900	100%
New York	56,286	56,286	100%
Ohio	43,759	27,025	62%

(continued on next page)

	OPEB Liability (in millions)	Amount Underfunded	% Underfunded
Pennsylvania	10,048	9,956	99%
Texas	29,340	28,611	98%
Virginia	3,963	2,621	66%

It looks odd, but the underfunded status of half of these plans is 100%, meaning they have saved absolutely nothing for what is a multibillion-dollar liability! Looking at the two combined makes the picture clearer.

STATE TOTAL FUNDING STATUS			
	Combined Liability (in millions)	Combined Amount Underfunded	% Underfunded
Arizona	$ 42,153	$ 8,679	21%
California	516,422	121,955	24%
Florida	132,277	1,283	1%
Illinois	159,106	94,329	59%
New Jersey	194,707	103,334	53%
New York	197,541	45,858	23%
Ohio	191,820	46,527	24%
Pennsylvania	115,330	23,680	21%
Texas	177,934	42,392	24%
Virginia	69,127	13,344	19%

Florida is the one star in this sample group. New York, which was doing so well on its pensions, is now more than 20% underfunded. Illinois and New Jersey are so far behind, having only 50% of what they need, that there is no road map or plan for how these funds can recover. It simply does not exist. Because there is no plan or path, there will be an intense period of blame shifting as different groups try to off-load any responsibility to anyone they can.

Taxpayers are waking up to the situation, as could be seen in the elections of 2010. Articles began to surface laying bare the responsibilities that taxpayers face in terms of shoring up unfunded public pensions, which caused a backlash from unions that represent municipal workers. On October 22, 2010, the *Wall Street Journal* ran an article about a group that was the largest spender on advertising for the midterm elections. It was the American Federation of State, County and Municipal Employees (AFSCME), which had spent almost $100 million in elections around the country. The goal? To protect the interests (read here: benefits) of its members. When asked about this level of spending, AFSCME president Gerald McEntee replied: "a lot of people are attacking public-sector workers as the problem. We're spending big. And we're damn happy it's big. And our members are damn happy it's big—it's their money."

It's whose money? Right now the money belongs to taxpayers, but it is owed, through unfunded liabilities, to public workers. To act like these liabilities stop at the state or the city makes no sense. These entities must get the funds from somewhere, and cities and states don't make products or create profit. They tax.

The full set of numbers can be found at the Pew Center's website, www .pewcenter.org. This organization also wrote a report on the subject entitled "The Trillion Dollar Gap: Underfunded State Retirement Systems and the Road to Reform," February 2010. This report can be accessed online as a PDF. It outlines this problem in great detail and shows the figures for each state. Obviously, Pew's estimate is of how far states are underwater is $1 trillion, as I referenced at the beginning of the chapter. This is not the total liabilities of state retirement systems, it is just the amount by which these funds are short! And it gets worse. Once you figure out how these liabilities are calculated, you will begin to see the overwhelming nature of our problem.

Calculating Long-Term Liabilities: Figuring Out What You Owe in the Future

If you owe someone $100 in two years, you might not think much of it. It's only $100, after all. What if you owed them $1,000 or $100,000? This would be more likely to get your attention. You might save a little bit of money, or even a lot of money, every month in order to pay off your debt, kind of like a car payment in reverse, where you save first and then make the payment at the end. You might even put the money into an interest-bearing account in order to have some growth on the funds over time. The interest you earn serves to lower what you must contribute to the account. If your interest-bearing account earns 4% per year, then in order to have $100,000 in two years, you have to put only $92,455 into the account today, assuming you will not make payments. The $92,455 is the net present value of your $100,000 future liability when it is discounted back to today at 4% (the assumed rate of growth). So to figure out long-term liabilities in today's dollars, you need to know:

1. The amount that has to be paid in the future (the pensions, or liabilities)
2. When those liabilities are to be paid in the future (how many years away)
3. What payment or contributions will be made into the pension fund
4. What rate of return will be earned on the fund between now and the payment dates (the discount rate)

Items 1, 2, and 3 are pretty straightforward mathematical computations. It is number 4 that is the source of problems. In the previous example where you earned 4%, it took a $92,455 contribution to have $100,000 in two years. However, if you had earned 8% it would have taken a contribution of only $85,733 to pay your debt. Earning an extra 4% allowed you to save over $6,700 in contributions. It's magic! Actually, it's not magic, but it is the power of interest earned and compounding. Consider this on the scale of pension funds, which is to say in the billions.

This is where things get sticky. The only thing that is known about pension funds is what must be paid at the end, or the liability (unlike health care benefits, which are also a moving target). The actual rate of return that is earned will change year to year. Some years are good, some are not. So states have to make an educated guess or assumption about what rate of return they will earn in order to calculate how much of a contribution they must make in order to have enough funds to pay the pensions when they come due. It is this assumption of a rate of return that is the root of all evil in pension funding calculations.

If a state assumes that it will earn 8% on its pension fund (called the discount rate, or rate of return), then the state will have to make much lower contributions than if it had assumed a discount rate of 5% or 6%. Because these liabilities stretch out for decades into the future, the compounded difference between 6% and 8% can be tens or even hundreds of billions of dollars, changing the required contributions of the state. It is in the state's best interest to assume the highest rate of return possible, therefore making its current-day liability (and also its current-day required contribution) as small as possible. But then reality shows up in the form of what actually happens. If the state assumes a rate of return of 8% per year and over 10 years the fund earns a rate of only 4% (comprising some good years and some bad), then the difference is racked up as unfunded liability in addition to any shortfall in contributions. As you might imagine, this is exactly what occurred over the last 15 years.

The last decade and a half has seen tremendous stock market gains (the late nineties) and some devastating losses. Along the way, interest rates have gone up and down in a narrow band but remained historically low. The combination of these two things has led to poor returns in pensions around the country. These poor returns are the result of pension funds having exposure to risky assets, like stocks. The reason that pension funds hold stocks is because, while they have the potential for loss, they also have the potential for gains well beyond what could be had in Treasury bonds. Pension funds are relying on potential gains in stocks to provide outsized returns so that states have lower required contributions. When pensions underperform over a long period, as they have recently, it underscores the risk of holding such assets.

There is a school of thought that says pension assets should be only as risky as their liabilities. Because pension liabilities are a guarantee of the state, then the assets held in these pensions should be guaranteed as well. This would require the pension funds to hold only Treasury bonds or other government-guaranteed securities. If pensions were to do this, then their assumed rate of return would be closer to 5% than the 7% to 8% that cities and states assume they will earn today. This change would create on paper a much greater unfunded liability because they assumed the contribution of the investments inside of the pension fund between now and when the payments are due would be smaller—guaranteed, but smaller. This seemingly small change would bring the unfunded liability of state pension funds from $1 trillion to just over $3.5 trillion.

So what is a state to do? If pension funds remain invested in risky assets, there's the potential for loss, which must be made up for in some way that involves higher taxes and fewer services for constituents, or diminished benefits for retirees, or a combination. If pension funds instead change their allocation to more guaranteed securities, they will lock in a much higher unfunded liability and still be left calling upon taxpayers and municipal workers to make up the difference. It is truly a case of damned if you do and damned if you don't. And none of this addresses the blatantly irresponsible actions of states that did not make their required contributions, thereby compounding an already difficult situation.

Tough Choices Facing States

No matter what course these governments choose, the impact on budgets is obvious: there will be less money available for everything else. This brings us all the way back to the pro-cyclical nature of pension funding. These funds need much higher contribution rates at the exact time that governments cannot afford it. Because of where we are in the Winter Season of the economy, cities and states don't have much reason to believe that they will see a pickup in economic activity and, therefore, tax revenue. Over the last several years tax revenue has fallen from where it was in the mid-2000s. Now property tax revenue seems likely to fall given the extended decline in property values. The year 2010 saw a slight positive uptick in tax revenue from 2009, but that was due to increased tax rates, not a dramatic move higher in economic activity.

The Nelson A. Rockefeller Institute of Government (www.rockinst.org) tracks state finances and shows how revenues have changed over the past several years in **Chart 4-1.**

While it looks like tax revenue has made a dramatic recovery, remember this is only the percentage change from the prior year, so a move back above zero simply means that revenues are no longer falling. Actual tax revenues are still well below what they were three years ago, and that is not adjusted for inflation, nor does it take into account the tremendous increase in claims on state services over the last three years in terms of Medicaid and unemployment benefits. All of these claims on states come at the exact time they cannot afford them.

Every day, every minute, retirement benefit liabilities are growing. They don't stop unless there is a change in the calculation of what recipients will receive. With a cloudy economic picture and taxpayers struggling to not only stay afloat but to prepare for their own retirements, it is difficult to

Chart 4-1: Percentage Change in State Tax Collections vs. Year Ago

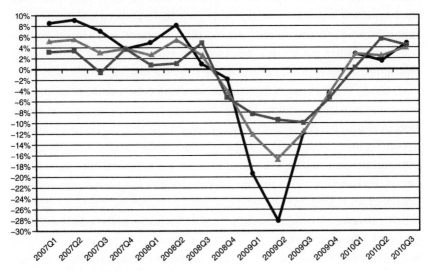

Data Source: **Rockefeller Institute**

see a good ending to this situation. The only good thing that can be said about this situation of owing at least a trillion dollars more than you have is that you are not the biggest deadbeat around. That award, hands down, goes to the US government.

The Greatest Unfunded Liabilities of All: Social Security and Medicare

The backstory to Social Security (Old Age, Survivor's, and Disability Insurance, or OASDI) is littered with Machiavellian motivations and broken promises. The program was instituted under Franklin D. Roosevelt not as an annuity to hard workers so that they could retire in comfort, but as part of a forced retirement system that was meant to make room for younger workers. The program was supposed to be voluntary, never take more than 1% of pay, never be taxed, and never were the funds to be commingled with other US government funds and spent by the government. So much for any of that! The story on Medicare is a little truer to its current form. It was always meant as a way for seniors in our country to access health care. It was not supposed to run a deficit, and certainly not meant as an open invitation to get any and all treatments available no matter what the cost. What was true about both of these programs from the beginning is that they were always pass-through programs where current workers paid for current retirees. They were not, and are not, savings programs. What got us into trouble were two things: the changing age distribution of our population and the runaway cost of health care.

In the 1930s, there were 16 workers for every retiree and Social Security was running a large surplus. The baby boom generation brought an explosion in young people who eventually joined the workforce and paid into Social Security as well. This worked wonderfully in terms of paying for retiring workers through taxes on current workers until the baby boom ended. By the mid-1970s it was obvious that the long-term prospects for the program were grim. We would reach a point where the large group of retiring boomers would claim more out of Social Security than the smaller group of younger workers was paying in. Ronald Reagan once said that Social Security is like a man who has jumped off of a 100-story building. At the twentieth floor someone says, "How's it going?" The man replies, "Pretty good so far!" Unfortunately, it won't end well. As the boomers move toward retirement, and we have fewer young workers entering the workforce, there simply won't be enough taxpayers to fund Social Security. The pyramid of many young workers with few retirees that existed from the 1930s through the 1960s has been changed into something of a square. So what about that surplus? It doesn't exist. Well, it does on paper.

The Social Security Administration is the proud owner of trillions of dollars of . . . US government bonds. By regulation, when Social Security runs a surplus (which it did every year it existed until 2010) it was required to buy US Treasury bonds with the extra money. This means that when Social Security needs to spend down some of its surplus in the years ahead, it will have to redeem its bonds. The US government has no money, so it must access the bond markets and find other buyers. For all intents and purposes, Social Security has no savings whatsoever. Any deficit run by the program when current taxes do not cover current disbursements must be made up by the US government incurring more debt.

The situation with Medicare is actually worse. This program began running a deficit in 2005 and will for the foreseeable future, spending down its stash of US Treasury bonds. As more boomers move into retirement, the health care system in America will have a very difficult time keeping up with services, much less payment for services rendered.

This brings up the question of money. Given that Social Security and Medicare ran surpluses for decades and now hold trillions of dollars in US Treasury bonds, how underfunded are these programs? The numbers are so big as to defy understanding.

Social Security is estimated to be $16 trillion underfunded, whereas Medicare is estimated to be roughly $30 trillion underfunded. These figures are from the US government and unfortunately are woefully inaccurate. They are way too low! The Medicare number is such a figment of political imagination that the actuary responsible for calculating the figure would not sign off on it. The actuary was required to use current law in his calculation, but he believed that the law would be constantly adjusted. He was proven right. Just a few short months after the new health care law was passed, Congress once again approved the "Dr. Fix," which postponed cuts to the payments made to doctors for Medicare services.

Independent analysts have pegged our unfunded liabilities at anywhere from $70 trillion to over $100 trillion (www.usdebtclock.org). While we believe the US government's figures are too optimistic, the best estimate comes from Mary Meeker at $66 trillion. But does it matter? At $66 trillion, our unfunded liabilities are 4.5 times our GDP!

The numbers are so large, so daunting, as to be incomprehensible. And they grow every day. In the world of, "I can't believe we just did that," the US government voted in December of 2010 to cut Social Security payroll taxes by 30% for the year of 2011, an estimated $120 billion reduction in contributions. The reason was to put more money in the pockets of consumers who might then spend it. When addressing the fact that this adds to the shortfall for Social Security, White House advisor Jason Furman said, "The payroll-tax cut has absolutely no effect on the solvency of Social Security."* Furman is absolutely correct, of course. The program is insolvent, period. A $120 billion inflow or outflow will not materially change the funding status of a program that is $16 trillion underwater. Unfortunately, it is small enough to be a rounding error considering the scope of the program.

While these numbers are horrific, they represent only part of the prob-

---

* "Payroll Tax Cut Worries Social Security Advocates," *USA Today*, 12/12/10.

lem: the compounding promises that we must pay in the future. This is different from simply going into debt so that you can spend more money today than you take in as revenue, as you would on a credit card. To get a sense of what that problem looks like, we have to review the US annual deficit and total debt. Needless to say, this picture isn't pretty either!

The Growing Monster That Is Our Debt

Periodically, governments run deficits, incurring small or large amounts of debt to meet their annual obligations, depending on the circumstances of the moment. Typically, large deficits are run during wars or periods of economic contraction. The origins of the US as a country took substantial funding, resulting in $80 million of US debt by 1792, when the GDP was $220 million, or a 36.36% debt-to-GDP ratio. There can be periods of prosperity where the debt is paid down; however, to totally eliminate debt is uncommon . . . but not unheard of.

President Andrew Jackson was determined to completely eliminate US debt in the late 1830s and he did just that. Jackson had dismantled the Second Bank of the United States and firmly believed that credit was evil. For several years after the elimination of all US debt, the United States had neither an annual deficit nor a national debt. It didn't last long. His successor was Martin Van Buren, who won the election of 1836 and took office in 1837, right in time for the worst downturn of the Republic to that time. Van Buren felt the same way about debt as Jackson, so when the economy started to contract, Van Buren remained true to the idea of a solvent nation, cutting expenses and selling assets to remain in the black. Many argued that the fiscal restraint kept the nation in an economic downturn longer than necessary. In the years after Van Buren, the debt and deficit returned ever so modestly, but then came the Civil War, which required massive amounts of debt to finance. In the decades after the war, the debt was paid down some, only to move higher after the Bank Panic of 1907 and then explode during World War I. The annual deficit of the United States has ebbed and flowed over time while the debt remained tame well into the late 1900s. It is only recently that we have gone on a spending binge.

The table opposite shows the US deficit and debt, and also shows those figures as percentages of GDP to give some perspective on the numbers. The negative figures in the deficit column show periods of surplus. The US debt as a percentage of GDP shows that debt has grown and contracted over time, showing the effects of major wars. This back-and-forth existed until the 1980s, after which time our national debt grew dramatically both nominally and as a percentage of GDP. The explosion in national debt is due to the continued budget deficits run by the federal government. From 1792 to 1950, the United States ran deficits in one-third of the years, or 51 out of 159 years. Starting in 1951, the United States has run a deficit in 50 out of 60 years, or more than 80% of the time!

HISTORICAL U.S. DEBT AND DEFICITS					
Year	US GDP	US Deficit	Deficit as % of GDP	US Debt	Debt as % of GDP
1792	0.22	–		0.08	36.36%
1830	1.01	(0.01)		0.05	4.95%
1840	1.56	0.01	0.64%		Debt-free
1865	9.88	0.96	9.72%	2.68	27.13%
1900	20.60	(0.04)		2.14	10.39%
1910	33.40	(0.04)		2.65	7.93%
1920	88.40	(0.60)		25.95	29.36%
1930	91.20	(0.87)		16.19	17.75%
1940	101.40	3.06	3.02%	42.97	42.38%
1950	293.70	1.27	0.43%	257.36	87.63%
1960	526.40	(2.52)		286.33	54.39%
1970	1,038.30	2.84	0.27%	370.92	35.72%
1980	2,788.10	73.83	2.65%	907.70	32.56%
1990	5,800.50	221.04	3.81%	3,233.31	55.74%
2000	9,951.50	(236.24)		5,674.18	57.02%
2008	14,441.40	458.55	3.18%	9,986.08	69.15%
2010	14,623.90	1,555.58	10.64%	14,153.00	96.78%

Note that the current debt and deficit numbers do not include unfunded liabilities, and therefore they are not the result of Social Security and Medicare! These two programs ran surpluses until only recently

(Social Security, 2010, and Medicare, 2005), after which they required contributions from the US government in the form of repayment of the bonds that each trust fund holds as discussed above. Instead, the current deficits are being run in order to fund the day-to-day operation of the government plus the recent stimulus programs ($168 billion in 2008, $800 billion in 2009, $100 billion in 2010) and the increase in unemployment benefits to cover those who are unemployed more than 27 weeks. There are many areas in the US budget that can be argued—defense spending, education, homeland security, etc.—and rightfully all areas should be examined.

To run such deficits, growing our national debt, requires that investors continue to buy US government bonds. It is idiotic to claim that just because investors around the globe have bought our bonds in the past that the will continue to do so in the future!

US spending is wildly out of control, with the US budget deficit in 2010 reaching $1.4 trillion and representing 10% of GDP in just that one year! This was the second year of trillion-dollar deficits, and, unfortunately, the forecast is for huge deficits in the years to come.

Using the US government's own projections, we are expected to run deficits of $1.3 trillion in 2011, falling to $724 billion in 2014, then rising to $1.25 trillion in 2020. And this is based on not just rosy, but naïvely optimistic assumptions! **Chart 4-2** shows the president's budget projections.

Chart 4-2: Estimate of the President's Budget

	2009	2010	2011	2012	2013	2014	2015	2016	2017	2018	2019	2020	2011–20
Revenue	2105	2118	2460	2808	3095	3341	3504	3693	3869	4036	4211	4416	35434
Mandatory	2094	2034	2156	2091	2176	2322	2454	2636	2752	2871	3084	3267	25808
Discretionary	1237	1375	1401	1334	1301	1303	1323	1355	1381	1407	1446	1487	13737
Net Interest	187	209	244	298	365	440	520	596	675	755	834	916	5644
Total	3518	3618	3801	3723	3842	4065	4297	4587	4808	5033	5364	5670	45189
Deficit	−1413	−1500	−1341	−915	−747	−724	−793	−894	−939	−997	−1153	−1254	−9755
Public Debt	7545	99221	10512	11579	12467	13329	14256	15297	xxxxx	xxxxx	xxxxx	xxxxx	xxxxx
GDP		14236	14595	14992	15730	16676	17606	18421	19223	xxxxx	xxxxx	xxxxx	xxxxx	xxxxx

Data Source: **Congressional Budget Office Presidential Budget**

Notice the revenue line at the top. This is the amount of tax revenue that the US government forecasts it will receive from personal income tax, Social Security tax, corporate tax, etc. In 2009 and 2010, the numbers are flat at around $2,100 billion. But a funny thing happens on the way to 2011: the government assumes it will see a 16% rise in tax revenue, from $2,118 billion to $2,460 billion, and then the revenues will rise between 5% and 13% in the years from 2012 through 2020. This type of tax revenue growth assumes the US economy will rebound quite strongly and show 4% to 5% growth year after year in the decade ahead. Given everything we know about the debt hangover we have today, this is not just questionable; these types of estimates are pure fantasy.

Instead, we believe that the US will move sideways for a period and then suffer another contraction. After that, we will most likely see muted growth for years as we work off the excess debt that we have at every level in our system. Instead of a "small" budget deficit of $1,254 billion in 2020, which assumes that tax revenues will be over 100% higher than 2010, our internal estimate is that our deficit will be closer to $3,000 billion, or $3 trillion, as reflected in **Chart 4-3.**

Based on our muted view of economic growth after another downturn, we see the US economy simply retracing its steps back up to revenues

Chart 4-3: Projected Federal Deficit of United States in 2020, per CBO and HS Dent

at Varying Revenue Levels ($Billions)

	CBO	HS Dent Optimistic	HS Dent Realistic
Total Revenues	$4,416	$3,029	$2,524
Mandatory Expenditures	$3,267	$3,267	$3,267
Discretionary Expenditures	$1,487	$1,487	$1,487
Net Interest	$916	$916	$916
Total Expenditures	$5,670	$5,670	$5,670
Deficit	($1,254)	($2,641)	($3,146)

Data Source: **Congressional Budget Office Presidential Budget**

of $2,500 billion, which was the high back in 2007. If we are a bit more optimistic, we could potentially see revenues jumping 50% above 2010. However, we don't see the possibility of government revenues increasing 100% over the levels of 2010 that would require a 7% growth rate every year!

With such massive liabilities, the US government is very limited in what it can do to assist in the current financial crisis, which we will discuss more in a later chapter. Right now, the important point to recognize is that the US government has created its own financial straitjacket, just as the states have done, and just as the private sector has done. We are smack in the middle of a crisis created by too much debt at every level!

Restructuring Debt

The current financial crisis is what is referred to as a balance sheet crisis. There is a breakdown between what is held as assets and brought in through revenue and what is owed as liabilities. Many cities, most states, and the US government all take in less than they spend and have gigantic, growing unfunded liabilities. In this instance, an individual company or person might go bankrupt, taking a full accounting of what they own and what they owe, and then apportioning to creditors according to their pecking order and how much is available. This is not what is usually done by public entities. But this is not a normal time. What will most likely come to pass is a massive restructuring in taxes and benefits for those who pay for and receive government retirement benefits. It won't be pretty, it won't be fun, and it won't be cheap. States such as Wisconsin, Ohio, and Florida recently took a stand against public employee unions and their benefits, much as Governor Mitch Daniels of Indiana did years ago. This is a start, but it is not enough.

We will throw away any pretense of Social Security being anything but a redistribution of wealth, means-testing out higher income individuals. Medicare will follow the same path, requiring those with means to pay more for coverage in retirement. There will be massive restructuring of current expenditures at all levels of government, which will require asset sales, office closings, employment freezes, and firings.

All of this works against any economic recovery and, just like the balance sheet restructuring that will happen with individuals, it points more toward deflation than inflation. Understanding deflation is hard. Chapter 5 will outline not only the traits of deflation, but also the role of money and money creation, so that you can see why government policies are ineffective and trivial compared to the massive issues that we face.

Deleveraging and Deflation: It's All About Money and Restructuring of Debt

The Rise of the Consumption Haters

As most of us (those older than 30) went through high school, college, and even grad school, Japan was a thing of envy. To appropriately refer to the country was not by a geographic designation—the country of Japan—but instead by its economic nickname, Japan, Inc. The theory that Japan would conquer the US without firing a shot, essentially out-manufacturing and out-engineering the great Western nation, was the subject of many books. For those of us in business school, studying Japan and its meteoric rise was required. From the ashes of WWII through the 1980s, it had grown to be the second largest economy in the world. It was only a matter of time before Japan eclipsed the US, and along the way the country would continue to accumulate large sums of US debt. It looked like the tide had turned in favor of the East. Then suddenly things changed.

Beginning in 1989, Japan began to feel the effects of decades of consumption and a rising property market built on debt. The wind came out of the sails of its real estate bubble in 1990–1992, leaving giant holes in the balance sheets of Japanese banks. The Japanese government tried to gloss over the problem at first, lowering interest rates and telling everyone that things were "fine." But they were not fine. Property values kept falling, as did interest rates and credit, business activity, and consumption. Japan was in a deflationary contraction. No amount of government borrowing or stimulus could pull it out. The country had turned a demographic corner that was easy to see, as long as you were looking.

We forecast the decline of Japan using the same simple but powerful research outlined in Chapter 2. The small island nation peaked in births in the late 1940s, and then suffered the 1960s, which would logically lead to economic decline starting 46 years later, or approximately 1992. Even Japan's rebound in births was small. The downturn in Japan that was expected in the early 1990s started slightly earlier, brought forward by a debt bubble based on property values that ended in a credit crisis. Sound familiar?

Today, 20 years after the start of its meltdown, Japan is still suffering deflation. An entire generation of young people has come of age knowing nothing but falling prices, a lack of employment opportunities, and a government that continues to favor the elderly at the expense of children and education, all the while piling up government debt that has now reached 200% of GDP. Hisakazu Matsuda, president of Japan Consumer Marketing Research Institute, calls the twenty-somethings "Consumption Haters," putting them in stark contrast to the previous generation that showed ultimate refinement by throwing around money at nightclubs and karaoke bars. Members of this young generation have watched prices fall their entire lives, making the idea of purchasing anything seem witless. They have looked on as people have purchased condos for $500,000 only to sell them for less than half that a decade later. The average home price in Japan currently stands exactly where it was in 1983. Jobs are retained by the older set as they simply wait to retire, leaving little for young, ambitious new graduates to do anything but work for modest salaries with no benefits or emigrate. Continually falling asset prices, stagnant and falling wages, and a quickly graying population are all feeding deflation. The force of deflation slowly and steadily eats away at the standard of living in Japan.*

We have often referenced Japan in our work, as it is the only modern-day example of deflation that existed until 2008/2009. We need people to understand that governments can try to change the economic tide,

---

* Martin Fackler, "Japan Goes from Dynamite to Disheartened," *New York Times,* Oct. 17, 2010, p. A1.

and they might even succeed for a very short period of time, but ultimately the force of demographics will overwhelm their efforts. The
Japanese ran up their property values in a debt-fueled frenzy just as
their large demographic group was reaching its peak in spending.
Even though the rest of the world was on fire through the 1990s and
part of the 2000s, Japan kept falling further and further into a deflationary funk! How do people think that the US will stay out of deflation
with overwhelming debt and the largest group in our population trying to pay down debt and save more? We won't! To see why this is a
foregone conclusion, all you need to do is follow the money. The creation and destruction of money, to be exact.

Do you know that you have the power to create money? It's true! In fact,
anyone who takes out a loan, spends on credit, or in any other way bor-
rows money from a lending institution creates money. The reason has to
do with a process called "fractional reserve." Modern banking is founded
on the idea of lending. A saver will take his money to a bank and put
the money on deposit. But the money does not stay at the bank. Instead,
the bank lends out most of what the saver deposits, keeping only a small
amount of the deposit, or fraction, on reserve. The bank earns interest on
what it has lent out, which is typically lent at a higher rate than the bank
pays savers. This is how banks traditionally make money.

The key focus here is that a bank lends out most of the deposits that it
receives from savers. If the bank receives a $1,000 deposit from John, the
bank will record on the books that it owes John $1,000. Then the bank
will loan out roughly $900 (in the US the reserve requirement is 10%, so
banks hold back 10% of deposits), say, to Susan. At this point the bank will
record that it has lent $900 to Susan, who owes that amount back to the
bank. John still "owns" his $1,000 and can withdraw it at any time, and yet
Susan now has $900 to spend as she wishes. In effect, the $900 that Susan
received was lent into existence, as two different people (John and Susan)
claim ownership of that money at the same time. The money simply did
not exist before the bank lent it to Susan. Now that she has it, Susan is free
to spend it, for example, to pay a tailor. If the tailor then deposits the $900
in his own bank, then his bank will lend 90% of that amount, or $810, to
another borrower. This situation continues until the original $1,000 rep-
resents $10,000 in the economy; $9,000 was simply created out of thin air
through fractional reserve!

Through fractional reserve, or the requirement that banks keep only a small fraction of their deposits on hand, our economy allows for the expansion of money supply through lending. The larger the amount of lending in the economy, the greater the expansion of money supply. As money supply increases through credit, consumers have a greater ability to spend, thereby driving the economy ever higher. This is exactly what happened during the 2000s! We funded new spending on houses, cars, boats, televisions, furnishings, education, eating out—just about everything under the sun—by finding new ways to expand credit!

Consider the combination of all of the different types of debt in our economy: consumer, corporate, financial sector, and government. **Chart 5-1** shows the growth of each of these layered on top of each other. At the top in 2008, the total outstanding debt in the US was $56 trillion!

This total debt amount represented an increase of just over 100% from 2000 through 2008, and a large portion of that increase was centered in the financial and the consumer sectors. As discussed in Chapter 3, many factors contributed to the explosion of private debt in the US, which was

Chart 5-1: Total US Debt

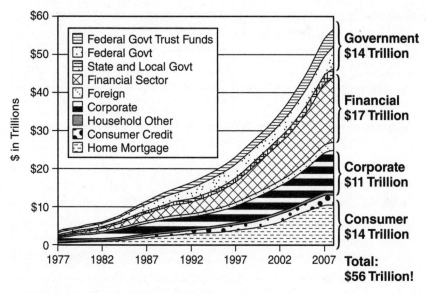

Data Source: Federal Reserve Flow of Funds Report

Chart 5-2: Total Mortgage Debt

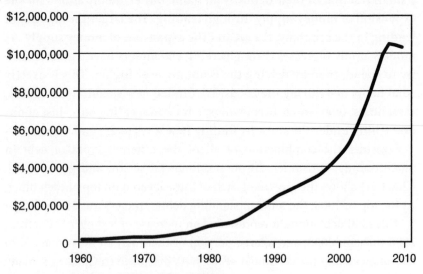

Data Source: **Federal Reserve Z1 Flow of Funds Report**

Chart 5-3: Total Revolving Consumer Debt

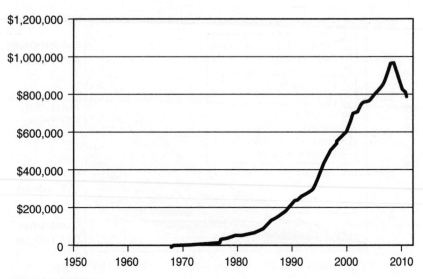

Data Source: **Federal Reserve**

mainly centered on the housing market in both primary and secondary loans. Total mortgage debt is shown in **Chart 5-2.** The total US debt also includes hundreds of billions of dollars worth of credit card debt and other revolving debt, as well as installment debt, such as car loans and student loans. **Charts 5-3 and 5-4** show total revolving debt and total non-revolving debt, respectively.

As we grew our dependence on credit to fund our spending desires in the economic Fall Season, we also were expanding the money supply in the US by trillions of dollars. Institutions such as investment banks got in on the act and were leveraging to the hilt, much more than commercial banks. While traditional banks were limited to 10× leverage (keeping only 10% of deposits, lending the rest), investment banks were leveraging at 25× and 30×, meaning that for every dollar of capital they had, they lent out $30! Money was created at a dizzying pace! Thus, the financial sector exploded with debt creation (new borrowing) during the 2000s! **Chart 5-5** shows the change in debt in each section of the economy from 2000 through 2010.

Chart 5-4: Total Nonrevolving (Installment) Consumer Debt

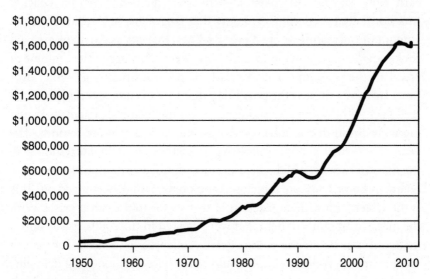

Data Source: Federal Reserve

Chart 5-5: Change in Debt Outstanding, 2000–2010

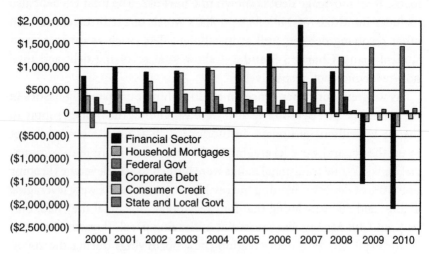

Data Source: **Federal Reserve Flow of Funds Report (FRB Z1)**

Notice the huge increases in the financial sector leading up to 2008. These steady increases in borrowing are the same thing as money creation, leading to spending that is greater than we could sustain just on what we earn. Now ask yourself, "What happens when the money gets paid back?" In a normally functioning economy that is growing at a steady rate, the amount of borrowing rarely if ever declines. Instead, as old loans are paid back, new loans are made to new borrowers. This keeps the amount of credit in the economy at least steady, if not consistently growing, over time. However, there is the possibility that we can enter a period in which credit actually declines, wreaking havoc on the financial system and causing widespread disruptions. We have entered one of those periods. The years 2009–2010 show the massive reductions in debt outstanding in the financial sector, which correspond with huge write-downs across the board, as home loans are foreclosed and credit card debt charged off. This is the violent, immediate reaction in this sector to the credit crisis. With the massive amounts of debt that were created in the 2000s, it was only a matter of time before the house of cards collapsed in on itself. The earned income in our economy simply could not service the amount of debt outstanding. The rate of default on mortgages, credit cards, home equity lines of credit (HELOCs), and all other types of loans exploded. Each default represents a reduction in the amount of money outstanding, or money destruction, unless another loan is made to make up for the contraction. However, new loans are not being made at the same rate that other borrowing is being paid back or simply written off. Instead, we have entered a period in which banks, financial institutions, businesses, and consumers are working to pare down debt, not to take on more.

Look again at **Charts 5-2, 5-3,** and **5-4**. These numbers reveal a sea change, wherein the steadily rising tide of debt in the past has given way to a new era of flat and falling credit on the consumer front. The importance of this cannot be overstated! When our population as a whole chooses to reduce the amount of debt it has outstanding, the money supply in our economy shrinks! Like turning an aircraft carrier, this change is slow, but it is steady and almost unstoppable.

A contraction in the amount of money available in an economy leads to deflation, which creates a very difficult economic situation. The amount of money available to buy the goods and services that are available literally is falling, which leads to falling demand. This slack demand leads to a loss of jobs, which leads to even less demand. Thus, governments will do most anything to avoid deflation. Unfortunately, as the Japanese found out, those efforts rarely work. But they do leave behind a legacy: a government whose finances are in shambles. The US government has embarked on a program of deficit spending as in no other time in history except during major wars. Their purpose is to rekindle our economy by having the government make up for the lack of consumer spending, but it's not working. As **Chart 5-5** above shows, the US government has barely maintained the level of debt in our economy, as it has borrowed roughly the same amount that the private sector has shed! While this has staved off some deflation for the short term, at what price? The US deficit and debt are now putting the US government at risk, so a different approach has to be used. This is where the Federal Reserve takes the stage.

Money is created in two ways: it is lent into existence, as we discussed above, or it is printed out of thin air, which is the purview of the Federal Reserve (the Fed), the central bank of the United States. The Fed is responsible for maintaining the currency in the US. As such, the Fed can use its unilateral, unchecked power to create new money any time it wants to. Why would the Fed create new money? To create inflation, of course!

The Fed's Failed Efforts to Manufacture General Inflation

The baby boom generation and the Gen X and millennial generations all came of age at a time of ready access to debt. Home lending was a growing industry not just during the 1990s and 2000s, but has been since the 1940s. Credit cards, once the purview of individual stores offering credit, moved into the bankcard realm and then finally severed that tie, becoming the preferred method of transaction over checks by the 1990s (how many times do you see checks written at retailers anymore?). Cars, boats, vacation condos, education (student loans), elective surgery, daily shopping, holiday gift buying—it all became easily attainable through credit issued either directly in the form of unsecured personal debt (credit cards) or taken out as a secured loan in some form (a home equity loan, car loan, boat loan, etc.). It got to the point that your dentist would (and probably still will) offer you an easy-pay credit program to get that teeth-whitening treatment that will make you successful at work and attractive to the opposite sex!

Low interest rates were fueled by falling inflation in the Fall Season, and then were fueled even further by the Federal Reserve, which made these transactions ever more palatable, as monthly payments fell and leveraged asset prices rose. If you take out a home equity line of credit (HELOC, discussed in Chapter 3) and then your house subsequently rises in value, it's as if you got free money. As boomers went through their predictable stage of rising consumption in the Fall Season of the economy (1982–2007), not only did spending rise year after year, but also asset prices seemed impervious to the normal business cycle, rising year after year and suffering nothing but short-lived declines. Asset bubbles and falling interest rates are the hallmark of the Fall "bubble boom" Season. In this environment, lending to consumers or businesses or against assets like commercial and home real estate seemed like a no-brainer. Now, of course, we are dealing with a much different scenario.

The recent downturn has highlighted the risk of lending and the risk of borrowing. Roughly 28% of all mortgages in the United States are underwater: the current market value of the home is less than the mortgage on that home. The situations in some hard-hit areas are much worse than the national average. In Florida, just under 50% of homes with mortgages are underwater. Despite the stimulus and recovery, 2010 set a record in terms

of the number of foreclosures for the nation, and that included a period
of almost no foreclosures, when the "robo-signing" scandal brought about
a moratorium on foreclosures near the end of the year. The new Frank-
Dodd Wall Street Reform and Consumer Protection Act calls for mortgage lenders to keep a portion of home loans on their books if the down
payment is small. This requirement is causing banks to be even more
reluctant to make loans than they already were in this market.

In 2010, over 90% of new mortgages were guaranteed by the government through the US Federal Housing Authority (FHA), the Federal
National Mortgage Association (FNMA, or Fannie Mae), or the Federal
Home Mortgage Loan Corporation (FHLMC, or Freddie Mac). Buyers
are waiting out the cycle to see if prices will continue their fall, and so far
they have been right. Zillow, a real estate valuation company (www.zillow
.com), reported in January 2011 that home prices have fallen 26% from
the top, outpacing the drop in real estate prices from 1928–1933, during
the Great Depression. Homeowners who must sell are competing with
short sales and foreclosures, which push prices even lower than they otherwise would be. Commercial property is faring worse. Companies such
as JP Morgan have reneged on billions of dollars in loans, because they
have realized that the costs of the mortgage payments and other expenses
will far outstrip any reasonable estimate of future rents and capital gains.

In the realm of credit cards, companies went through a period of
charge-offs in 2008 and 2009, culling from their books the slow-pays and
no-pays and shedding billions in uncollectible debts. Companies such as
American Express and Capital One became more stringent in their lending standards, and many card companies lowered the amount of credit
available to borrowers. GMAC, the finance arm of General Motors that
waded into the subprime lending arena in the heyday of that market,
required a bailout from the US government. The entity became Ally Bank
in order to qualify for and receive the bailout. In an odd, ironic twist, a
recent advertising pitch for this same company was all about being truth-
ful with customers.

The financial sector, which created all of this debt, is shrinking. As
shown in Chapter 3, the financial sector ramped up its own debt from
$7.5 trillion to $17 trillion in just 8 short years. Municipal debt, discussed
in Chapter 4, is roughly $2.8 trillion, which doesn't include another
$1 trillion (a very conservative estimate) of unfunded retirement benefit

liabilities. Tax revenues fell sharply and have recovered only partially; cities and states simply cannot afford their current levels of debt. The US government is grappling with $1+ trillion deficits, with no end in sight. Their own rosy, everything-will-get-better-soon estimates show that we will run ruinous deficits for the foreseeable future, with our national debt ballooning from its current $14 trillion to $25 trillion by 2020, according to Congressional Budget Office (CBO) estimates that assume a doubling of federal revenues by 2020. Our view is that the outlook is much grimmer, as we discussed in detail in Chapter 4.

We are at the point at which the largest group of consumers, the baby boom generation, wants to pay down its debt and save for retirement. This coincides with a forced reduction in credit outstanding in the financial sector through mortgage foreclosures, credit card write-offs, etc., and a time of financial crisis at all levels of government. With consumers, businesses, banks, investment banks (shadow banking industry), cities, and states all at a point of reducing their debt, or deleveraging, a period of credit contraction for everyone but the US government is all but certain, and even the US government will be restrained by market forces eventually. What accompanies deleveraging is an unusual economic occurrence: deflation.

Everyone is familiar with inflation, a period of generally rising prices; however, deflation is a rare occurrence in modern economic times in the Western world. It typically occurs only once in a human lifetime, currently about every 80 years. Back in the 1800s, it happened about every 60 years. Deflation is the other hallmark of the Winter Season, as last occurred from 1930 to 1942. The reason that deflation is so uncommon is that it stands in direct opposition to what central banks want to have happen. With the rise of central banks and the decoupling of currencies from any linkage to hard assets such as gold and silver, governments have been able to steer monetary policy to avoid deflation in almost every case, until now. As the story on Japan shows, demographics are the overwhelming force that even the government cannot overcome.

Inflation Is Manageable, Deflation Is the Devil

Inflation is a period that is marked generally by rising prices and usually by rising wages. As is always the case, wages tend not to rise as quickly as prices, which creates an uncomfortable situation for consumers, who will experience a constant erosion in their standard of living, or their purchasing power, which is their ability to buy stuff with the dollars they have. Rising prices might sound like a nagging, bad thing. After all, who wants stuff to cost more? In the world of economics and politics, you might be surprised to find out that governments want this. Most governments not only desire inflation, they desperately *need* it. Moderate inflation is supposed to create interesting motivations for companies and consumers as well as give governments a break on their debt. Deflation is a period that is marked by generally falling prices and falling wages. While falling prices might sound good to consumers, they are very bad for businesses. Falling prices tend to lead to high unemployment and make debt more expensive, which are bad outcomes for governments.

The Theory of Monetary Inflation and Deflation

Suspend your internal view of the world for a moment (you think that things are getting better or getting worse, you need to save for retirement, you are worried about job security, etc.) and focus only on prices. If you believe that prices will go higher in the next year, will you buy more stuff now or will you wait? It's a silly question, of course. If everything else is taken off the table for you in terms of making economic decisions and you think that prices will go higher in the future, then you will buy all that you can right now, locking in the lower prices of today. This is the simple theory of how inflation is supposed to affect the buying decisions of consumers and businesses.

There is also the other side of the economic coin to consider: the money that you use to buy stuff. If the money comes from savings, then you have to compare the interest rate on your savings to the expected price increase. If you have money in a savings account earning 4% and prices are rising by only 3%, then you would be better served by saving your money right up until you need something, because you are earning money faster than prices are rising. If you are earning 2% and prices are rising by 3%, then you should withdraw your savings and buy stuff immediately. If you are borrowing money, then the comparison is between the interest rate on your loan (or credit card) and the expected rate of inflation, or price increase, of whatever it is you are going to buy. If your loan cost is higher than the inflation rate, then you are better served by waiting to purchase.

Notice that with inflation, the rational consumer is expected to use interest rate comparisons (either the savings rate, if it is money he or she already has, or the borrowing rate, if it is money he or she will take out in a loan) to make a determination about when to spend. It is no accident that this variable is one of the central tools controlled by governments through central bank activities. If the central bank (the Fed in the US) believes that inflation is heating up and prices are rising too quickly, it can raise interest rates. This increase in rates should make savers choose to spend less because they are earning more and should make borrowers spend less because they have to pay a higher rate for a loan. Since interest rates can be increased to very high levels (such as the 20% short-term rates that prevailed in the early 1980s), the theory is that government action always can tame demand-based inflation. Demand-based inflation is inflation caused by an upward movement in the prices consumers are willing to pay for goods and services and is fed by expansion of credit, or borrowing. This type of inflation is different from inflation that reflects an erosion of purchasing power caused by the printing of money. We'll get to that shortly.

The government would like to see moderate inflation, because that is supposed to motivate rational consumers and businesses to engage in robust economic activity, which creates jobs and generates tax revenue, both of which are good for economies. Another benefit to inflation is that it makes debt cost less. If you have a car loan that costs $400 per month and you make $4,000 per month, then the loan payment is 10% of your monthly income. If, through general inflation, you get a raise of 5% this year, then you are now making $4,200 per month. The car loan, however, did not change; it is still $400 per month, but now represents only 9.5% of your income. Fixed payments cost less over time in periods of inflation because of rising incomes. Most governments operate at deficits, meaning that they must borrow money. In periods of inflation, their interest costs are expected to represent a declining percentage of their tax revenue simply because tax revenues are expected to go up as prices and wages go up. This is the old axiom of paying back debt with cheaper dollars in the future, because, due to inflation, the dollars won't buy as much (falling purchasing power). As you might expect, interest rates paid to savers tend to trail inflation, meaning that there is usually a constant erosion of the purchasing power of dollars that people have saved.

Deflation works exactly the opposite of inflation and is the scourge of governments. Return to our theoretical world in which everything else is being ignored for the moment. If prices are expected to fall, then consumers and businesses have good reason to put off purchases. There is no complicated comparison of rates of return or cost of borrowing, because these numbers cannot go negative (unless the government begins confiscating unspent funds by taxing savings). The government cannot lower interest rates below zero. Therefore, the ability of the government to control an economy that is faced with deflation using normal central bank tools is very limited, unlike its ability to raise interest rates to dizzying heights during periods of inflation. Also, debt becomes more expensive in times of deflation because incomes are falling.

In the inflation example above, a car loan was cheaper in relative terms because, as income grew, the fixed payment of $400 represented a smaller piece of the monthly income. In periods of deflation, the $400 still remains constant, but income falls. If the borrower's income falls from $40,000 to $38,000, then the $400 car payment now represents 10.5% of his monthly budget, leaving fewer funds to spend on other things. The same is true for the government. In periods of deflation, tax revenues fall as lower prices generate less sales tax and corporate income tax. Lower property values cause falling property tax, and falling incomes lead to falling personal income tax. Meanwhile, the interest and principal payments owed on outstanding government debt remain the same. They must be paid. As tax receipts fall, these debt payments represent a larger share of the government's funds. This situation is the opposite of what happens during inflationary times; it is an example of paying back debt with more expensive dollars (a time of rising purchasing power, in which dollars can buy more because prices are falling).

Periods of strong inflation, considered to be anything above 4% to 5% per year, can be painful for consumers, given that rising prices will make it difficult to maintain a standard of living. If a household's income does not keep up with rising prices, then choices have to be made about what to purchase and whether savings or debt should be used to supplement income. Inflation robs everyone of purchasing power by making existing dollars less valuable. You simply cannot buy as much. This is particularly hard on those who rely on a fixed income, like most retirees, who do not have the ability to move from job to job in search of higher income. Their days become a long, slow decline in the standard, and quality, of living. Strong inflation is not what governments want. Instead, they work toward that Goldilocks range of inflation, roughly 2%. They want the boiled frog effect. If the purchasing power of consumers is eroded slowly, it gives spenders a nudge to create more economic activity, which creates jobs, lessens the impact of debt, and makes people feel good about the assets they own. Thus, it is highly unlikely that most people—like that frog—will notice and/or complain about the temperature of the water that is rising so slowly that the frog does not notice! Of course, the outcome is the same. In economics, you still lose your purchasing power; the frog still ends up just as dead.

The winners in a period of mild inflation are those who own assets (more motivation to spend), those with incomes rising faster than inflation, and those who owe debt, as repayment becomes cheaper in the future (more reason to borrow). It is true that prices are gently rising and that there is a cost to borrowing (interest rates are not near zero), but all in all, things are good in the eyes of the government. An economic period that allows governments to pay back debt with cheaper dollars, encourages consumers to spend more, rewards those who buy hard assets, and has the kicker of rewarding those who use debt to leverage their purchases is definitely preferred, as long as it doesn't get too hot. This scenario creates what is called the Virtuous Cycle of Growth.

Virtuous Cycle of Growth
- As spending increases, sales increase and profits rise.
- Rising profits lead companies to hire more people and pay more, as well as to reward business owners and shareholders.
- Rising incomes and profits lead to greater spending.

The Virtuous Cycle is one of ever-increasing demand, employment, income, and profit. Utopia! In general, populations are happy. Their jobs are secure because of growing economic activity, their income is on the rise, and their standard of living might even increase if their income and borrowing are increasing.

Think about who this situation benefits: those who are currently working, those who are borrowing, those who are lending, and those who are investing in growth assets (equities, real estate, etc.). Looking at the spread of the population in the US over the past 25 years during the Fall Season, this would have been the baby boomers, who were working and raising their children, as well as retirees who owned real estate and held some equities and finance companies that were lending against assets that were rising in price. For those who were retired without growth assets and relied on fixed income, the last 25 years were difficult. Steady inflation eroded their standard of living as interest paid on simple savings was not enough to keep up with prices.

Deflation, on the other hand, is typically seen as a punisher. A period of falling prices leads to shrinking companies and rising unemployment. Corporate margins fall dramatically, leading to a "survival of the fittest" rout, with many business and bank failures. Those lucky enough to keep their wages steady and to maintain their wealth through simple savings can increase their standard of living during a deflationary period. However, to those who lose their income, like the millions of Americans who have found themselves unemployed since 2008, or those who hold growth assets such as real estate and stocks, deflation is a monster. In times of deflation, cash and cash flow are king. Economic theory tells us that as prices fall, consumers choose to buy less, waiting on even lower prices. This slack demand causes prices to fall further, reinforcing the decision not to buy. Unfortunately, it also causes sellers to cut back on production, thereby leading to higher unemployment. With fewer people able to buy things, demand falls further, adding to a Vicious Cycle of Deflation (falling demand) that causes economic contraction and causes demand to fall further.

Vicious Cycle of Deflation
- As demand slows, prices fall.
- Falling prices lead to consumers holding off on purchases, waiting to see if prices fall further.
- Lower demand leads to sellers cutting prices and buying less inventory.
- A slowdown in production and selling leads to job losses.
- Job losses lead to fewer people buying, or a further reduction in demand.
- The further reduction in demand leads to prices falling again, thereby completing the cycle.

Deflation causes strife and uncertainty in economies. Workers are worried about job security. Home prices fall, stock values plummet, and economic activity slows. Populations caught in deflation become agitated and demand government action.

You can get free access to Harry's very popular webinar "Understanding the Economy and What Lies Ahead" by visiting and registering at http://www.hsdent.com/webinar.

While the widespread sentiment in times of deflation is negative, there are those who do well. In addition to those who keep their current income, as noted above, deflation rewards savers who either hold cash or receive steady streams of income. In our population, that group includes those still employed without a cut in pay and retirees who have most of their wealth in fixed-income or simple savings. As prices fall, these groups do not see a commensurate fall in their wealth and can purchase more with their dollars, especially assets that fall much more than consumer products and services. A first-time home buyer or perhaps a retiree who rents but is contemplating a move to Florida or Arizona can afford a better home today than he could 5 years ago or can buy the same house as 5 years ago for a lot less money. The result is the same. For a homeowner thinking of moving to a home that is similar in size and quality to his existing home, the loss on the existing unit offsets the new, lower price on the next home.

As mentioned above, falling prices render interest rates ineffective against deflation, which removes the main tool that most central banks use to steer economies. With interest rates compressed to near zero and deflationary forces still at work, governments turn to their other source of firepower: the printing press.

The Other Tool Used by Governments: Money Creation Through Printing

As explained above, governments use interest rates to encourage economic activity and to steer the credit system of money creation (saving and lending). If they push rates higher, they are trying to slow down an economy by rewarding savers and punishing borrowers. If they lower interest rates, then they are attempting to invigorate the economy by punishing savers and making loans easier to pay. In addition to interest rates, governments (or central banks) also have another tool: the creation of money itself. This topic is very difficult for people to grasp. It seems unimaginable, but in the US a small group of people, the seven members of the Board of Governors of the Federal Reserve and the five voting members of the twelve regional Federal Reserve Bank presidents, simply can choose to create what the rest of us work so hard to acquire.

However, the Fed does not look at money in the same way that workers and consumers do. To workers a dollar is the value received in exchange for their time and efforts. To consumers a dollar is a storehouse of value with three potential uses: savings, consumption (spending), or debt repayment (which is neither saving nor spending). The Fed views dollars not as earned vehicles for saving, spending, or debt reduction, but instead as fuel for the engine of the economy, to be injected or removed as necessary. If you want the economy to move faster, then you add more fuel, or money. If you want the economy to slow down, then you simply reduce the amount of fuel. How this actually happens will cause your brain to hurt a little.

The Fed maintains a balance sheet of US Treasury bonds. If the Fed wants the economy to slow down, it will sell bonds out of its inventory and it will receive the cash. This removes cash from the economy and is assumed to have the effect of slowing the economy down. Conversely, to speed up the economy, the Fed will print money out of thin air and buy bonds, which takes bonds out of circulation and injects more cash into the economy than was available before, thereby adding fuel. This is what the Fed has done since late 2008; it has added more fuel to the economy, first by lending more to commercial banks than it had previously and then by printing money out of thin air and buying securities.

Some will argue that the Fed does not literally print money, i.e., currency and coin. That is true, but it misses the point. However, to address this rebuttal, here is how it works. Financial institutions maintain accounts at the Federal Reserve. If the Fed wants to inject money into the economy, it will inform the markets of what bonds it wants to buy. Financial institutions then make an offer to sell those bonds to the Fed, which in turn buys what it wants from those institutions. Because these institutions maintain accounts with the Fed, the Fed will simply increase the accounts of the institutions from which the Fed bought bonds. So if Bank of America (NYSE: BAC) had $6 billion in its account at the Fed, and BAC then sold $200 million in US Treasury bonds to the Fed, the Fed would simply click a few keys to increase BAC's reserve account from $6 billion to $6.2 billion and would receive the bonds it purchased into its inventory. Voilà! Two hundred million dollars were created out of thin air. Was it printed into physical existence? No. Is it real? You bet. If you or I bought those bonds from BAC, we would have to use cash or sell another investment. The Fed does not do that.

At this point, the newly created funds are not cash; they are simply part of BAC's account at the Fed. However, now BAC can choose what to do with the funds. BAC can leave the funds on reserve at the Fed, at which point BAC would have excess reserves, which does nothing to stimulate the economy. BAC could lend the funds to borrowers who would spend them (consumers, home buyers, businesses, etc.), or BAC could use the money to buy other assets for itself, like bonds, stocks, etc. Other than leaving the money sitting at the Fed as excess reserves, the other actions that BAC might take all lead to the reserves being turned into cash. So while the Fed doesn't actually print money when it buys bonds, it certainly creates money digitally, which serves to increase the money supply in the economy.

The Inflationary Effect of Printing Money

If all other things are held the same, when the money supply is increased, the prices of goods and services will go up. This happens for two reasons. The first is that more dollars are available to buy the same amount of stuff. If BAC has more money to lend, then lending should increase. If BAC has more money to use for its own purpose of buying assets like stocks and bonds, then the prices of those assets are likely to go higher. Thus, the wealth of other investors will increase, allowing these investors to spend more. This increase in lending and increase in general wealth leads to more spending by borrowers and the holders of assets, thereby pushing prices higher.

The second reason prices go higher is dilution of value. Money as we think of it today is not tied to any hard asset like gold or silver. Instead, money in a country is generally said to represent the value of goods and services in the economy at the time. Allowing this definition to stand for a minute, you can see where if new money is created out of thin air without a corresponding increase in the goods and services, then all of the money in the system must be worth a little less. This is the exact point of printing money and the desire of the government when it does it. Its goal is to make money lose a little bit of its purchasing power, which affects all those dollars currently outstanding—including those in your pocket and in mine. Every time the Fed prints a new dollar, it sweeps some of the value from all the dollars already in existence to the new dollars, which is the same as a tax. However, this tax is not voted on, not deliberated, and not apparent. The government does not demand a payment from you outright. Instead, the government works to diminish what you can buy with the dollars you are holding on to, all in an effort to motivate you to spend so that the economy will grow again. This is the very definition of inflation: a period of rising prices that diminishes the purchasing power of currency. When central banks print money, they are attempting specifically to manufacture inflation that was not taking hold on its own.

This approach is what Fed chairman Ben Bernanke was describing when asked what he would do if he was faced with deflation. His answer was that he would "drop dollars from helicopters," meaning that he would make money very easy to get through low interest rates and by creating new money. Looking back at the last two and one half years, we say that he has been true to his word. As our economy has faltered, the Fed first lowered short-term interest rates dramatically and then injected massive amounts of newly created money into our system. The Fed's balance sheet, shown in **Chart 5-6**, reveals how the Fed has tried desperately to stimulate our economy using money, or monetary policy, to create inflation.

This chart shows a huge increase in the "Other Securities" category in late 2008, when banks were in desperate straits for cash. These banks had already sold or pledged their "good assets," meaning Treasury bonds, and most of the assets they had left were quickly sinking mortgage-backed bonds. Needless to say, in the fall of 2008 there wasn't much of a market for these securities. The Fed changed its lending standards to allow banks to pledge mortgage-backed securities in exchange for cash. This step was called qualitative easing, because the Fed lowered the threshold for the

Chart 5-6: Federal Reserve Balance Sheet ($ trillions)

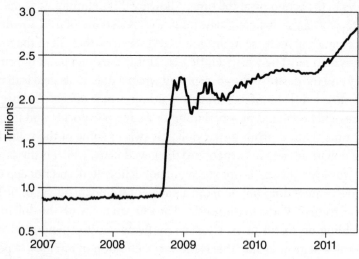

Data Source: **Federal Reserve**

quality of securities it would take as collateral for a loan of newly minted cash. Banks pledged this junk by the billions. Unfortunately, the markets did not cooperate by bouncing back quickly.

In April 2009, the Fed announced that it would straight out purchase over $1.25 trillion of mortgage-backed securities, thereby allowing banks to unwind their loans with the Fed and simply to sell the questionable mortgage-backed bonds to the Fed. This approach of printing money out of thin air to buy securities in the open market is called *quantitative easing* (QE), because it involves the Fed putting an increased quantity of new dollars in the hands of banks so that they can, presumably, use the infusion of cash to make new loans. But the banks did not make new loans. Instead, banks held on to their newly found cash, keeping it in their own accounts that they maintain at the Federal Reserve. Commercial banks are required to hold a small amount on account at the Fed, known as their reserve requirement. Anything above the required amount is called excess reserves. Over the course of 2009 and 2010, banks held approximately $1 trillion in excess reserves, as shown by **Chart 5-7.**

What motivates banks to hold the money instead of lending it? More bad loans on their books that they need to hold reserves against? No cred-

Chart 5-7: Excess Bank Reserves Held at Fed

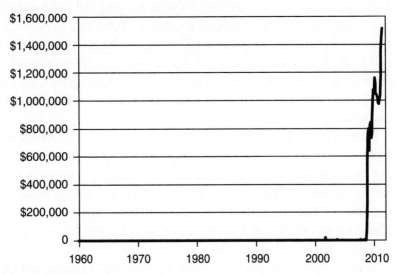

Data Source: Federal Reserve

itworthy borrowers? Low loan demand from consumer and business borrowers who are too much in debt from the last bubble? Obviously, the
banks hold the money due to some combination of these factors, but the
primary factor is likely to be low loan demand! No matter what the reason
for holding back the funds, the end result is that the cash is not finding its
way into the economy.

Throughout this new program of buying mortgage-backed securities,
which became known as quantitative easing 1 (QE1), the Fed created
more than $1.4 trillion. When the program came to an end in April 2010,
the credit markets were still a mess and the economy was limping along.
There was no sign of moderate inflation except in the rapid rise of the
equity markets and the rising prices of commodities. The general mood
and the equity markets in the US both turned sour in the summer of 2010
after QE1 ended, so the Fed went at it again. In a program called QE Lite,
the Fed announced that it would use all principal and interest payments
on the mortgage-backed bonds it held to buy Treasury bonds in the open
market. This gave the stock market a little boost, but it was short-lived.

By this time it was August 2010. Short-term interest rates were near
zero, 30-year fixed mortgages had been below 5% but were creeping

higher, and yet inflation was not widespread, unemployment remained high, and banks were not lending! So what does the Fed do? It once again goes on a buying binge, pledging another $600 billion in newly created money, this time for the purpose of buying US Treasury bonds. The goal was twofold: not only was it to put more money into the economy to create some inflation, but it also was to increase the demand for US Treasury bonds, with the intent of causing long-term interest rates to fall, to make mortgages cheaper.

In total the Fed printed and committed to print over $2.3 trillion. The Fed set overnight interest rates at 0% to 0.25%, which made the cost of borrowing almost nothing. The Fed now is using all of its newly printed money to buy US government bonds, effectively buying down interest rates so that generally loans and specifically mortgages, which key their interest rates off of Treasury bonds, are cheaper. All of this activity definitely is causing some inflation, but not in the way that the Fed wants.

Instead of a benign general rise in prices that causes an uptick in spending and wages, the economy is suffering through an unstoppable deflationary rout accompanied by high prices for natural resources and select assets. In short, the long-term trend of deflation is plodding along at a slow, deliberate pace, while the fleeting forces of inflation have reacted quickly to newly printed money and uncertainty over the value of money. However, this trend will not last. As time goes on, it will be readily apparent that the Fed, using monetary policy through creating money, is essentially bringing a knife to a gunfight. Not only will consumers not react the way that the government would like, but the problem is so big that a mere—that's right, a *mere*—$2 trillion to $3 trillion is like using a garden hose on a forest fire.

The Wrong Outcome: Rising Commodity Prices

During 2008 and 2009, the economy of the US splintered. The Fed did what it could to manufacture inflation out of thin air by keeping interest rates exceptionally low and printing money. This move was supposed to motivate consumers to spend more and banks to lend more, to make homes go up in value, to create more jobs, and to push wages gently higher; however, those things did not happen. Instead prices are rising on gasoline, canola

Chart 5-8: Jump in Commodity Prices, 2009–2010

Oct 2009–2010 Year-Over-Year Change

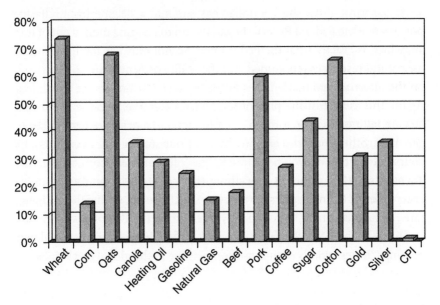

Data Source: Casey Research

oil, copper, gold, silver, wheat, sugar, steel, coal, oil, corn, and cotton. **Chart 5-8** shows the change in some commodities from 2009 to 2010.

Three things that we purchase at the grocery store or the gas station cost more, but our wages are not going up, jobs are not coming back, and our home values remain depressed. How is this possible? It is because of the difference between local and global markets.

Natural resources are priced on international markets and reflect the constantly changing relationship of currencies as well as supply and demand around the world. Local markets react only sluggishly to changing currencies (manufactured inflation), but they react swiftly to local supply and demand. While the United States has been mired in a deep economic crisis, other nations have rebounded in terms of their growth rates, particularly emerging and developed nations such as China and India. These two countries are the most populated in the world and are in the process of urbanization. As their economies grow, their demand for natural resources grows as well. This puts pressure on the demand side for those items that all nations consume (such as natural resources) that can be bought and sold on the global markets. While US gasoline consumption is down, global consumption is higher.

At the same time, the US dollar has suffered a decline in purchasing power since the Federal Reserve began its run of creating money out of thin air, which is exactly what the Fed wanted. So not only has foreign demand for natural resources rebounded, but the ability of Americans to buy goods on the international markets has fallen because our dollars are worth less. Again, this is part of the plan of the Federal Reserve, because if our dollars are falling in value, it means that foreign currencies are getting stronger. Thus, other countries can buy more of our stuff (a rise in exports). Of course, along the way you pay more for gas, olive oil, beef, corn, wheat, rice, Toyotas, shirts—just about everything that comes from another country, except China. China pegs its currency to the US dollar, so that the exchange rate remains constant. Consequently, every time the Fed prints more dollars to make the US dollar fall, it also makes the Chinese currency go down, making Chinese goods even more competitive in the global marketplace.

The Final Judgment: Is It Working?

The mountain of debt in the private sector, including the financial sector, households, and corporations, began to cave in on itself in late 2007 when credit became tight. By late 2008, it had become a massive implosion. The financial sector saw the collapse of three of the five investment banks—Bear Stearns, Lehman Brothers, and Merrill Lynch—while the other two quickly snapped up bank charters so that they could receive bailout money. Commercial banks were zombies, loaded with billions of toxic assets that were not performing and could not be sold. Consumers were recognizing that their houses, those really big ATMs that had generated so much "free" cash for years through HELOCs, were losing value fast. Home sales stopped. The lending-borrowing-spending game was over. The credit-based process we had developed to expand our money and dramatically increase our spending broke down. Loan values were trashed, and asset prices were trashed.

Like a junkie without his next fix, without the constant feed of new credit, our economy started to go into debt withdrawal. It was ugly. Foreclosures, credit card write-offs, falling sales, falling prices, closing stores, dying companies (General Motors, AIG, Citi, etc.) became the norm. Deflation had begun. Then, in rides the Federal Reserve (we'll talk about the Federal government programs in another chapter) with a mandate to maximize employment. With interest rates near zero, they dust off the printing press and fire it up! If the private sector will not generate new money through renewed lending, then the Fed will do it the old-fashioned way, by simply (electronically) printing new money!

What happened next was like something out of a movie. Everyone claimed that a miracle had happened! The US equity markets shot to the moon, large banks were suddenly making a profit, and unemployment stopped going up! It seemed so good! In fact, this massive inflow of newly printed dollars created another, short-term bubble. However, just like the credit bubble of the early 2000s, this one is not sustainable either.

The Fed injected massive amounts of new money into our economy by printing money and using it to buy bonds. This caused commodities, stocks, and junk bonds to skyrocket. **Charts 5-9, 5-10,** and **5-11** show examples of indices in these markets, and you can clearly see the recent bottom in each market and the subsequent move higher as the Fed began printing in March 2009, and then announced its most recent round in August 2010.

Chart 5-9: Dow Jones Industrial Average, 2008–2011

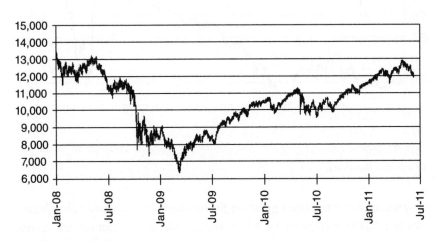

Data Source: Yahoo Finance

Chart 5-10: CRB (Commodity) Index, 2008–2010

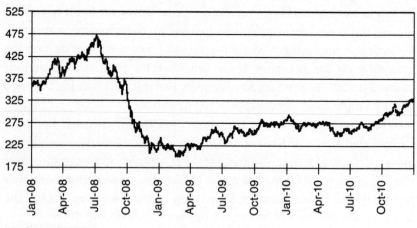

Data Source: **Bloomberg**

Chart 5-11: iBoxx High-Yield (Junk Bond) Index, 1998–2010

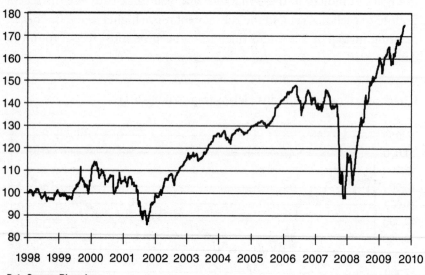

Data Source: **Bloomberg**

  This response has been great for those who own such assets, but it cannot last. These moves are based on ruining the dollar, not on productive gains in output. Are we willing to push our dollar to zero? Are bondholders of US Treasuries, as well as our international trading partners who receive dollars when they sell us stuff, going to stand by and let that happen? Of course not! The voting members of the Fed are not stupid. They understand that they are walking a very fine line between attempting to restart our economy and destructive currency devaluation. Just as when the credit boom was exhausted and collapsed on itself, the initial thrust and seeming success of the QE programs will falter and fail.

The Federal Reserve simply printed $2.3 trillion, effectively taxing trillions of dollars away from American citizens and corporations in an effort to mitigate the falling housing market and generate employment. Unfortunately, most of the benefits went to the banking system, not to consumers. To put this into context, in fiscal year 2010, the US government received the following amounts in taxes:

Personal Income Tax	$935 billion
Social Security Tax	$874 billion
Corporate Tax	$156 billion
Other (estate, gift, etc.)	$208 billion
Total	$2,173 billion

Numbers are from the US Office of Management and Budget

The Federal Reserve has now printed more dollars than the US government received in tax revenue in fiscal year 2010, and unemployment remains stubbornly high and housing remains weaker than it was during the Great Depression.

The monetary policy used by the Federal Reserve to manufacture inflation has failed, and failed miserably. The program has swept value from savers as dollars lost their purchasing power, and it has made daily life more expensive for all Americans by pushing up the cost of the goods we use in daily life (food, energy, etc.). How can the Fed, which controls a printing press and answers to no one, fail so badly in its quest to beat deflation by manufacturing broad inflation? It's simple. The Fed is fighting two battles that it cannot win: one against demographics and the other against a wave more massive than any we have ever seen in history—the implosion of private credit and the weight of unfunded liabilities.

Demographics Don't Give In

As described by us in countless articles and speeches, as well as in several preceding books and in Chapter 2 of this book, people are extremely rational and predictable, as long as you are looking at the right measurements. The US government and most economic theory would have us believe that people, as consumers, are motivated simply by price movement and interest rates. This is idiotic. Of course the decision to save or spend is more complicated. Unfortunately, economic models cannot handle variables like "I'm scared of losing my job," or, "I have to save every nickel for retirement because Social Security won't be there," or "My house is now underwater so I have to save even more," or even, "Gee, I make $60,000 per year but have debts of $800,000 and no one will lend me more money." Because economic models cannot incorporate such variables, there is the assumption, as we outlined above, that consumers behave "rationally," making decisions in a vacuum in which price and/or interest rates are the main factor. Once we get rid of that silly assumption, the world gets clearer.

With the largest generation in America firmly in their peak saving years as we go through the economic Winter Season, it only makes sense that we would experience a period of falling and slack demand. On average, consumers are trying to deal with a change to "less" as they use the next decade to prepare for retirement by saving more and paying down debt. This is easy to see in your own life. Ask yourself, as the Federal Reserve has pushed interest rates to almost zero, have you reacted "rationally"? Have you rushed out to spend more simply because what you earn in your savings or money market account has dwindled? Are you rushing out to borrow more, now that borrowing costs are lower? Of course not! If you were already in the market to buy an asset—a house, car, television, Blu-Ray DVD player, laptop, iPad, etc.—then perhaps you were nudged in the direction of making a purchase. But if you were not in the market to spend more, then it makes no sense whatsoever to assume that a change in price or interest rates will suddenly make you a buyer! Yet this is the theory on which our government is operating. Our officials are busy passing laws, creating stimulus plans, and, through the Federal Reserve, printing trillions of dollars in order to affect changes according to a theory that has no basis in reality. In addition to this fight against the personal goals of consumers (which cannot be won), the Federal Reserve is facing another foe that is just as daunting: existing debt.

Reducing a Lifetime of Debt

The snowball effect that created the greatest debt bubble in centuries took years to form and a number of participants, as described in Chapter 4. **Chart 5-12** shows the distribution of debt in the US in 2008, 2009, and 2010. Notice that in 2008, at the top of debt accumulation in the US, the government (federal and municipal) accounted for only $14 trillion of $56 trillion. The rest is spread among the financial sector, consumers, and corporations. The largest of these is the financial sector at $17 trillion in 2008, with most of that from government-sponsored agencies like Fannie Mae and Freddie Mac, which guarantee over $7 trillion of mortgage debt in the US and which have already lost over $130 billion, with hundreds of billions more to go. The financial sector is the exact group that was manu-facturing debt at a record pace in the 2000s in order to finance anything and everything through securitization.

Chart 5-12: Distribution of Debt, 2008–2010

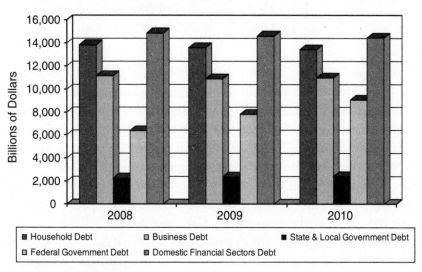

Data Source: **Federal Z1 Report**

In just two years' time, the amount of debt outstanding in the financial sector has declined by $2 trillion . . . but there is still $15 trillion outstanding! This includes outstanding Lehman Brothers debt, securitized second mortgages sitting on the books of BAC, home mortgages on the books of Citi and JPMorgan, and of course the FNMA and FHLMC debt. Most of the debt in this sector is tied to housing. With $15 trillion still left to deal with, we anticipate at least another $7 trillion in reductions as we go through the continued foreclosures, write-offs, and write-downs that we have been working through for the last three years. So while the Federal Reserve has been exploding its balance sheet, printing money with abandon, and creating as much money as the US government received in tax receipts in 2010, it has barely kept pace with the rate at which the private sector is destroying credit. This is a huge game of tug-of-war being played out in our economy.

On one side, the Fed is creating money at a hurried pace, desperate for consumers to borrow and spend and, in the meantime, diminishing the purchasing power of the US dollar in an effort to create inflation. On the other side, consumers are paying down debt and saving more, and the financial sector is slashing debt at every turn through foreclosures and write-downs. Compare what is outstanding:

Private Debt	Fed Printing
$42 trillion	$2.3 trillion

Now consider the insurmountable problem of unfunded long-term liabilities. There is no question that benefits owed to those who have not yet retired will be reduced, but in many cases pension benefits to current retirees—such as state workers—are guaranteed by governmental constitutions and cannot be changed. Cities and states will have to go through continued austerity measures, slashing benefits and raising taxes, to find a balance among what they spend today, what they receive in taxes, and what they owe in the future. Every dollar that is taxed away from constituents and contributed to a savings plan like pensions is a dollar *not* used to grow our economy through consumption. When states slash services, they tend to slash payments to the least among us, those who were availing themselves of government services in the first place. They also fire workers at all levels—administrators, teachers, inspectors, etc.—which adds to the rolls of the unemployed. Again, firing workers might assist in cutting costs, but it's a tough way to grow an economy. And then there's the US government with Social Security and Medicare.

Unfunded by over $50 trillion, our government cannot provide the level of pay currently on the books. However, the compromise will not be one-sided; taxes will be higher and benefits lower. It is that simple. What is not simple are the questions of "Who pays what?" and "Who gets what?," which of course have not even begun to be sorted out. If you are reading this book, the chances are that you will be in the former group (payers), not the latter group (receivers), unless you are already retired.

To get a sense of the magnitude of the issues we are facing compared to the efforts of the Federal Reserve, look at **Chart 5-13**, which puts the unfunded liabilities of the US, the total amount of private credit outstanding, the US deficit, and the amount of money printed by the Fed all on the same chart.

In this war of debt and money creation, the Fed is simply outgunned. It cannot create enough money to fend off deflation without ruining the currency. It is that simple.

With debt repayment and credit contraction as the order of the day and

Chart 5-13: US Debt Creation, 1980–2009

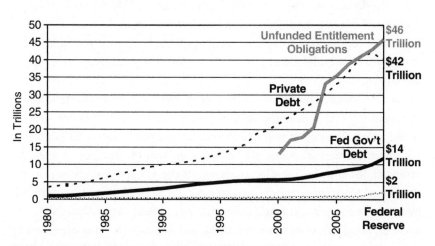

Data Source: The Chart Store, St. Louis Fed, Treasury Direct, US Treasury

much larger in scope than any printing of the Federal Reserve, deflation will continue to drive the US economy lower in the areas of housing and employment and will eventually engulf and drive lower commodity prices as well. The game of tug-of-war between the repayment and cancellation of private credit, which makes the US dollar stronger and increases purchasing power, and the printing efforts of the Fed, which has the opposite effect, was over before it began. Due to the size differential, private credit reduction will dwarf the efforts of the Fed; it's just a matter of time as to when the economy sets back into a deeper downturn. While government entities at all levels would like to intervene through public spending, they have no ability to act, because the debts they have accumulated over the years now threaten to take down the government itself!

This painful process of shrinking credit is accompanied by all the bad side effects that are the opposite of when the credit is extended. Just as people lived well beyond their means when taking on the credit, now they must live within their means, only now it includes the cost of debt repayment. We do not simply pull back to a "normal" level of spending fueled by debt plus income; we must drop below that level. As for lending, we've already discussed that the sources of credit that got us here are simply not available. As demand tapers off or simply moves sideways, the negative implications grow larger. Those who are unemployed remain so; those using social services call for more. Governments struggling with lower tax revenue receive the same or less, and property values fall. Companies fight to gain any sort of pricing power, unable to raise prices as consumers simply change consumption to lower-priced goods. All of this leads to even greater unemployment (government and private), which leads to less spending and the continuation of the vicious cycle we are already in.

As this steady march of deleveraging continues and the temporary effects of the Fed printing money wears off, the vicious cycle will pick up speed again. The dollar will rise in purchasing power as credit contracts, commodities will fall in response and then will fall further as fears are renewed about a double-dip recession, in the US specifically and in the developed world in general. Of course, it's not a double dip. It is a continuation of the same decline and crisis that began years ago. We simply took another, bigger dose of the same drug that got us here, spending money we don't have in 2009, 2010, and 2011 for a brief respite. In the end, savers will have their day and will be rewarded for their fiscal conservation. For everyone else, it's going to hurt.

Of course, this is not what the government wants. The government wants inflation—not a lot, mind you, but definitely inflation. To this end, the government took many steps in the last three years to shore up our economy and to move us forward, meaning greater economic activity. This included a lot of US debt and stimulus spending of many types. Unfortunately, none of these programs addresses the underlying concerns that are leading us down the deflation path. The government's approach, like that of the Fed, is destined to fail. In the next chapter, we will outline what the federal government has done and why its programs will lead to nothing more than skewed short-term outcomes, actually making our eventual deflationary Winter Season worse than it already is!

CHAPTER 6

Why the Government Stimulus Plan Will Fail: The Recovery Is Not Real

By January 2008, the US economy was looking dicey. Gross domestic product (GDP) growth had stalled, the housing market was at a standstill, and it appeared that the nation was falling into a recession. The credit markets were seizing up, making it harder to get loans for just about everything, which, of course, translated into falling demand. The US government came up with a plan: give (almost) everyone money.

Speaker of the House Nancy Pelosi sponsored bill H.R. 5140, the Economic Stimulus Act of 2008, which carried a price tag of $140 billion. The purpose of the bill as stated in the legislation was "to provide economic stimulus through recovery rebates to individuals, incentives for business investment, and an increase in conforming and FHA loan limits." The bill passed in an overwhelming vote, was sent to the Senate where it was modified to be slightly bigger ($160 billion), and then was sent back to the House of Representatives. The House passed the bill, and President George W. Bush signed it in February 2008.

Help was on the way to Americans, expected to arrive in the form of tax rebate checks by the summer. Each household would receive between $300 and $1,800, depending on the number of people in the family. The benefit also was subject to an income cap. If an individual made over $75,000 filing alone or $150,000 filing jointly, then the benefit started to decline and eventually went to zero. The IRS estimates that roughly 130 million families and single adults received this payment, and the average received was $950.

The goal of the program was pure economic "stimulus": an attempt to create economic activity beyond what was possible with the current level of income and credit in the system. The US government did this by going deeper into debt in order to send money to people, hoping that people would buy more stuff than they otherwise would have, so that companies would have more orders, businesses would earn more profits, more jobs would be created, and families could keep paying their bills. In short, this was a very deliberate attempt to steer the economy. It was good timing because by the spring of 2008 it was clear that we had issues. Bear Stearns seized up in March of that year, leading to a forced sale of the company to JPMorgan for pennies on the dollar. The markets were confused, moving up and down with great volatility. Rebate checks went out the door by May, with tens of billions of dollars hitting the bank accounts of average Americans a few hundred bucks at a time. According to a study by Kellogg School of Management professor Jonathan Parker, we as Americans did the right thing: we spent it . . . or at least, we spent half of it.* Unfortunately, that is all the government ever expected. When the checks were mailed out, the government hoped that out of $160 billion, we would spend $80 billion on consumption. What happened to the other $80 billion? We saved it. Or paid down debt. Either way, we did not use the money to drive the economy higher. So did it work? That depends on what you consider success.

According to Parker's analysis, we most likely got the hoped-for $80 billion of spending out of the plan, with roughly 12% to 31% of the total going to nondurables (gas, food, etc.) and the balance of what was spent going to durable goods, mostly cars and trucks. In short, the stimulus checks shored up demand for the brief months following their arrival. Unfortunately, this does not mean that the stimulus checks achieved their true goal, which was to revive demand in a way that would lead to lasting growth. The checks did nothing to rekindle a desire for continuous spending or to return us to a path of growth, to create jobs, to persuade business owners to expand, or to reach any other long-term economic goal. Without the onetime booster shot of the Economic Stimulus Act of 2008, it is probable that the United States simply would have tipped into this Great Recession faster. Of course, we also would have saved ourselves as

* J. Parker, "What Happened to the 2008 Stimulus Checks?" Kellogg School of Management, August 3, 2010. Available at: http://www.kellogg.northwestern.edu/News_Articles/2010/spent.aspx. Accessed January 19, 2011.

taxpayers an additional $160 billion in US government indebtedness. This is the heart of the problem with stimulus spending and government plans that are designed to motivate, steer, and otherwise manipulate economic activity. Outside of short-term effects, most plans fall miserably short of their goals, but they do end up achieving one thing: greater debt for the United States, which must be dealt with down the road.

The stimulus actions taken by the government are meant to influence external forces that consumers and businesses contend with, like prices, interest rates, and taxes. While these factors do have an impact on consumption decisions, they are neither the only considerations nor the main considerations when it comes to consumers choosing whether and how to spend. Still, governments insist on attempting these programs. Instead of the desired result, they simply get more debt, which is exactly what our most recent efforts have achieved!

Program After Program, Money (and Debt) as Far as the Eye Can See

The stimulus of 2008 was just the beginning. As 2008 wore on and 2009 began, it became apparent that a generic gift of cash to consumers would be woefully inadequate. Economic deterioration was all around us. Soon the US government was fighting fires at all levels, creating initiatives on the fly. After the stimulus of 2008, we continued that summer with a blockbuster: the government takeover of Fannie Mae (FNMA) and Freddie Mac (FHLMC). These two entities, which had bought up trillions of dollars in mortgages from banks for decades, were now dealing with a previously unheard of situation: record defaults that were threatening their solvency. While most of the loans owned by these two entities were prime loans, some nonconforming loans also were on the books. However, in the end it didn't matter. The default rate for all types of loans soared. FNMA and FHLMC were both leveraged just like other financial institutions, as discussed in Chapter 3. Thus, when part of the loan portfolios for these entities tanked, their real capital was wiped out quickly. They were flat broke. The government assumed control of the entities and wiped out common stockholders and preferred shareholders but guaranteed the bondholders 100% of their money. Essentially, what had been an implicit government guarantee for these programs became an explicit guarantee overnight. Why make the bondholders whole? Because the government wanted more of their money. The goal of the government was to keep credit flowing, in hopes of making bond buyers comfortable enough to purchase more FNMA/FHLMC bonds, which would give these entities the money necessary to buy mortgages from banks that then could make more loans.

This was a concerted effort to keep home financing available for potential borrowers. What happened? We are now three years down the road and facing record low housing starts and record high home foreclosures. FNMA and FHLMC own hundreds of thousands of homes on which they have foreclosed and have become landlords, as they test programs to keep delinquent owners in their homes on a lease-to-purchase program. Buyers for homes are not materializing. There is simply a lack of demand. Through FNMA and FHLMC, the US government spends $10 million a month simply to mow grass. The cost of upkeep on foreclosed homes in 2009 was over $1 billion.*

This bailout of the home loan guarantee programs has not been free. At first, the bailout was expected to cost $30 billion to $50 billion. However, that estimate quickly grew. The government eventually set a limit at FNMA and FHLMC on how much in losses it would cover: $400 billion. This limit was an eye-opener, as it signaled to people that there could be massive losses in these programs. Then, on Christmas Eve 2009, the US taxpayer got an unwelcome present. On that very quiet news day when people were distracted with the holidays, Congress approved a measure to remove the cap on what it would guarantee in these programs, meaning that now the losses are limited only by the dollar amount of mortgages these entities hold, roughly $7 trillion. No one expects 50% or 60% losses in conforming loans held by FNMA and FHLMC, but of the $7 trillion in mortgages backed by these entities, there is the real possibility of 5% to 10% in losses, or $350 billion to $700 billion. Naturally, these losses will be covered by the US taxpayer.

As the fall of 2008 wore on, the financial picture grew darker. In September 2008, Congress failed in an attempt to pass a bill that would bail

---

* B. Appelbaum, "Cost of Seizing Properties Surges for Taxpayers," *New York Times*, June 19, 2010. Available at www.nytimes.com/2010/06/20/business/20foreclose.html?page wanted=all. Accessed January 19, 2011.

out the financial sector. It turns out that the US Congress was not a fan of a three-page letter from then Secretary of the Treasury Henry Paulson requesting three-quarters of $1 trillion. The measure was rejected and the proposal rewritten, and then the measure passed. The United States suddenly had a $700 billion lifeline to throw to financial firms that represented the backbone of the credit and payment system in America and, indeed, the world.

This issue was not a small one, like an out-of-control campfire. This was a raging forest fire that was threatening massive destruction. These institutions had borrowed short term (30-day renewable borrowing) and had used the money to lend long in the housing market. As their loan portfolios suffered because of the housing market implosion, these institutions lost access to credit. Oddly, the lenders were all lending to each other, but since no one knew what anyone else's real financial situation was, the system simply froze up. As their balance sheets deteriorated, it was questionable who had any money left to lend! Through the financial bailout, the taxpayer made loans to businesses that had run themselves into the ground. While this might sound bad, it actually turned out to be a great deal, as long as you were one of the financial institutions. Their values were falling fast, no one trusted them, and their portfolios were in question, but the group that controls the printing press and US government debt was willing to lend them money in whatever amount they requested! This access to an unlimited amount of financial backing made these companies seemingly invincible. They suddenly had no risk, because if they got into trouble, all parties knew what would happen—Uncle Sam would come to the rescue!

As Chapter 3 outlines, it took several different groups to create the housing-lending-credit bubble of the 2000s, but the risks and rewards did not flow equally among all parties. When the dust settled, the Fed had egg on its face and it has been desperately trying to pump up the economy ever since. The consumer received some reward through inflated sales prices in the high-flying years but is now suffering from falling property values, a debt hangover that includes underwater mortgages, and unsalable property. The US government and other taxing authorities enjoyed record tax receipts, but those days are over. The one group that came out of this well was bankers. They might be hated, but they are getting rich, insured by taxpayer guarantees!

Lending institutions were an essential part of the development of the credit crisis, but unlike homeowners and the government guarantee programs, these institutions cashed out large percentages of their profits every year. When the crisis finally exploded in late 2008 and early 2009, there was no way to take back bonuses and profit sharing that had been booked and distributed in prior periods. That money was simply sucked out of the system, locked into the hands that had received it. Without that cash in their coffers to cushion the blow of the credit crisis, the very existence of these firms was threatened, which is why the government went to such lengths to save them. This lifeline gave these companies an advantage without compare: who would not lend to a company if they knew that the US government stood behind that company in bad times?

This is where the phrase "privatized profits and socialized losses" comes from. In the good years, the profit flowed to the owners of the financial institutions and their employees. When things fell apart, it was the US taxpayer who came to the rescue. This type of situation is the very definition of "moral hazard," in which a person or group receives the potential benefits of their actions, but any losses are incurred by someone else. In this type of situation, you can see how people would be motivated to take the biggest risks possible, because if it works out, they make a bundle. If their endeavor fails, they suffer no losses. Welcome to the financial industry, circa 2000–2010. Now that this industry is back on its feet, the record profits (and bonuses) are flowing again. Of course, that money doesn't flow to the US taxpayer (the one who recently socialized the losses through bailouts), just to the owners of the institutions and their employees.

At the same time that we were doling out hundreds of billions of dollars to strapped lending institutions, we were also lending money through the Federal Reserve. As **Chart 5.6,** shows, the Fed's balance sheet exploded in the fall of 2008, as it allowed banks to pledge lower-quality assets in exchange for loans. Again, this is a "wolf in sheep's clothing" bailout. It appears innocuous, but who else was going to lend cold hard cash with housing bonds as collateral in October 2008? Through government programs of different sorts, we ended up guaranteeing, bailing out, and back-stopping not billions of dollars, but *trillions* of dollars in private credit!

The goal of the US government was not just to ensure the survival of these firms, but also to ensure that the credit system in the US remained intact so that consumers could access credit in order to spend. While the financial system did recover, the level of access to credit did not return or was not used. These firms, which received hundreds of billions of dollars in aid as well as trillions of dollars in guarantees, did not resume lending as they had in the boom years, and they still have almost $1 trillion in excess reserves sitting on their books. While credit might technically be available in the private sector, it is shrinking, not growing, as outlined in Chapter 5.

This largesse quickly spread outside of the financial sector and into the auto industry. In December 2008, just as no one would lend to financial companies, no one was very interested in lending to car companies, either. Ford had mortgaged itself to the hilt in 2006 and 2007, so although the company was saddled with over $30 billion in debt, it did have the liquidity it needed to survive. Not so for GM, which lost $30 billion in 2008, and Chrysler, which also was bleeding profusely. These companies showed up on Washington's doorstep and told Congress that without government intervention they would not be able to meet payroll. Hundreds of thousands of union workers would be out of a job, along with all of the workers at ancillary businesses like parts suppliers and raw materials companies. Congress responded with billions of dollars. Eventually, the government gave Chrysler and GM almost $30 billion and demanded that the companies provide viable, long-term business plans. If the companies could not deliver such plans, then at the end of the 90-day period (March 2009) they would be required to repay the loans they had received. Really? Who believed that? These companies were running on empty, pardon the pun; they were bankrupt. They were hemorrhaging cash, had no access to debt, and were booking record losses! There would be no paying back. Instead, the companies asked for even more loans and were told to pursue bankruptcy. The bankruptcies of the car companies, and the way that bankruptcy law was ignored in order to favor very specific special-interest groups, is the subject of many books, so we will not pursue the topic here. Suffice it to note that the US taxpayer stepped in to pay again.

As the lead story in this chapter shows, bailout/stimulus funds were often aimed at everyday Americans as well. The December 2010 Tax Relief, Unemployment Insurance Reauthorization, and Job Creation Act (H.R. 4853) extended current tax rates for 2 years, extended current emergency unemployment benefits for 13 months, and cut the amount workers pay into Social Security by one third. There is no doubt that all of these items are directly aimed at individuals, in hopes of providing some sort of economic boost through greater spending of monies not paid in taxes or the spending of monies received in unemployment benefits. Of course, this bill also brings with it debt of approximately $850 billion.

Given the number of programs, bills, and proposals, as well as the fact that we are dealing with both the US government and the Federal Reserve acting separately, it is understandable if you have difficulty tracking all the different aspects of the stimulus/bailout/tax cut initiatives of the last 3 years. Here's a cheat sheet of the different programs through 2010.

US GOVERNMENT FINANCIAL SECTOR BAILOUT (TARP: TROUBLED ASSET RELIEF PROGRAM)*		
Recipient	Committed	Invested
AIG	$70	70
Asset guaranty	12.5	5.0
Auto-related companies	5.0	3.5
Loans to autos	80.1	77.6
Capital purchase	218.0	204.7
Consumer lending	70.0	20.0
Making Homes Affordable	50.0	27.4
Public-private investment	100.0	26.7
Targeted Investment	40.0	40.0
Less funds repaid	(118.5)	(118.5)
New initiatives	172.9	0
Total TARP	$700	$356.2
Federal Reserve bailout		
Bank of America loan-loss backstop	$97	$0
Bear Stearns	29	26.3
Citigroup loan loss	220.4	0.0
Commercial paper funding	1,800	14.3
Foreign exchange dollar swaps	unlimited	29.1

(continued on next page)

Recipient	Committed	Invested
Federal Reserve bailout (*cont.*)		
GSE debt purchases	200	149.7
GSE mortgage-backed securities purchase	1,250	775.6
Money market investor funding	600	0
Term asset-backed securities loan	1,000	43.8
Term auction facility	500	109.5
Term securities lending	250	0.0
US government bond purchases	300	295.0
Fed total	$6,400	$1,500
US government stimulus (directed at consumers, states, and some businesses)		
2008 stimulus	$168	$168
Unemployment benefit extension	8	8
Student loan guarantees	195	195
American Recovery (2009 stimulus)	787.2	358.2
American technology vehicles	25.0	8.0
Cash for Clunkers	3.0	3.0
US government stimulus total	$1,200	$577.8
Other programs		
AIG	$182	$127.4
FDIC bank takeovers (2008 and 2009)	45.4 (cost of funding)	
Credit unions and temporary liquidity	1,700	366.4
Other housing initiatives	745	130.6
Total other programs	$2,672.4	$623.8
Grand totals (rounded)	$11,000	$3,000

* Numbers are in billions of dollars and are from Bailout Tracker, CNN Money, accessible at http://money.cnn.com/news/storysupplement/economy/bailouttracker/.* Accessed January 19, 2011.

Over the course of two years, our government and our central bank have committed to $11 trillion of bailouts, backstops, and stimulus measures. Of that $11 trillion, we currently have $3 trillion outstanding!

To put these numbers into context, consider the following list of the top ten countries in the world, as ranked by GDP (in trillions of dollars):

United States	$14.6*
China	5.7
Japan	5.4
Germany	3.3
France	2.5
United Kingdom	2.2
Italy	2.0
Brazil	2.0
Canada	1.5
Russia	1.4
India	1.4

At $11 trillion, the authorized stimulus of the United States is larger than the GDP of every country in the world except our own. Our currently pledged, used, or expended stimulus, at $3 trillion, is larger than all but the four largest economies on the planet. There can be no doubt that the government efforts of the United States have been massive in scale and have been used to address many different areas and levels of our economy—cities, states, consumers, companies, financial institutions, and green initiatives, just to name a few. With such force at work in so many different areas, you'd think that we would be exploding!

The government is guaranteeing loans, guaranteeing assets, handing out cash, and printing record amounts of new capital. New growth should be everywhere. We should be running at full speed, with unemployment under 5%, GDP growth at 5% to 7%, and hours worked and wages moving up sharply. But none of that is happening. In the face of the largest

* List of countries by GDP, *Wikipedia*. Available at: www.wikipedia.org. Accessed January 19, 2011.

stimulus growth initiative in the history of the world, we are barely moving sideways. The stimulus so far has failed, mainly because most of the efforts were not intended to "stimulate" the economy at all, but instead were meant to stop the bleeding of different entities and sectors. While some attempts have been made to stimulate economic activity, the United States will not alter the demographic pattern of changing consumption by the boomers (as described in Chapters 2 and 5), and our efforts so far have failed to address the two monsters in our economy: unemployment and housing.

Insanity: Doing the Same Thing Repeatedly but Expecting a Different Result

In early 2009, the State of California was staring down a bad set of facts. The state was fast approaching the time of year when the budget for the next fiscal year, July 1, 2009, through June 30, 2010, would have to be adopted. The problem was that California was facing a bit of a budget gap. For the coming fiscal year, when the state expected to spend $86 billion, California expected to receive only $41 billion in revenue. In just one year, the State of California was facing a budget gap of a whopping $45.5 billion, or 52% of its one-year budget. This gap was just for the budget for one year; it was not the state's full debt, which is hundreds of billions of dollars! California, like many other states, took a knife to its spending, but it also did something else. Like all other states, California got in line to receive its share of the US government stimulus money, which turned out to be $85 billion for the Golden State. The money did not flow in all at one time. California tracks its 2009 Recovery Act dollars on a website designed for that purpose, www.recovery.ca.gov, whereas of September 30, 2010, the state reported that it had received $51 billion of the full $85 billion allotted to it. So what became of the $51 billion received so far? It went into "business-as-usual" spending.

Unemployment insurance, Medi-Cal (state-provided health care for low-income families), education (teacher salaries, etc.), and a state "fiscal stabilization fund" (read: we don't have enough of our own money so we used yours to plug the gap) are among the largest recipients of the US government monies sent to California. This division is fairly representative of how monies were used by most states that received part of the 2009

Recovery Act funds, which means that the hundreds of billions of dollars that US taxpayers have sent to cities and states have been used in an effort to tide them over until the larger economy recovers. These actions are not stimulative. Most of these dollars were not spent to create new jobs, open new factories, fund new infrastructure projects, or for any other purpose that would be considered additive. Instead, the dollars were spent to shore up funding in areas for which the states and cities had shortfalls, like payroll in education, depleted unemployment insurance funds, and empty Medicaid copayment (the states' required payments) funds. Cities and states were hoping and praying that things would get better before the US government money ran out.

Things have not gotten better. California's Legislative Analyst's Office (LAO) reports on the fiscal health of the state and also provides an outlook based on budget projections and current law. Mac Taylor, trusted analyst at the LAO, reported in November 2010 that California had the same dismal 5-year forecast ($20 billion per year deficits . . . per year! Not cumulative!) that it had in 2008. His numbers are in the table below.

LAO REPORT OF THE CALIFORNIA BUDGET FORECAST, 2011–2012, AS REPORTED IN CALIFORNIA'S FISCAL OUTLOOK, NOVEMBER 2010	
Year	Budget surplus/deficit, billions of $
2011–2012	−25
2012–2013	−22
2013–2014	−20
2014–2015	−20
2015–2016	−19

The amazing part of these numbers is the backstory. The current year deficit of $25 billion includes a carryover of $5 billion from the year before. The state simply did not pay all of its bills. The next year (2012–2013) includes $2 billion for a loan repayment to California cities. In 2010, the State of California forced its cities to lend the state $2 billion by withholding property tax payments that flow through the state but are lawfully meant to go back to municipalities. The state has to repay such a forced loan in two years, which would be by 2012–2013. The 2015–2016 estimate of a declining shortfall is due to an estimate of a growing economy. As bad as these numbers are, they don't tell the whole story.

In this LAO report, Mac Taylor points out that the "[p]rojections likely understate the state's fiscal woes." He goes on to explain that the numbers do not include any cost-of-living adjustments (pension increases), inflationary pressures on department budgets (like health care costs), or provisions to address the monstrous underfunded pension and retirement health care benefits owed by the state. The large pension funds run by the state already have shown that billions of dollars more are needed in contributions.

California is a shining example of how years of "stimulus" funds have been used simply to shore up existing spending plans rather than to stimulate anything. But California is not alone. The Center on Budget and Policy Priorities (CBPP) reports that in the past 3 years states have relied on over $150 billion in stimulus money to help offset record budget gaps. The problem is that the stimulus money is coming to an end, but the budget gaps are not. While the CBPP estimates that more than 40 states will have budget gaps totaling over $140 billion this year, the Government Accountability Office (GAO) shows a rapid decline in what states and cities will receive from the US government as the Recovery Act comes to a close. Through the end of the year 2010, just over $192 billion in Recovery Act funds were disbursed to cities and states since the beginning of the program.* **Chart 6-1** shows the flow of money by year and what is expected in the years ahead.

From this point forward, very little money will be flowing from the US government to the cities and states to assist with closing budget gaps. While many people have talked about the recovery of the US economy, such terms are not used in state capitols around the country. They talk about austerity. The future looks grim.

All of the 30,000-foot-view conversations about stimulus, bailout, and fiscal woes dance around the real topic: people. Monies that cannot be paid by states or companies eventually mean lost income to everyday, ordinary people. It is this loss of income, which translates into less spend-

* US Government Accountability Office, *Projected vs. Federal Outlays to States and Localities* (report online). Available at: www.gao.gov/recovery. Accessed January 20, 2011.

Chart 6-1: Flow of Money by Year to Cities and States (Estimates)

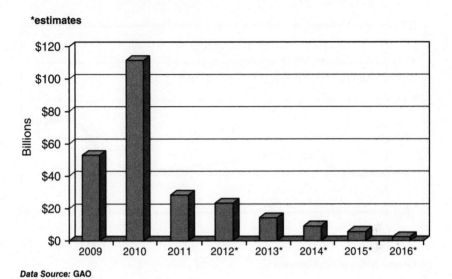

Data Source: GAO

ing, less repayment of credit, and less new credit extended, that is the heart of the matter.

The Largest Fallout in Both the Private and Public Sector: Jobs and the Income Those Jobs Provided

As credit dried up, consumers cut back, companies sold less, and governments received less in taxes, the immediate response from most sectors was the same—fire people. Starting in late 2007, we did exactly that. The unemployment rate in the United States, as reflected in **Chart 6-2,** shot higher, from a low of 4.4% in 2007 to a high of just over 10% in the fall of 2009. At the end of 2010, the official rate of unemployment, called U-3, sat at 9.4%.

The unemployment problem we are facing in this downturn is not just that people are losing their jobs, but that they are not finding new ones. Just looking at the rate of unemployment is a wake-up call, but when you also look at the duration of unemployment—meaning how long those

Chart 6-2: US Unemployment (U–3), 2000–2011

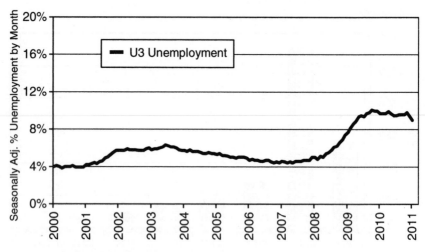

Data Source: Bureau of Labor Statistics

who lose their jobs are out of work—the crisis takes on an entirely new dimension. **Chart 6-3** shows the number of unemployed who have been out of work more than 6 months.

When workers are not quickly added back to the labor force, they can see their work skills begin to fade, which makes it all the more difficult to find the next job. In addition, the longer a person is out of work the more likely it is that he or she will receive less income in their next position. So the rate of unemployment, the number we see posted everywhere, is simply a starting point in understanding the current job crisis.

This number, the headline unemployment rate, which was at 9.4% at the end of 2010, gets thrown around all the time. Let's try to give it some perspective. Let's talk about real people, in terms of the number of people being affected, and how these numbers are developed. In doing so, you'll soon understand that our employment situation is much worse than you are being told!

The Bureau of Labor Statistics conducts two surveys every month, the Current Population Survey (CPS), referred to as the Household Survey, and the Current Employment Statistics Program (CES), or Payroll Survey. The Household Survey consists of a monthly telephone survey of

Chart 6-3: Unemployed Longer Than 6 Months,
January 1948–February 2011

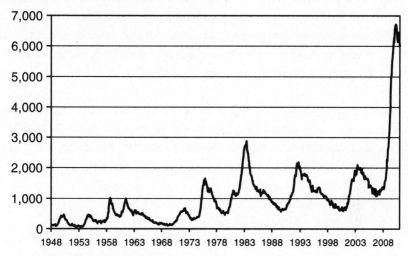

Data Source: **Bureau of Labor Statistics**

about 60,000 households used to figure out who is working and who isn't, along with demographics, such as race and age. The Payroll Survey covers 140,000 businesses and government entities and tries to determine the size of employment in the country along with hours worked and wages paid. Both surveys classify employment by sector of the economy. Both surveys suffer from data manipulation that makes the numbers look better than they are.

Household Survey

In the Household Survey the BLS asks respondents if they are 16 or older, and then determines whether they are employed, unemployed, or neither. You would think that figuring out if you are unemployed would be simple. If you get a paycheck, you are employed, right? Maybe, but maybe there are qualifying factors. Are you working full time or are you perhaps working part time because you cannot find a full-time job? Are you working as a janitor while you continue looking for a job in another field of education and experience, such as aeronautical engineering, for example? Even though you get a paycheck, your employment might not reflect either your desire for more work or your capabilities and past level of earning.

Qualifications that you might not be aware of also exist for determining whether you are unemployed. If you don't get a paycheck but you want to be working, you'd think that you fit the definition of unemployed—but not so fast!

The BLS goes through a series of questions to make its determination of whether a person is unemployed. First, the survey uses questions to try to figure out whether someone is in the labor force (part of a group that can and wants to work). These questions include the following:

> *Are you 16 or older?*
> *Are you institutionalized (school, prison, etc.)?*
> *Are you able to work (handicapped, disabled, etc.)?*
> *Are you caring for a relative or in some other way unable to hold a job?*

So far so good. If you are over age 16, not institutionalized, able to work, and able to hold a job, things seem promising for being in the workforce. The questions continue:

> *Are you employed?* (This one asks more detail, like, Did you work for family?, etc.)

If you say yes, then you are not only counted as part of the labor force, but you are also marked down as employed! The survey goes on to ask whether you are in your field of expertise and whether you are working full time or part time, and, if you are working part time, whether that is because you cannot find full-time work. These are good things to know, but for the headline U-3 report, you are considered employed.

If you say no to the question of employment, then there are more questions.

> *Do you want to work?* (This one ferrets out retirees and homemakers, who are considered neither employed nor unemployed, and therefore not in the labor force.)

If you say yes, meaning that you currently are unemployed and want to work, then that might seem to be the end of it, meaning that you are part of the labor force but are currently unemployed. Not so fast. The survey has more questions, and this is where things get very interesting. The government wants to know what you are doing about your situation. The next series of questions is meant to determine whether you are putting any effort into finding a job.

Have you been out of work for less than 4 weeks?

If so, you instantly count as unemployed and as part of the workforce. If you have been out of work for more than 4 weeks, things get dicey.

In the last 4 weeks, have you taken steps that would lead to employment, such as filling out applications, reviewing jobs at union halls, attending job fairs with employers present? (This does *not* include reviewing help wanted ads in the paper or on the internet!)

If you answer yes to this question, then you count as unemployed and as part of the labor force. This group is the last to qualify, which leaves a big group of people, those who did not take such specific steps in the last 4 weeks, who simply "disappear" in the eyes of the government. These people are defined by the government as "marginally attached to the labor force" and are considered "those who currently are neither working nor looking for work but indicate that they want and are available for a job and have looked for work sometime in the past 12 months."* A subset of the marginally attached are the "discouraged workers," or those who "have given a job-market-related reason for not currently looking for work,"† such as a belief that no jobs are available or that the worker is being discriminated against because of age or some other factor. Marginally attached workers and their subset of discouraged workers are still counted, but they simply are not added to the total of the labor force or to the number of unemployed workers for the headline reports (U-3). Thus,

---

* United States Department of Labor, Bureau of Labor Statistics, *Alternative Measures of Labor Utilization* [economic news release]. Available at www.bls.gov/news.release/empsit.115.htm. Accessed February 17, 2011.
 † Ibid.

when you look at the unemployment rate in **Chart 6-3,** you are not seeing millions of Americans who want to work and are able to work but have not looked in the last 4 weeks.

In addition to this group that is not reported in the headline U-3 number, another group also simply is not reported anywhere: those who are not working and say that they want to work but have not looked in the past 12 months because they believe no jobs are available or that they will not be hired. Once you cross over the 12-month threshold, the government no longer lists you in any employment report. You are completely dropped from the labor force rolls and are part of the population considered not participating in work. You want a job, you want to work, and you are able to work. But you don't count. This fact goes a long way toward explaining some glaring discrepancies and oddities within the current government reports about employment, which we will go through below.

The Size of the Workforce: Getting Smaller?

The BLS reports that currently about 153 million people are in the US workforce, as shown in **Chart 6-4.**

Chart 6-4: Number of Americans in Workforce, 2000–2011

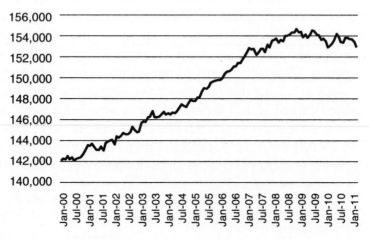

Data Source: Bureau of Labor Statistics

According to this chart, since the depths of our recession in October of 2008, the size of our labor force actually has declined! In fact, in October 2008 the BLS counted 154,953,000 people in the workforce, including 144,778,000 employed and 10,176,000 unemployed people. Since then, the numbers have changed a little. Today the BLS shows 153,690,000 people in the workforce, with 139,206,000 working and 14,485,000 unemployed, as shown below.

	October 2008	December 2010	Change
Employed	144,778	139,206	(5,572)
Unemployed	10,176	14,485	4,309
Total	154,953	153,690	(1,263)
(Numbers are in thousands)			

According to the government, we have the same number of people in the labor force today that we did in August 2007. What makes this odd is that we know that roughly 100,000 new workers are added to the labor force every single month, because the children of the boomers are graduating high school and college (hence, reaching the workforce) faster than the boomers themselves are retiring. This is why you often hear that we need to add 100,000 new jobs a month to the economy simply to stay even. If this is true, then how can our labor force be the same size that it was in 2007, and how could we have lost workers in the last two years? **Chart 6-5** shows a stacked chart of the employed and unemployed in the US.

The trend line over the past decade is consistent with the notion of 100,000 people joining the workforce each month. After the peak in total labor force in October 2008, you can see the decline in the measured labor force as well as what we are missing in terms of counted workers by looking at the white space under the trend line. We are missing these people because we have dropped them from the measurement. As described above, these people are neither employed nor unemployed. They simply do not count. In the eyes of the government, they are the same as retirees or homemakers. But of course, that's not true. This missing group includes the "marginally attached" and the subset labeled "discouraged." This missing group even includes the workers who have no name, those who have

Chart 6-5: Employed and Unemployed in US, CPS

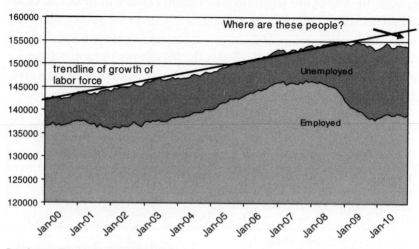

Data Source: Bureau of Labor Statistics

been "discouraged" for more than a year. These are people who still have to live. They have to eat. They have to provide for their families. They still have mortgages, car loans, credit cards, etc. But by not counting them, we are able to change the arithmetic on the reported unemployment figures. With a smaller labor force and a smaller number of unemployed, the unemployment report magically shrinks, which is why our rate of unemployment recently dropped to 9.4% even though the number of people working did not increase appreciably. Instead, we simply shrank the size of the labor force and number of people who count as unemployed. The result was instant success in terms of falling unemployment! Never mind that the people we dropped off the list of unemployment are still, well, unemployed.

The Problems Get Worse

The headline unemployment number of U-3 is the prettiest, most uplifting number the government can report. It cuts out the marginally attached, the discouraged, and the unnamed group of people who have not looked for work in more than 12 months. This number also does not distinguish among the employment of those working 40 hours a week at a good job, those working 20 hours a week stocking shelves at night for minimum wage because they want a full-time job but cannot find it, and those working minimum-wage jobs because there are no openings in their field. All of these descriptions, as described above, are captured in the Household Survey. These numbers get reported, but the mainstream media does not focus on them. This total group (except the unnamed, who get counted nowhere) is called the "unemployed and underutilized" and is reported by the BLS as U-6. Tracking U-6 (**Chart 6-6**) looks a lot closer to what we see around us in unemployment.

According to U-6, unemployment and underutilization shot up to 17.4% in October 2009, and had fallen back to only 16.7% by December 2010. This number suggests that 1 in 6 Americans are unemployed, underemployed, or marginally attached. If we plot U-3 and U-6 on the same chart (**Chart 6-7**), we can see where the big discrepancy began.

What typically was a 3% to 4% difference between the two numbers is now over 7%. Keep in mind that 7% of the US labor force is over 10,000,000 people—people who want to work.

Chart 6-6: U-6 Unemployment, 2000–2011

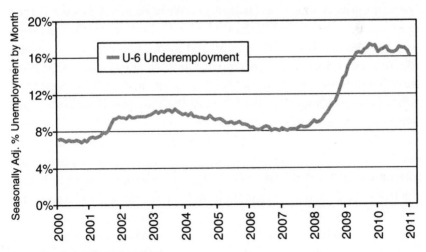

Data Source: **Bureau of Labor Statistics**

Chart 6-7: U-6 vs. U-3 Unemployment, 2000–2010

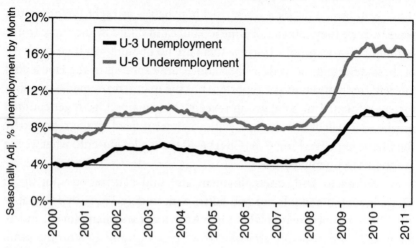

Data Source: **Bureau of Labor Statistics**

The Worst of It

That final group, the "unnamed" group of people who are not employed, are not homemakers, are not retired, and have not looked for work in the last 12 months, don't have a classification. We have no way to identify their exact number and how it has changed over the years. These are the people who have seen jobs leave their cities and towns, never to return—places like Youngstown, Ohio, and, of course, Flint, Michigan, where unemployment has been high for years. John Williams of Shadow Government Statistics (www.shadowstats.com) is one of the only people we have found who tries to estimate this group. His best estimate is about 6% of the labor force. If we add that 6% to the U-6 number of 16.7%, we get a December 2010 all-in unemployment, underutilized, and long-term discouraged estimate of 22.7% of the labor force. This is, indeed, the worst of it from the Household Survey. The Establishment Survey holds its own secrets.

Current Employment Statistics Survey (CES): Sector Analysis and a Little Distortion

The Current Employment Statistics Survey attempts to give us a broad picture of employment in the US by asking questions of employers (establishments) instead of employees (households). The goal is not only to find out whether we are growing or contracting, but also to identify areas of growth or contraction by zeroing in on jobs in each sector of the economy. As expected, construction continues to struggle in recent years, and manufacturing has been in a long slump. Health care keeps growing, as the need for more caregivers shows no sign of slowing down. A very interesting part of sector analysis is what is happening in the area of government employment. When looking at the overall picture (are we creating or losing jobs?), a built-in distortion mechanism keeps the numbers skewed to the positive.

Cities and States Cutting Back

One area of employment that tends to remain steady or even rise during recessions is government work. These jobs are more secure because they are backed by taxes, which usually don't fluctuate like private company revenue. Not anymore. With the current destruction of the budgets of cities and states due to greatly reduced tax revenue and skyrocketing expenses, these entities are shedding jobs just like the private sector, albeit not at the same rate so far. **Chart 6-8** shows employment numbers at city, state, and local levels. Only the US government is adding jobs, and that's because it has a printing press! It seems like every month we get an employment report showing losses in city and state jobs; the change is gradual, but consistent.

The description of California at the beginning of this chapter, along with the information in Chapter 4 regarding the budgets and liabilities of cities and states in general, points to a continuing deterioration in the fiscal health of government bodies. The city of Camden, New Jersey, laid off half its police force in January 2011 because it could not come to terms with its employee unions regarding cuts to current contracts. Without a reduction of what is paid to current employees or a reduction in benefits

Chart 6-8: City, State, and Federal Employment

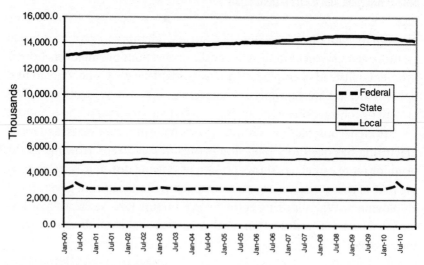

Data Source: **Bureau of Labor Statistics**

to current retirees, cities, counties, and states will be forced to continue whittling down their payrolls. The results will be fewer teachers, firemen, policemen, sanitation workers, inspectors, administrators, etc. An area of the economy that was once seen as boring and secure is now volatile and uncertain.

Questionable Growth

As noted, the CES strives to give us not only sector analysis but also a big-picture look at what is going on in employment. This is the report that comes out the first Friday of the month that commentators are quoting when they say, "We added 100,000 jobs this month," or "Nonfarm payrolls contracted by 35,000 jobs this month." The CES is based on tabulated results of a survey sent to 140,000 businesses or entities (governments) around the country. The questions on the survey concern how many people were on the payroll in the previous month and whether that number represents an increase or decrease from the preceding month. But what happens when a company does not return the survey?

When it comes to bankrupt companies, the BLS has a problem. If a company goes under and doesn't return the survey, do you count all of those jobs as lost? The BLS doesn't think so. Instead, the BLS makes the assumption that the employees of bankrupt companies either go to work at existing small businesses or start their own small businesses—which creates another issue, because the BLS does not survey small businesses. So where does that leave the CES regarding these previously counted but now not-identifiable workers? With an assumption. Using what is called the birth/death model, the BLS assumes that every single worker in the bankrupt company found employment elsewhere. The name of the model stems from the "birth" of new companies arising from the "death" of old ones.

If our economy is growing, then there is some logic to this. If the BLS simply counted all employees at a bankrupt company as lost jobs, then it probably would undercount employment in good times. However, assuming a 100% gainful employment rate for those who were at bankrupt companies certainly overcounts employment in tough economic times. In the current environment, it is arguable that this overcounting is to the extreme! The BLS does attempt to make better estimates of the "birth" of new companies, but they are still missing the boat according to their own reports and revisions.

Each year in February the BLS reports on revisions to its benchmark estimate of jobs that goes back to the previous March. Which means that in February 2010 the BLS reported revisions to its jobs benchmark back to March 2009, and the report in February 2011 referred back to the benchmark in March 2010. Why this accounting takes so long is anyone's guess. The point is that the revisions in the last several years have all been all to the downside, and sometimes have been huge. The last three revisions are below:

2009 revision (2008 benchmark)	−89,000 jobs
2010 revision (2009 benchmark)	−902,000 jobs
2011 revision (2010 benchmark)	−378,000 jobs

Thus, in the year leading up to the benchmark, the BLS overestimated job creation by the revision amount. In the year ending March 2009, the

BLS had overestimated by almost 1 million jobs! In the year ended March 2010, the BLS had missed its mark by over 375,000 jobs! The problem with revisions is that few pay attention. Who was reading this information? All of it is published for the world to see, but since the numbers adjust what happened in the past, no one really cares. But these numbers do have meaning. This information is not just about the inaccurate reports of the BLS concerning jobs in the US; this information reflects how many people in our economy are working, earning, paying bills, paying off debt, and saving for tomorrow. The greater the numbers of unemployed, under-employed, and underutilized people, the greater the problem we have in restoring our economy to growth.

In the world of employment, there aren't many places to hide. Corporations have returned to profitability, not by growing sales dramatically, but by cutting costs (people) to meet the new, lower level of demand. Without new demand, there is no reason to hire, which keeps pressure on wages, as there remains an imbalance between those looking for work and the number of jobs available. Unlike during previous downturns, even cities and states are cutting jobs. The BLS is reporting stubbornly high unemployment for a record period of time, and even those numbers undercount the real size of the problem.

As described above, the current government stimulus programs were not stimulative in nature at all. Instead they were meant to tide over city and state governments as well as to bail out certain private companies, in the hopes that after the economy was stabilized it would rebound on its own, leading to increased demand and therefore increasing employment. That recovery has not happened. After spending or guaranteeing $3 trillion in stimulus, we still have at best 15 million people unemployed, and probably closer to 30 million if we count properly. The current stimulus plans do little to address this. As the unemployed watch the days go by without finding work, their debts become harder to pay. Savings accounts dwindle, and retirement accounts get raided. Part of what is getting sacrificed is homeownership, because traditionally a house is the largest asset owned by American families.

Housing Remains in a Deep Freeze

Chapter 3 reviewed the asset bubble in housing, which addressed the excessive debts that our nation took on as prices went through the roof. After the collapse of the housing market and the ensuing financial crisis, we were left with more than just a lot of debt we could not pay. We were left with an overhang of housing inventory and a massive buildup of foreclosure and preforeclosure inventory on the books of banks. **Chart 6-9** shows the buildup of inventory of existing homes.

As sellers try to get better prices, buyers simply wait. Of course, those would be the few buyers who qualify. For those who own a home, the prospect of selling their current house before buying the next one, either across town or across the country, is now daunting. You cannot assume that the home will sell near the estimated value. How do you determine the value of your home when a short sale or foreclosure might pop up next door, skewing the market? And the foreclosure market appears to be growing, not abating. **Chart 6-10** shows foreclosures and delinquencies in the United States.

Notice that while delinquencies flew higher in the last part of 2010,

Chart 6-9: Inventory of Existing Homes for Sale

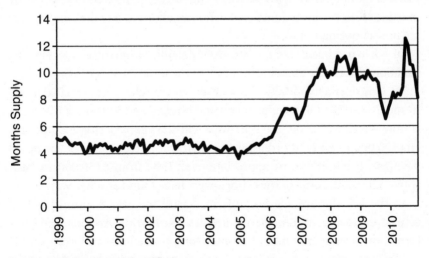

Data Source: National Association of Realtors

Chart 6-10: Foreclosures and Delinquencies, 1995–2010

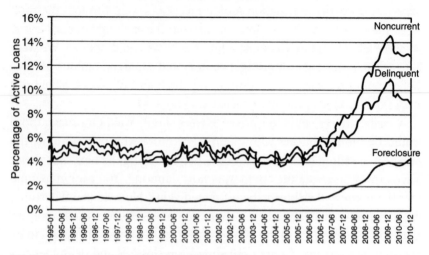

Total Delinquent and Foreclosure Rates by Month

Data Source: Information provided by LPS Applied Analytics

foreclosures flattened out. This was the result of the "robo-signing" scandal. As banks took measures to ensure that their foreclosures were in proper order, they took a break from foreclosing in general. None of this changes the underlying factors—millions of people cannot pay their mortgages. In addition, borrowers who can afford to pay their mortgages are now choosing not to.

In what has been termed "strategic default," a borrower looks at his situation objectively and determines that the repayment is a losing investment. Consider a hypothetical borrower who purchased a $250,000 home by making a $50,000 down payment and borrowing $200,000. If the home is now worth $150,000, the borrower will start considering his options. His $50,000 is gone. In order for the borrower to regain any of his down payment, the home must appreciate over 33%, from $150,000 to back above $200,000. Some of these borrowers have found another way.

In the US, the average home is in default for over 8 months before actual foreclosure. In some hard-hit states, like Florida, Arizona, and California, the average number of months for a home to be in foreclosure is 20. This means that a defaulting borrower can stay in her home for almost

2 years without making a single payment. Thinking about the borrower in the example above, if her payment was $2,000 per month, she could save $40,000 simply by not paying her mortgage and instead putting the money in the bank! At the end of the ordeal the borrower usually can rent a home near her existing home at a rental rate lower than the payment on her old mortgage. Her credit is drastically impaired, and chances are that she will not be able to buy another home for at least 7 years, but does that matter? All sorts of legal and moral issues are tied up in this, but the dilemma is obvious. The homeowner lost her investment, and the banks, which were bailed out by the government, are demanding repayment. Many homeowners are simply saying no.

We are at a point at which not only are the unemployed and underemployed defaulting on their mortgages, but borrowers who see no hope of either recouping their down payment or building equity in their home also are defaulting. These foreclosures add to the existing foreclosure market and keep a lid on home prices for the entire market. This logjam in the housing market has brought a major piece of our economy to a standstill. We are not employing people to any degree to build or sell homes, we are not building equity for current owners, and we are not using our stimulus approach to change the status quo. The government has made small attempts to change this situation, such as when the Federal Housing Authority (FHA) raised the size of loan that can be financed under its auspices and when the federal government made a halfhearted attempt to prod banks and servicing organizations into modifying existing loans. The problem with modifying existing loans is the securitization discussed in Chapter 3. Because most home loans no longer reside at one bank, but instead are sliced into small pieces and sold through pools, then no single entity now is available to negotiate with the homeowner. The person at the other end of the line from a homeowner in distress is not the lender or lenders, but is instead a loan servicer, who has a much different set of goals.

Lenders want to be paid their principal and interest. Servicers want their fees. A lender gets principal and interest when a borrower makes timely payments. Servicers, the group that actually receives payments from homeowners and sends the monies to the right places, get some fees when borrowers pay on time, but they earn a lot more when borrowers are delinquent or default. When a borrower stops paying, the servicer will make payments to the lenders on the borrower's behalf and will start assessing the borrower late fees and interest. This continues until the borrower defaults and the property is foreclosed on. At this point the servicer maintains the property and oversees the sale. Any proceeds from the sale of the foreclosed property go first to pay all of the costs incurred by the servicer and then go to the lenders. In a sense, the servicer, who is the one the borrower actually can speak with, has a built-in motivation to see the borrower fail, which is exactly the opposite motivation of the lenders.

The stimulus program in February 2009 included the Making Homes Affordable (MHA) program, which included the Home Affordable Modification Program, or HAMP. While HAMP and other programs inside of the MHA are well intentioned, they were doomed from the start because of the conflicting roles played by lenders, who want modification, and servicers, who don't. There is little incentive for servicers actually to take a home loan through modification instead of through foreclosure. As the special inspector general of the Troubled Asset Relief Program (SIGTARP), Neil Barofsky reported in October 2010 that the 1.6 million loans that entered the HAMP program represent less than half of the number of loans that the government had hoped for. Of that 1.6 million, only 640,000 remain in the program. The rest have fallen back to delinquency or otherwise have not made it through the trial period.

The result is that we are pretty much where we started, trillions of dollars in debt on housing and with roughly 1 in 4 home mortgages underwater. Even after the government has doled out trillions of dollars in bailout and stimulus, the former biggest asset for most American families has become an anchor around the neck of the household, not a bedrock of savings and security.

Another Round of Pain

Many of the loans that are in trouble are subprime, as discussed above, and have an adjustable interest rate. Depending on the specific terms of the loan, the interest rate might adjust once after two years or five years, or the interest rate might adjust every six months. The variations on this are almost endless. The point is that the monthly payment of many of the most vulnerable mortgage loans outstanding are dependent on interest rates. If interest rates move higher, then these adjustable mortgages will see their required payments move higher as well. This is part of the reason that the Fed has worked so hard to keep interest rates low: in addition to making borrowing cheaper, they want to keep the payments on adjustable mortgages as affordable as possible. With the stimulus plan losing its power, this is getting harder. Rates are moving up. With higher rates will come another round of pain as adjustable rate mortgages ratchet up.

Chart 6-11 shows the wave of resets in the US. Our original forecast was for the wave of resets at the end of 2009 and again in 2010 to cause significant disruptions. The moves by the Fed kept that from occurring. Now with interest rates moving higher in spite of Fed actions, there is not much anyone can do to change the wave of resets.

The Failure of the Stimulus Plans

Most of the government programs listed earlier in the chapter were meant to "tide people over" to wait for a better day. Except for making those in

Chart 6-11: Wave of Mortgage Resets

Trigger for the Next Financial Meltdown

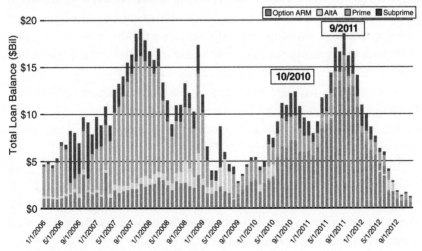

Data Source: **Loan Performance, Amherst Securities**

financial institutions even richer through privatized profits and social-ized cost, the effects have been to kick the very large proverbial can down the road. The Keynesian goal of restoring confidence so that consumers suddenly began spending more was not met and was unrealistic to begin with. There was little recognition on the part of the US government that we have changed our standing as consumers, taxpayers, and savers. While the stimulus plans might have worked in the economic Fall Season, when growth seems to be busting out at every turn, this same approach should not have been taken in the economic Winter Season, for which the goal is to conserve and save in recognition that economic growth will return, but not today.

By using the approach that it did, the US government enabled many actors—banks, states, cities, and even federal agencies like Social Security and Medicare—to ignore their problems for a little while. The idea was that if we could only kick-start growth, then we could begin to address these problems from a much stronger point. Unfortunately, that stron-ger point is not going to arrive anytime soon. Americans are not about to jump back into more debt, they are not at the point of buying bigger homes, and their goals are changing from spending to saving as they age. All of this adds up to the same thing: weak economic growth and even contraction in the years ahead. If we are interested in addressing our eco-nomic issues, we first have to recognize our starting point. We are not a young, aggressive population. We are aging. A younger generation is coming of age, but the older, driving force in our economy, the larger baby boom generation, is changing what it will do and what it wants. Because their goals are no longer centered on higher levels of spending, we cannot rely on this type of economic activity to pull us out of our slump. Almost since their birth we have been dealing with a generation that did not seem to know the meaning of the word no. They gave in to every vice and desire, so much so that they were named the Me Generation. That time is over.

This economic Winter Season will see the boomers move on. They won't like it, and they are currently doing everything they can to put it off, but in the end they will follow in the footsteps of their parents. Facing down the brutal reality of where they are, the boomers will learn to push away from the table of consumption.

While we have focused on the issues facing the economy—debt, unemployment, housing, misapplied stimulus—we have not focused specifically on the typical boomer, the person who has driven this economy for decades. In the pages ahead we will outline exactly what the typical boomer is up against in his effort to build a reasonably comfortable retirement for himself, and what his struggle for his own situation will mean to the economy at large.

CHAPTER 7

Consumers Are Too Much in Debt: The Credit Cycle Will Not Come Back

Consumers in the Winter Season—A Long Period of Deferred Gratification

It was just a marshmallow. One small, fluffy treat. But in the context of the experiment, it meant everything. In 1972, a researcher at Stanford University, Walter Mischel, conducted an experiment to test deferred gratification. This was no ordinary test. This was a test on children. His subjects were 4- to 6-year-olds from the Bing Nursery School on campus at Stanford. The setup was simple. A child would be asked to choose which treat he liked best: an Oreo cookie, a marshmallow, or a pretzel stick. The child would be led into a room free of distraction and sat down in a chair. On the table in front of the child would be the treat that he had chosen. At that point, the child would be given a choice: he either could eat the treat immediately or, if he could wait 15 minutes, he could have two. What happened next was a study in comedy.

Some children immediately ate the treat. Some covered their eyes so that they could not see it. Others fiddled with a treat—mashing it, rolling it, stretching it, and sniffing it—using all of their willpower and distraction methods to resist eating it. Some ate the treat before the researcher had left the room. Others agonized over it, and a few tried to nibble the edges without really making a mark. This study has been reproduced many times, and the results have been videotaped. Examples can be found online by searching YouTube with the term "marshmallow test." The results of similar, more recent tests have been comparable to those of Mischel. Roughly a third of the 600 children in the experiment were able to defer gratification long enough to get the second treat.

What is amazing is the follow-up research conducted by Mischel. In 1990 he was able to contact many of the original test subjects. Not only did the parents of the children who were able to defer gratification note that their children were more competent than other adolescents, but the SAT scores of this subset were higher than the SAT scores of the rest of the group.

There is a connection between the ability to defer gratification and success. In the context of everyday life, the most common example of this is saving up monies to use for a purpose rather than incurring debt. Most of us think of this idea as a blinding glimpse of the obvious, and yet this concept has significance for us today. Baby boomers are in a difficult spot. They have spent the last two decades growing their spending. Now, as they enter what should be their highest earning and saving years, the US is in the midst of the greatest recession of our generation, which affects not only the earnings and ability of all consumers to save, but also dramatically reduces the value of what is for many consumers their biggest asset, their home. Meanwhile, the government wants something from them—more spending, in order to jump-start the economy, to bring down unemployment, and to boost tax revenue at all levels.

Where is the personal payoff in that trade? What is the "marshmallow" that we are reaching for? Another DVD player, iPad, or television? How does having that trinket or device compare with the notion of a grim retirement? Consumers are neither crazy nor stupid. As we pointed out in Chapter 2, consumers make very rational decisions based on their own set of needs and goals, most of which are roundly ignored by economic theory and government programs. The world is not so simple as "purchase/ don't purchase."

As we go through the years ahead, boomers will not be motivated by the needs of the greater economy. They will not respond to calls to simply "buy more" or "feel confident." The average boomer recognizes exactly where she is, sitting at the bottom of a very large mountain that must be climbed. The deal that was struck by the parents of the boomers, the Bob Hope generation, is not available anymore.

The Bob Hope group survived the Great Depression, won World War II, and then grew America through the 1950s and 1960s. As the New Deal programs took effect, this generation benefited tremendously because so many more young workers (the boomers) had been added to the economy. At the same time, the pensions and benefits that had been offered by private companies and governments were coming due and being paid. The golden age of retirement arrived. A place at the beach, rising Social Security checks, pensions with cost-of-living adjustments, and gold-plated health care benefits were common.

However, with 92 million baby boomers leaving the workforce in the coming years, there is simply no way for the US to maintain for the boomers the benefits that were enjoyed by their parents. Choices will be made. Benefits will be cut. Taxes will be raised. Boomers must fend for themselves. They know it. They will do it. But they are starting from a very difficult point—low savings, high debt, dwindling equity in their homes, and an economy that won't cooperate during what should be the highest savings years of their lives.

The predictable consumer spending patterns discussed in Chapter 2 illustrate why boomers, the reliable class of overspenders who coined the phrase "conspicuous consumption" to describe their behavior, will be motivated to save. As their children leave home, these parents will look to the next phase of life, being empty nesters. It is during this time that people prepare for their quickly approaching retirement. This preparation requires an assessment of their current condition, and it is here that we start to realize how big a problem the boomers really have.

Over the past decade the baby boomers and consumers in general got caught up in the heat of the moment, spending greater amounts through various credit mechanisms (credit cards, HELOCs, etc.) as credit became easier to obtain. Meanwhile, income levels remained stagnant, which means that consumers either were borrowing from the future (debt that had to be repaid) or spending down the equity of their homes or other savings. Either way, the outcome was the same: a worsening financial position. For the largest segment of the boomers, those born in the mid- to late 1950s through the early 1960s, this is an especially rude awakening. They have just started to prepare for retirement and find themselves starting near zero. Looking at the factors of their financial lives (savings, income, and debt), we get a clear picture of the severity of the issue.

Savings, Income, and Debt

A Wells Fargo survey in 2010 posed a number of retirement- and savings-related questions to middle-income Americans. For the survey, "middle income" was defined as those households with annual income between $25,000 and $100,000, to keep the results from being skewed by those who are barely getting by or those who are affluent. Among the respondents in their 50s, the median savings for retirement was $29,000. Their stated savings goal? $300,000. With less than 15 years to go before retirement, this group was a mere 90% short of its savings goal. For the forty-somethings, the problem was even worse. Those in their 60s and 50s were fairly confident about reaching their retirement goals, but they are also much more likely to have a pension (59% of those in their 60s, and 55% of those in their 50s).* For those in their 40s, only 36% reported access to a pension. The 50- and 60-year-olds were excited about approaching retirement, and those in their 40s were scared to death. The overriding concerns of those in their 40s were paying down debt and saving more. They think their future looks difficult. They are right.

This report basically reflects what we already know. Those in their early 60s and mid- to late 50s will share some financial characteristics with their parents. These people joined the workforce in the late 1960s and early 1970s, right at the end of the pension era in corporate America. For those who came along a little later, the bulk of the boomers born in the late 1950s and early 1960s, pensions belong to a bygone era. For this group, there is plenty to fear and very little from which to take comfort. Without a pension, the only security net is Social Security, which is $14 trillion underfunded, appears headed for curbs in benefits, and provides only modest supplementation anyway (around $1,200 per month). After that, future retirees know that they will be on their own. They will have to plan for their financial future on their own and have to estimate how things will look tomorrow. It is clear that the current retirement savings amounts accumulated by the boomers will not be sufficient. Of course, these retirement accounts are not the only funds that people have. In addition, people treat their homes as built-in savings programs. Lately, that hasn't worked

* *2010 Wells Fargo Retirement Study* [PDF], Wells Fargo Bank, N.A., 2010. Available at www.wellsfargo.com/downloads/pdf/retirementpartners/2010_Retirement_Study.pdf.

Chart 7-1: S&P Case-Shiller 20-City Home Price Index

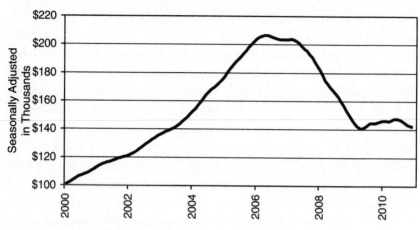

Data Source: Standard & Poor's Case-Shiller US 20-City Home Price Index

out so well. **Chart 7-1** shows the S&P Case-Shiller 20-City Home Price Composite Index. After rising over 100% from 2000 to 2007, the index has given back 60% of its gains so far.

We covered the reasons for this bubble in Chapter 3. If you owned your home throughout the entire period and did not borrow against it, then your situation might not be so bad. You purchased the home, made your payments, and saw the value skyrocket and then decline, but your home sustained a 50% gain and you've been paying it off. Unfortunately this does not describe many homeowners. During this same period of time, not only did the percentage of Americans who own homes shoot up, meaning that many homeowners are new to the marketplace, but loans were extended on very loose and questionable terms. Also, the American economy was flooded with home equity lines of credit (HELOCs) that allowed people to borrow against their home. This is the same thing as raiding your 401(k). **Chart 7-2** shows the explosion in HELOCs in the US during this period.

HELOCs, which barely registered at $100 billion outstanding in 1999, shot up 600%, to just over $700 billion by 2008. Over the course of 10 years we managed to borrow another $600 billion against our homes in order to fuel consumption. This type of action lowers the net value of homes in terms of assets on the books of homeowners, or rather in terms

Chart 7-2: Home Equity Lines of Credit (HELOCs)

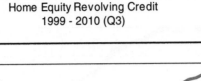

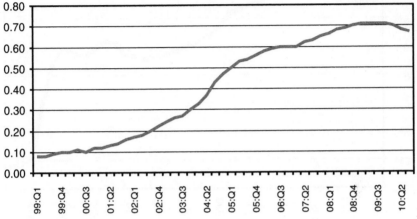

Home Equity Revolving Credit
1999 - 2010 (Q3)

Data Source: **Federal Reserve**

of the amount of equity the homeowner has. The Federal Reserve tracks and reports homeowner equity numbers. **Chart 7-3** shows homeowner equity as a percentage of home value.

Obviously the homeowner equity values have dropped dramatically in the last 10 years, as consumers have used more leverage to buy homes and as existing homeowners have taken out second mortgages and HELOCs. But there's even more bad news. The number above includes homeowners who hold their property free and clear, meaning that no mortgage exists. This group, which makes up about 30% of all homeowners, has 100% equity, which skews **Chart 7-3.** If we remove this group of homeowners from the calculation, then of those homes with a mortgage, the average equity in the home is 15%, as shown in **Chart 7-4!**

That's not much of a savings plan, especially as the values of homes continue to fall or go flat. Without a dramatic upturn in home prices, this asset is not going to add much to the balance sheet of people trying to save for retirement. The boomers are going to have to gather more assets. This leaves boomers two possibilities in their quest to prepare for retirement: to grow their income or to reduce their spending.

Chart 7-3: American Homeowner Equity

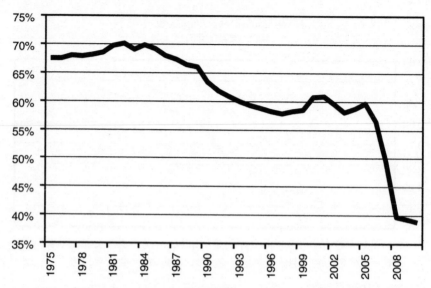

Data Source: Federal Reserve Flow of Funds Report (Table B. 100)

Chart 7-4: Homeowners' Equity Among Homes with Mortgages

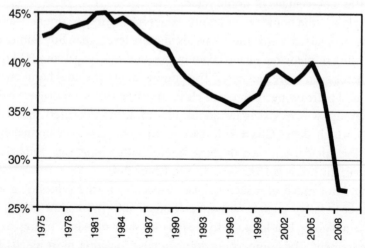

Data Source: Federal Reserve Flow of Funds Report (Table B. 100), adjustments based on US Census data and HS Dent

Income—Flat and Under Pressure

Income in America has been under pressure for over 30 years. Beginning in the early 1970s we faced international competition and stagflation at home, leading to a long period of flat income. As the baby boomers grew in their productivity and spending in the 1980s and 1990s, income grew, especially on a household or family basis, due to the formation of two-income households. As both parents went to work, total family income rose, but only to a point. The growth of family income continued until the late 1990s and has since remained stagnant, which is reflected in **Chart 7-5,** Median Household Income, 1975–2009.

It is interesting that median household income went flat as we entered the largest credit and debt boom in our history! What consumers could not generate on their own (increased purchasing power), they simply borrowed. Now that the financial crisis is here, with its attendant unemployment as described in Chapter 6, the possibility of incomes rising significantly over the next 5 to 7 years is remote. **Chart 7-6** shows the number of job seekers compared with the national number of openings.

The number represented above for November 2010 (the last date avail-

Chart 7-5: Median Household Income, 1975–2009 (2009 Dollars).

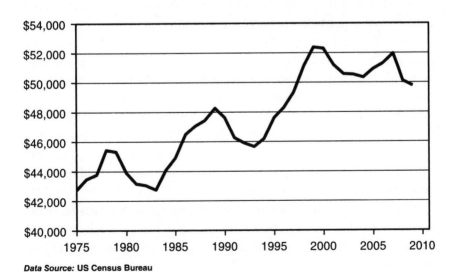

Data Source: **US Census Bureau**

Chart 7-6: Job Seekers per Job Opening

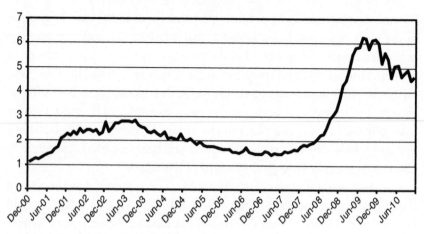

Data Source: Bureau of Economic Analysis

able) is 3.2 million job openings, compared with 15.0 million unemployed, or a ratio of 4.6 job seekers per opening. This ratio peaked at just over 6 job seekers per opening in 2009. Keep in mind that this chart represents the best face of unemployment put out by the Bureau of Labor Statistics, meaning that it is the lowest count of unemployment, reported as U-3 and discussed at length in Chapter 6. The U-3 number excludes anyone unemployed who has not looked for a job in the last 4 weeks (marginally attached). If we add back in this group, which represented over 2.1 million people in November 2010, then the ratio of job seekers to openings pops up to 5.3. Even this number does not tell the whole story, as it does not count the millions of unemployed persons who have not looked for a job in the last 12 months. How many people is this exactly? No one knows for sure, but as mentioned in Chapter 6, John Williams of www.shadowstats .com estimates this group to be roughly 6% of the labor force, or roughly 9 million workers. Adding this group to the ratio above would bring the job seekers per opening to over 8!

Adjusted for inflation, income has been flat for over a decade. In the current economic climate, businesses have cut their payrolls to match demand, and cities and states also have cut payrolls in response to falling tax revenue and rising costs. With an overhang of potential workers

and income levels flat at best, Boomers cannot rely on a future rise in income levels to reach their retirement goals.

What We Owe

In Chapter 3, we explained in detail the levels of debt in the private sector of our economy. Most of that description had to do with financial sector debt, which is the 800-pound gorilla when it comes to existing debt in our society and which will cause problems for years to come as we deal with debt. However, consumers have their own debt crisis. Consumer debt is worth examining to understand what sort of headwinds boomers face as they try to pay down this debt and move on to the next stage of life, retirement. With little savings and dim prospects of garnering higher-paying employment, debt plays an even more critical role in the equation of retirement planning than it previously did. At this point, boomers cannot assume that they will just "grow" their way out of their debt, earning higher amounts of income so that their debt payments are a smaller portion of their budget.

At first glance it might seem that we have good news, as the total consumer debt outstanding, as shown in **Chart 7-7**, appears to be declining.

Total consumer debt shot up from just over $5 trillion in 2000 to $12.5 trillion in 2008. Since then, the balance has fallen by almost $1 trillion, down to $11.58 trillion. This reduction in overall consumer debt is part of the deflation to which we keep referring. As consumers pay back debt overall, the money supply shrinks, unless another force (the Fed, US government borrowing, etc.) picks up the slack through its own borrowing or printing of money. The problem is that much of this debt reduction most likely did not come through voluntary repayment by newly converted misers. Instead, much of it probably came through the write-off of mortgages.

The total mortgage market in the US comprises most of the total consumer credit outstanding. **Chart 7-8** shows the size of this market, which rose from $3.6 trillion in 2000 to $9.3 trillion in 2008.

Since the peak in 2008, the mortgage market has fallen by $700 billion. RealtyTrac, an online tracking database of foreclosed homes and homes

Chart 7-7: Total US Consumer Credit Outstanding, 1999–2011

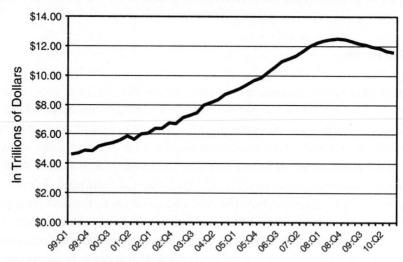

Data Source: **Federal Reserve Bank of New York**

Chart 7-8: US Consumer Mortgage Debt Outstanding, 1999–2011

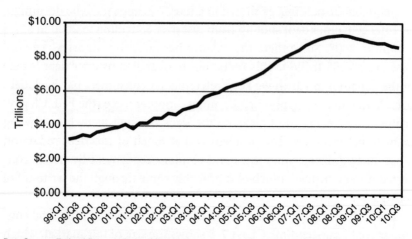

Data Source: **Federal Reserve Bank of New York**

for sale (http://www.realtytrac.com/home/), estimates that 2.3 million homes were repossessed from the time that the crisis began in late 2007 through 2010. This number does not include short sales. So between the mortgage write-downs on straight foreclosures and the losses taken on short sales, arguably more than $500 billion of the mortgage decline had nothing to do with voluntary repayment. However, it also could be argued that the mortgage industry has not suddenly chosen to begin marketing all of the crazy loans that it created in the 2000s, so fewer homeowners and a reduction in mortgage principal outstanding over time is exactly what we would expect.

At the same time that we are paying off and reducing mortgages, we are also chipping away at HELOCs, as shown in **Chart 7-2.** This category is being reduced much more slowly, down to $670 billion from $710 billion by the end of 2010, but it is still moving in the right direction. With so little movement, it is possible that the entire balance reduction was due to write-offs. The interesting part about the debt that we owe as consumers is what has happened in the other categories—credit cards, student loans, auto loans, and "other." **Chart 7-9** shows the changes in each of these, along with HELOCs.

Chart 7-9: Consumer Credit Outstanding, 1999–2011

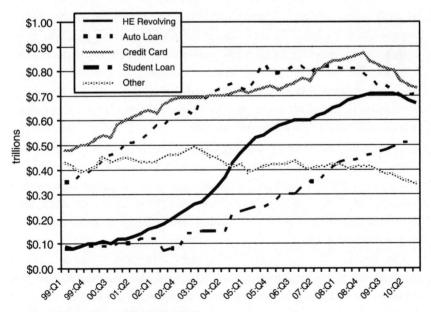

Data Source: Federal Reserve Bank of New York

Here is how the numbers fall out from their top in 2008 through the third quarter of 2010:

HELOCs	down $40 billion
Auto loans	down $80 billion
Credit cards	down $140 billion
Student loans	*up* $70 billion
Other	down $70 billion

Certainly credit card debt went through dramatic charge-offs as well as an effort by consumers to charge less, but auto loans? This reflects continued payments on existing cars coupled with a dramatic decrease in car sales. We bought fewer cars, while paying off the loans on the cars that we already have, equaling less debt.

The only category that showed an increase was student loans, by $70 billion. It is not surprising that this category is headed higher, given that the number of kids reaching college age has been rising since the mid-1990s (see Chart 2-1, The Immigration-Adjusted Birth Index), leading to millions of applicants vying for spots in colleges across the country. This competition has only been made fiercer by the addition of people who currently are trying to hide in academia because unemployment is so high. Until the crisis passes, there is no pressure on higher education prices to come down. This is arguably one of the last bubbles in the US. As the government has guaranteed student loans, it has encouraged a borrowing and spending boom that is reflected in the chart above: $500 billion in student loans outstanding. In exchange for the government guarantee, student loans are typically not discharged in a bankruptcy, making them almost impossible to wipe away. There is no "asset," like a house, that can be repossessed; instead the debt follows the borrower forever. The building anxiety in this sector is worth watching, as students are leaving college tens of thousands of dollars in debt (and their parents take out loans, too) but cannot find jobs. Look for a backlash in this area soon.

Our appetite for consumer debt topped out in 2008. We as consumers were not just at the breaking point of debt overload—we were past it. This is borne out by the foreclosures in housing and charge-offs in credit card debt. Now the trend is for less, and not just from the standpoint of the borrower. As we mentioned in Chapter 3, lenders do not have the same capacity to extend credit as they did in the 2000s, as exemplified by the investment banking world, where several of the firms no longer exist and the rest operate under charters that limit their leverage. At the same time, traditional banks have reduced capital, so they cannot generate the same levels of loans, either. This situation has led to a return to sanity in terms of how much debt is offered, which can be seen in two of the markets tracked above: HELOCs and credit cards. **Chart 7-10** shows the amount of HELOC debt outstanding as well as the HELOC debt limit available, and **Chart 7-11** shows the same thing for credit cards.

Both charts show a declining balance of debt, but this reduction is minimal compared to the tremendous cutback in available credit, which was reduced by $160 billion on HELOCs and was slashed by just over $1 trillion on credit cards. So in addition to the reduction in mortgage funding available, we have also seen a huge contraction in the availability of most other kinds of debt that consumers relied on during the 2000s to fuel their consumption.

While all of this is interesting and it appears that we are moving in the right direction, a quick look at a longer time frame will give you a sense of how big the debt problem of consumers really is. While total consumer

Chart 7-10: HELOC Balances vs. HELOC Limits

1999–2011

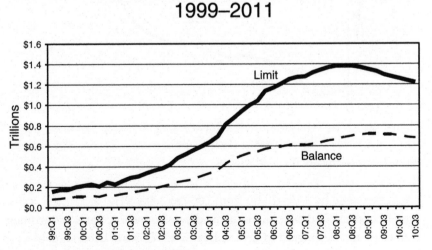

Data Source: Federal Reserve Bank of New York

Chart 7-11: Credit Card Balances and Credit Card Limits

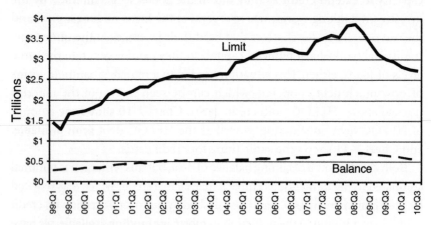

Data Source: **Federal Reserve Bank of New York**

Chart 7-12: Household Debt as Percentage of Disposable Income, 1980–2010 (Q3)

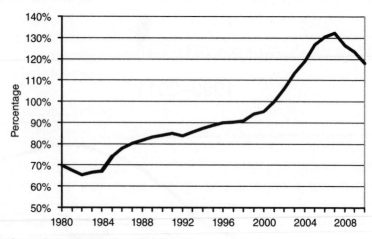

Data Source: **Federal Reserve Z1 and BEA Table 2.1**

credit increased by $7.5 trillion from 2000 to 2008, a rise of 150%, it is the ratio of household debt to income that drives home how the US consumer is maxed out with regard to debt. **Chart 7-12** shows household debt as a percentage of disposable income.

The US ratio of total household debt to disposable income remained fairly constant through the 1950s, 1960s, and 1970s, but then started to move higher in the mid-1980s. This makes sense, as it is exactly when the boomers were putting down roots and taking on the most debt relative to income in their lives—by buying their first homes. However, as a society we were not content merely to take on more debt; we more than doubled our debt as a percentage of disposable income compared with the previous generation! This measure exploded from roughly 64% to over 135%. It has fallen some since 2008, but we have a long way to go to get back to some semblance of normal as reflected in prior decades.

Through force (foreclosures and charge-offs) and choice (reducing net debt) we have begun to chip away at our mountain of personal debt, but we have a monumental, multitrillion-dollar task in front of us. Paying down debt will assist boomers by lowering their burden in retirement, but it makes building savings that much harder!

"We Have Met the Enemy, and He Is Us"

The above quote is from an Earth Day poster, circa 1970. It featured the comic character Pogo, created by Walt Kelly. His point was that our actions were endangering our own lives by destroying the earth through pollution and the excessive consumption of nonrenewable energy and minerals. This is a great analogy for where the boomers are today.

Through our own actions and decisions over the last decade, we have put ourselves in a much worse position than we otherwise would have been. The largest generation in our economy responded to its desire for consumption and its lack of income growth by taking on massive amounts of debt. The excess debt created an artificial asset bubble that made this same generation feel richer than it actually was. Unfortunately, because this is the largest generation, it creates its own feedback loop, which during the economic Fall Season was positive. As this group spent more to raise families, that spending led to growth in various industries and sectors, which led to a growing, albeit modestly growing, economy. The steadily growing economy kept unemployment low and asset prices rising. The debt that was taken on eventually consumed the system just as this huge generation was on the verge of changing its focus from spending to saving. The credit crisis was not caused by this shift in focus; instead the credit crisis pulled this shift forward by a year or so.

As the bubble collapsed, the true value of retirement savings held by this generation was exposed, and it was close to nothing (the $29,000 discussed above). The credit crisis, the housing bubble, and the aging of the boomers all contribute to this current climate of self-reflection, in which consumers are asking themselves, "How do we get out of this mess?" Only now are people beginning to realize that there is only one answer: reduce consumption. Rising income is not available to make this problem go away. Consumers have no more appetite for borrowing to fuel consumption at anywhere near previous levels, and certainly banks and other lenders now have no ability to lend at those prior levels. The only proactive step that most individuals can take to strengthen their personal balance sheets, meaning to increase their savings and lower their debt, is to consume less. The trend has already started. It is not overwhelming yet, but it is there. **Chart 7-13** shows daily consumer spending as tracked by Gallup.

These numbers represent self-reported daily spending by consumers, not including the purchase of a home, RV, auto, or normal daily bills. In essence, this is discretionary spending. With the last 2 years as a guide, we are running about 20% below where we were in 2008.

Chart 7-13: Daily Consumer Spending, Gallup, 2008–2011

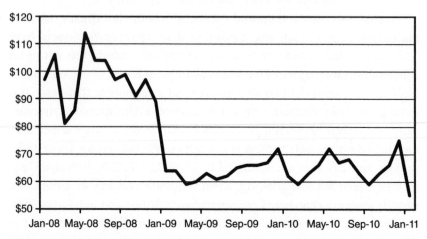

Data Source: Gallup, www.gallup.com

Keep in mind that spending does not go to zero! That is not the point. Consumers are going to spend, to be certain. However, they will be more judicious. This new way of thinking is creeping into our economic consciousness. It is reflected in both the declining debt and lower spending numbers outlined above. What is also abundantly clear from the information above is how far we have left to go, and what a difficult path it will be. Just as the economic Fall Season created a positive feedback loop for boomers, the economic Winter Season is creating a negative feedback loop—less will beget less.

Boomer spending has gone flat, while debt has started to decline. Incomes remain flat, and unemployment is high. Because the boomers are the largest generational group, as they continue whittling away at their debt and reining in their spending, it will only serve to slow our economy or to keep it on the path of tepid growth, leading to more pressure on incomes and unemployment, which will make debt reduction and saving for retirement that much harder. The government has spent trillions of dollars to nudge our spending levels higher and has succeeded only in keeping things level for a couple of years. When it comes to causing our economy to slow, we have seen the enemy, and he is us.

As the boomers continue to shift their focus from consumption to saving, the economy will continue to struggle to find its footing. The risks that stem from this will not be confined to just one or two industries, like housing and cars. Instead, it will reverberate throughout our system for years. Lower spending over time is like a slow-moving crisis; businesses slow, tax receipts fall, personal asset values erode, and opportunities for employment and success are few and far between. The next decade will be filled with many more risks than opportunities, and in order to avoid them you must recognize them now, before they show up on your doorstep! The next chapter will outline how this change of season from Fall to Winter, led by the changing focus on the boomers from spenders to savers, could impact the investments, employment, and opportunities facing all of us, as well as severely limit the options available to our government and corporate America.

Many people argue with us that this is only part of the story, as we are not alone on this planet. They are correct! There is more to this narrative than simply recounting what has happened in the US or even the developed world. But it is not what they think. Looking to the East, we

cannot rely on growth in Asia to balance out what is occurring in the developed Western world. In fact, when we analyze the East, and in particular China, we find that it will suffer a bubble burst and deflationary fall even greater than ours because it is so grossly overexpanded and inflated today! In Chapter 8 we will review emerging nations and highlight what to expect from these countries in the years to come. While the long-term outlook is quite positive, the short-term view is not!

The Last Great Bubble in China: Excess Capital Investment Means Global Deflation and an Emerging World Downturn

Ordos, Kangbashi, Zhengzhou, and Erenhot are four cities in China that have something in common: none of them has a population. The cities are empty. These are not small rural outposts that have seen their citizens move to urban centers for a better life. These are large cities built by the Chinese government for no purpose other than to keep building. In China, local politicians are rewarded on the basis of economic growth and employment. This system motivates local political party operatives to fuel growth in any way they can. When the downturn of 2008–2009 occurred, there appeared to be one giant way out of what could have been a slowing economy: build. Using explicit government backing in some cases and implicit government guarantees in others, China has been on a capital investment binge that has soared out of control. A December 2010 article, the *Daily Mail* (London, UK) showed satellite pictures of empty cities and reported estimates of up to 64 million unoccupied homes, with 20 new cities being built each year.* When this sort of overinvestment for its own

* Daily Mail Reporter, "The Ghost Towns of China: Amazing Satellite Images Show Cities Meant to Be Homes to Millions Lying Deserted," *Daily Mail*, Dec. 18, 2010. Available at http://www.dailymail.co.uk/news/article-1339536/Ghost-towns-China-Satellite-images -cities-lying-completely-deserted.html.

sake ends, the Chinese economy, as well as all those who feed it through commodities and equipment, will feel the pain.

In Chapter 6 of *The Great Depression Ahead*, we explained in great detail why the growth in the world was going to shift dramatically from the developed world of Europe, North America, Japan, and South Korea to the emerging world of countries like China, India, and Brazil. Growth in both the emerging world and developed world has been accelerating since the 1980s and 1990s, but that will not be the case from 2008 forward. Even though there will be another boom in North America and in Australia and New Zealand from 2023 forward, growth unquestionably will be centered in the emerging world. The reasons are simple and quantifiable well into the future:

1. Populations in the developed world increasingly are aging past the peak age for spending and workforce growth years, whereas the emerging world is just seeing the "demographic dividend" of falling birth rates and rising life expectancies that the developed world experienced in the last century. In countries like India more than 5 decades of workforce and demographic growth already have been set in stone as a result of past birthrates and growing life expectancy trends. The Middle East and Africa have even longer demographic growth trends if they continue to develop economically.

2. Developed countries have seen a plateau in urbanization rates between 70% and 80%. Our research has found that urbanization rates are the greatest generator of rising incomes and GDP per capita. Most emerging countries are still in the 30% (India) to 50% (China) range of urbanization, with decades of growth to come. The exception in the emerging world is Latin America, where urbanization rates have already hit 70% to 80%.

The long-term trends of growth clearly are strong in the emerging world. The strongest areas for growth are India and the Middle East, and Africa could prove even stronger if it joins the development party. These places will be the best places to invest in after the great crash ahead. The problems in the emerging world are threefold. Many such economies rely heavily on exports to the richer developed world, which is set for another decade-plus of slowdown, and that slowdown

is likely to be dramatic in the next few years. The developing economies increasingly are focused on supplying the Chinese economic bubble with materials and energy, and that bubble will burst in the next few years. Finally, our very reliable 29- to 30-year Commodity Cycle is peaking between mid-2008 and mid-2011. Lower commodity prices from 2020 to 2023, and especially around 2015, will hurt the exports of most emerging countries, particularly those in the Middle East, Africa, and Latin America.

The last major bubble boom in the world is occurring in China and it is unprecedented, just like everything else has been in this global bubble boom. However, China's boom will end soon. People often tell us, "No, it won't!" They are sure that China (like India) is growing due to a massive demographic trend that won't end for many decades! We agree, and indeed such demographic research is the cornerstone of our own investigations. But there are important trends to the contrary in the years and the decade ahead, as we explain below. If you don't see these trends, you could miss a catastrophic sell-off! Many of the exports from both the emerging world as well as developed countries like Canada, Germany, Australia, and New Zealand are going to China. China has become the manufacturing center for the world and the second largest economy on the planet. Today, more than half of all the construction cranes in the world belong to China. If the bubble in China bursts, as we have been forecasting and as we saw in Southeast Asia starting in 1998, then the whole emerging world will slow down, making this a global downturn. The developed world already clearly has entered an era of slower growth that will continue and intensify between 2012 and 2015.

China's real GDP growth was off the charts, at 13% in 2007. Growth rebounded to 12% in 2011 after dropping to a mere 6% in July 2009. This unprecedented growth spree has now been going on for 14 years, but China and even India are trying to put on the monetary brakes, as rising food and energy prices curb their growth. This inflation caused protests in India and even caused riots in many countries, especially in the Middle East. Maintaining growth at that level while trying to conduct normal business is not possible. The emerging countries in East Asia have deployed a new strategy of strong government capital investment (and foreign direct investment) to spur their growth from emerging-country status to developed-country status. That strategy is a good one, and it works to transition a country from an exporting support role on the world stage to a more sustainable consumer- and business-driven economy longer term. However, there is a limit to such growth. Government-driven strategies ultimately overexpand beyond even rapidly growing consumer demand, especially in infrastructures and export industries. This overexpansion causes major bubbles and currency crises, as happened in Southeast Asia from late 1997 into late 2002 and in Japan from 1974 to 1982. Despite the rapid rise in household income in China, income peaked as a percentage of GDP in 1999 at 90% and fell rapidly to 68% in 2008. The consumer is contributing less, while the government, through capital spending and exports, is contributing more to GDP over time. This simply is not sustainable, especially in a slowing world economy! How much is China's fixed capital investment contributing to its high growth rates in GDP? The answer is 66% and rising. See the story about ghost cities at the beginning of this chapter. This is nuts!

Pivot Capital Management issued a great research report on China in early 2010 showing the size of the government-funded fixed-investment bubble in that country. **Chart 8-1** shows how growth-fixed capital investment (GFCF) has averaged 50% of GDP for an expansion period of 12 years through 2009, which is far higher than the peak for South Korea (39% over 8 years, 1990–1997), Japan (36% for 6 years, 1968–1974), or the next strongest prior expansion, Malaysia (44% over 8 years, 1990–1997). Note that the last such bubble in Southeast Asia, from 1990 to 1997, ended in a 5-year bubble that lasted through 2002, with stock markets in those countries down more than 70%. For the United States, such capital investment averages more like 15%, with 70% from consumer demand and 20% from government. It is natural for such rates of growth driven by fixed capital investment to be higher in emerging countries, but rates of more than 50% are, again, simply not sustainable.

In addition to government-driven infrastructure building, China and many emerging-world countries have exports that are as high as 35% or more of GDP. Hence, a world slowdown affects them much more than countries that rely on selling to their own consumers. This is what caused the greater than 70% declines in the Chinese stock market in 2008, even though China's economy slowed to a mere 6% growth rather than undergoing a major recession and banking meltdown, as occurred in developed countries like the US, which suffered stock declines of more like 50%. Part

Chart 8-1: Intensity and Duration of Capital Spending Booms in Asia

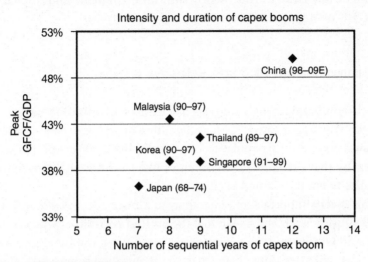

Data Source: **IMF, Pivot Capital Management**

of the fuel for the boom has been credit, which in China has been growing at a substantially faster rate than GDP. This capital investment strategy has led to excess capacity buildup in China's rapidly growing manufacturing industries. China's steel capacity outstrips every other country in total production, and its actual capacity is 20% above its actual production rate. China consumes more cement than any country in the world, with capacity that is at least 25% in excess of production and still growing. That is huge! Aluminum production and capacity is even more out of whack, with excess capacity near 40% and growing. As a report from Pivot Capital Management states: "At 1.35 [billion tons], China consumes more cement than the rest of the world combined. China's estimated spare capacity (about 340 [billion tons]) is more than the consumption of India, USA, and Japan combined."

China has become the largest manufacturing center in the world and the second largest economy. Such excess expansion and capacity from the strongest government-led capital investment boom in modern history clearly will lead to global price wars for commodities and manufactured goods. These price wars will lead to deflation in prices once the developed countries fall into the next great downturn,

between late 2011 and late 2013 or by 2014 at the latest. This represents another dimension to "the ticking time bomb of debt" and a deflationary crisis on a global basis.

Urbanization Trends Are Likely to Be Understated in China

Pivot's report also strongly suggests that China's urbanization statistics are substantially understated: "China's definition of an urban centre includes, amongst other things, population density of above 1,500 people per square meter. By that definition Western cities like Houston or Brisbane could technically not be counted as cities."

This is very important and may apply to a lesser degree to countries like India. Our research has shown that the greatest correlation with GDP per capita growth in emerging countries is rising urbanization. This correlation starts once two things come to pass: urbanization reaches 20% and the development path is clear. Urbanization tends to peak between 70% and 80% in most developed countries today. This correlation between urbanization and GDP growth makes sense, because when a household moves from a rural area to an urban one, its income and spending tend to roughly double! Brazil and Latin America have already largely attained 70% to 80% urbanization; hence, these countries will have less long-term growth than most would assume, although their demographic and workforce growth trends will be strong into the 2030s or so, as we will show ahead. Most emerging countries have decades more to come of such natural urbanization growth, which happens on a very predictable curve.

Chart 8-2 shows past and future projections for Chinese per capita GDP vs. rising urbanization rates. At present, China's urbanization is just shy of 50%, with per capita GDP at just over $5,000. Projected per capita incomes are approximately $8,800 at 80% urbanization, which is projected to occur just after 2050. However, if measured by international standards, China's urbanization rate is probably closer to 60% to 65% today. Such a populous country easily could top out closer to 70% than 80%, as Japan did, especially given how rapidly the Chinese population is aging and because China has limited flat land for urban development. Older people are much less likely to migrate to new places or urban areas than people in the 20- to 34-year-old age range.

Chart 8-2: China, GDP Per Capita vs. Urbanization

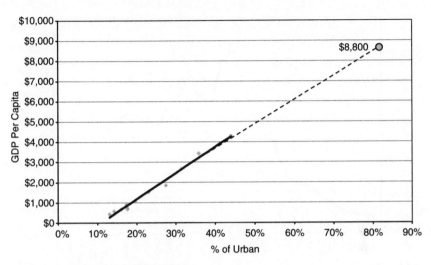

Data Source: **United Nations, Angus Maddison**

If the process of Chinese urbanization has matured more than is being reported, then China will not have strong growth prospects past the next few decades (likely into around 2035), unlike India and most emerging countries outside of South America. The more critical issue in the future for China is its workforce growth level, or lack thereof. Workforce growth correlates better with demographic spending trends in emerging countries than with the Spending Wave (46-year lag on births) in developed countries. China's demographic trends will peak around 2015, plateau around 2025, and then slow for decades to follow (**Chart 8-3**), much like Europe (but not as fast) and clearly more than in the United States. Even the stretch of economic growth for the Spending Wave shows a more dramatic top around 2015, a downturn into 2025, and a final, secondary top around 2035 followed by a decline for decades to follow.

Given such extremes in overexpansion from an unprecedented government-stimulated capital investment boom rather than from an off-the-charts private credit bubble, China's economy may reach something of a long-term peak by late 2011. However, China's demographics will not peak until 2015. By the time that excess capacity in infrastructure, real estate, and production is worked off, demographics

Chart 8-3: China, Workforce Growth vs. Spending Wave, 1950–2095

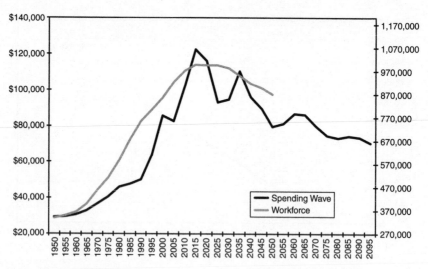

Data Source: **United Nations**

in China already will be peaking. China should continue to urbanize (at a slower rate) for a few decades to come, but its urbanization could be closer to peaking near term than most mainstream analysis would suggest. This confluence of events in China gives more credibility to the idea that India and Southeast Asia will be the greater boom region of the world in the coming decades and to the idea that the Middle East, Latin America, and Africa will feed that boom with natural resources.

China's Rapidly Growing Real Estate Bubble

Unlike most developed countries, China's real estate bubble accelerated rather than burst after the crash of 2008. **Chart 8-4** shows home prices compared to income in China, which have surged incredibly since the summer of 2009. The growing upper class in China increasingly is getting the same "real estate is the best way to create wealth" urge that we got from 2000 into 2006. This desire to own real estate is occurring even though, in China, credit standards for mortgages are much less liberal than in the United States. Many upper-class households put down 50%

Chart 8-4: Land Prices in China

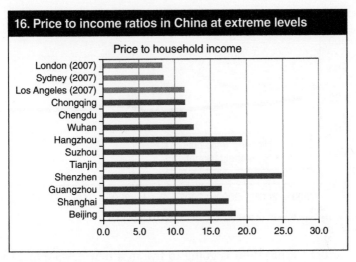

16. Price to income ratios in China at extreme levels

Price to household income

Data Source: **Nomura, Demographia, Pivot Capital Management**

in cash on a mortgage. However, the combination of strong government stimulus and "speculation fever" is creating a glut in real estate in China—yet another example of excess capacity that will lead to deflation in prices ahead. It's not like there isn't enough housing for China's growing middle class. China has more residential space per household than Hong Kong and South Korea, but not quite as much as Japan, Singapore, and Taiwan, despite much lower average income. Again, the growing upper middle class is driving this boom, and they will retreat much as happened in the US once the real estate boom finally ends in the years ahead.

Chart 8-5 tells a story that is consistent throughout China's economy. China has experienced a growing glut of home building in excess of household formation since 2001, with 2 million units per year in excess since 2005. The government is allowing and encouraging the building of residential and commercial real estate to keep economic and job growth up. As referenced at the start of the chapter, there is a city in central China, Ordos, where the entire infrastructure for 1 million people has been built—housing, apartments, stores, offices, etc.—but no one is living there! Many of the apartments and condos have been bought, but for speculation, of course. This is occurring in many smaller develop-

Chart 8-5: Housing Units vs. Household Formation

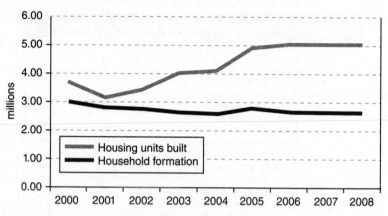

Data Source: National Bureau of Statistics, Pivot Capital Management

ments across China. Who is going to live in a new development where no one else lives? When will the speculators realize that this is a bubble and flee?

In China, the ratio of home prices to average income is very high compared with the same ratio of home price to average income in the most expensive areas of the US. Even if adjusted for higher income vs. average buyers, homes prices in China clearly are as high or higher than in major US cities; this is also true for major cities throughout the emerging world, such as Mumbai, India. The price ratio indicates that the Chinese real estate bubble is not sustainable, especially given that lower-income households, which would have to be the next buyers, would not be able to afford such prices. Thus, the last major bubble to burst around the world is likely to be in China, followed by the bursting of smaller bubbles in the major cities of India and throughout the emerging world.

In addition to the real estate and industrial capacity gluts, the Chinese direct stimulus program mostly was directed into infrastructure such roads and railways. China's initial $585 billion stimulus represented 14% of GDP vs. 6% in the United States. If China's urbanization trends do slow in the coming decades as we expect, then China probably is overbuilding its infrastructure for many years to come, especially in light of the global depression and slowdown that we forecast.

It is likely to take at least a decade to work off the excess capacity in industry, real estate, and infrastructure in China, especially in a slowing global economy. By the time this occurs, possibly in early 2020, China's demographics will be slowing (from 2015 to 2025 on). China's urbanization rate is likely to be slowing as well but still will be creating a low rate of growth and progress. China is not going to be the growth engine it has been for the last few decades, although it will be the second largest economy for decades. India is the only large country that can rival China or take its place, and India is likely to do so from 2050 forward.

We covered growth projections for the emerging world in great detail in Chapter 6 of *The Great Depression Ahead* over a monumental 77 pages. We looked at urbanization rates and workforce growth projections for all of the major regions and key countries around the world. We also looked at the growing megacities of more than 9 million around the world that increasingly will be concentrated in China and India, creating global innovation and dominance. We recommend that you read that chapter if you have any interest in global trends for investment, business, or career, as it is more than worth the price of the book. We won't repeat that extensive analysis here, as it would overwhelm this book's key focus on the deflationary downturn in the next decade or longer.

The summary insight is clear: the emerging world will dominate future booms, including the next one from around 2020–2023 through 2035–2036, as demographics slow in developed countries for decades to come. The overall global and emerging world boom is not likely to peak until around 2065, when world population is forecast to peak due to predictable birth and life expectancy trends.

Summarizing Global Insights and Trends

As demographics trend sideways in the United States (see Change in Spending at Each Age and Stage of Life, **Chart 2-2,** Chapter 2) in the coming decades, matched by similar trends in Canada, Australia, and New Zealand, demographics in Europe clearly are trending downward for decades to come (**Chart 8-6**). The weakest area in Europe is Southern Europe, and the strongest area is Scandinavia. Russia and Eastern Europe

Chart 8-6: Europe, Spending Wave vs. Workforce Growth, 1950–2095

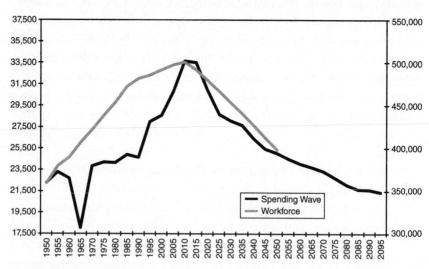

Data Source: **United Nations**

are similar to Southern Europe, with shrinking demographic trends second only to Japan.

An important concept to review here is the development of the S-curve, which we show in **Chart 8-7**. World growth has been accelerating since the Industrial Revolution in the late 1700s and early 1800s, and population growth has grown exponentially. In just over 200 years, the population of the world has grown from 1 billion to roughly 7 billion people, and it is still rising! More important, an increasing number of countries have developed middle-class living standards due to this revolution in productivity, which has continued to grow as a result of the Information Revolution. Great Britain led the Industrial Revolution and was the first to have growing urbanization rates. The rest of Western Europe and then North America; Australia and New Zealand; Japan; and South Korea, Hong Kong, Singapore, and Taiwan quickly followed. Now China is leading the industrialization trend in Asia. India is likely to follow, especially in the information and movie and entertainment industries, which would put it more in line with innovation trends in the United States.

The important insight is that the countries and regions that first innovate in new technologies tend to have higher living standards

Chart 8-7: The Wealth S-Curve

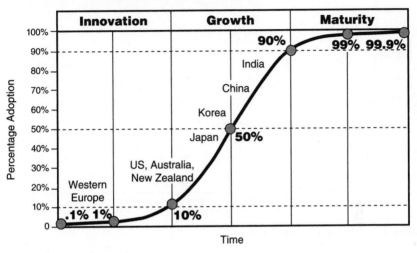

The S-Curve of Industralization/Urbanization

Data Source: **HS Dent Foundation**

and advantages over time than later adopters. This same phenomenon occurs with entrepreneurs; the top 1% to 10% of income earners in developed countries who tend to dominate 40% to 50% of the wealth. Emerging countries (with a few exceptions, such as Japan and South Korea, islands and island-like nations similar to Great Britain) are not likely to develop the levels of wealth attained by countries in the developed world (North America and Europe), because they have to compete at lower wage rates and lower margins over time. The United States and Australia benefited from innovations like railroads, electricity, and cars, which allowed their cultures, based on the ideas and ideals of England and Europe, to expand such technologies into much broader geographic areas. The genetic history and cultures in emerging countries that follow tend to lag in such skills and innovation.

The first paradox we noticed years ago was that leading emerging countries like Brazil (**Chart 8-8**) and almost all of Latin America had already achieved urbanization rates closer to those in the United States and Europe. At an 80% urbanization rate, Brazil had a GDP per capita of only $5,556 in 2000 and $10,900 by 2010. To continue increasing the standard of living

Chart 8-8: Brazil, GDP per Capita vs. Urbanization

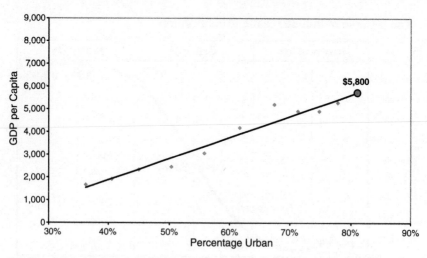

Data Source: United Nations, Angus Maddison

Chart 8-9: Latin America, Spending Wave vs. Workforce Growth, 1950–2095

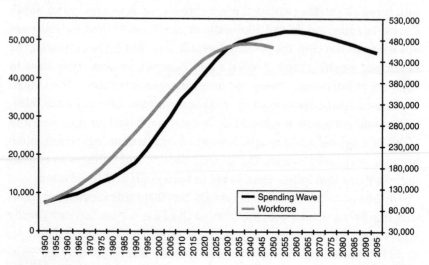

Data Source: United Nations

in the decades ahead, Brazil must increase the number of young people entering the workforce and expand its spending and income growth, as **Chart 8-9** shows for all of Latin America. Workforce growth will continue in Latin America until sometime in the 2030s—especially in the next global boom and commodity boom beginning around 2035–2036.

We have found that emerging countries don't have the same income, spending, and productivity curve as developed countries, because emerging countries are still focused on manual labor in agriculture, mining, energy, and construction industries. That is why workforce growth is a better gauge of economic trends in the emerging nations than peak spending around age 46, which is the standard for developed countries. However, these trends are somewhat similar, although workforce growth peaks earlier and is less extreme than the Spending Wave on a 46-year lag to birth. It takes longer for the cultures of these more traditional countries to adapt to new trends in technology and societal shifts. Present and past warlords as well as dictators tend to hold back progress to protect their interests, from the Taliban in the Middle East to the still-communist and unelected government in China (despite the massive growth of the Chinese middle class). Among the emerging nations, China has the largest young generation coming to adulthood, and it is the most likely to be able to challenge the older generation still in power.

One of the major trends we have been predicting for this Winter Season from 2008 to 2023 is that dictators and warlords in younger, emerging countries will be challenged or even overthrown, leading to more democratic and freer market economies over time, as has already occurred in the developed countries. As evidenced by recent protests, this trend has already begun to occur in North Africa and the Middle East. Expect much more unrest of this type in the years to come, spreading to Latin America and Africa.

These revolts will cause geopolitical crises and spikes in oil and commodity prices near term, but will be a positive factor in the long term for emerging countries, just as the American and French Revolutions marked major advances in the developed world in the late 1700s. Iran is a classic example of an emerging country, dependent largely on oil exports and wealth, that in the years ahead is likely to experience a revolution led by a progressive, educated younger generation to overthrow a backward government. The demographic growth trends in the Middle East are very favorable if such countries can move more into the modern world, as has the UAE (Dubai). However, overbuilding in the Gulf areas based on oil profits will cause a major setback and bubble crash in real estate in these countries, especially as oil prices are likely to peak in 2011 and trend downward to $10 to $20 per barrel by 2015. After rising for a few years following that drop, we see oil prices falling yet again in 2020 to 2023.

The largest country in Asia, India, has a very positive future that is indicative of the emerging world near its best. First, India's urbanization is close to 30%. Growth trends there started recently, in the 1990s. Urbanization trends in China are at 50% or higher. The projections for India's growth in GDP per capita are less predictable than for China and most emerging countries, because the recent bubble is likely to have exaggerated such trends. Currently India has per capita GDP of approximately $3,000, substantially lower than China. However, India's urbanization trends suggest growth for most of this century through the 2060s, and a range of per capita GDP of $8,000 at a minimum to as high as $13,500. The high end of the range could be achieved if India continues to see higher-middle-class growth as well as continued higher innovation in the technology and entertainment industries, which have higher potential incomes.

Chart 8-10 shows a very different story for India vs. China in the decades ahead. India's workforce growth doesn't start to peak and plateau until the 2050s, and its Spending Wave doesn't peak until around 2065, in line with global population peaks around then. If India's GDP per capita growth is more in line with China's, at $8,000 to $9,000 (in present-day terms), then its economy eventually will approach the size of China's and may eventually eclipse it as the second largest in the world. China's demographic growth slows after 2035, and its urbanization rates are likely to plateau by then as well. If India's economy approaches a level of GDP per capita that is between China's and South Korea's, then it could become the second largest in the world and even could start to rival the US economy between 2050 and 2065.

Now we will show the extremes in emerging country potential for urbanization and GDP per capita, with the same insight: these countries will not get as rich as the developed countries in our lifetimes. Malaysia (Kuala Lumpur is its capital) in **Chart 8-11** is near 70% urbanization, with GDP per capita near $9,000 and projected to be $10,200 at its peak in the decade or two ahead. That is about as good as it gets for an emerg-

Chart 8-10: India, Spending Wave vs. Workforce Growth, 1950–2095

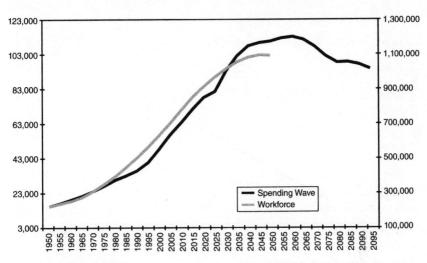

Data Source: United Nations

Chart 8-11: Malaysia, GDP per Capita vs. Urbanization

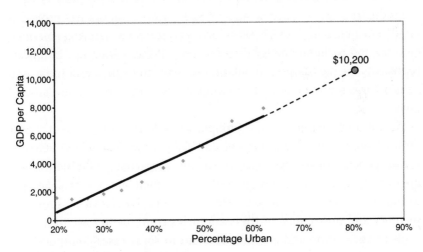

Data Source: United Nations, Angus Maddison

ing country in Asia, outside of nations like Japan, Singapore, Taiwan, and South Korea. Turkey has similar GDP per capita growth and projections. Indonesia **(Chart 8-12)** represents the typical achievement of an emerg-

Chart 8-12: Indonesia, GDP per Capita vs. Urbanization

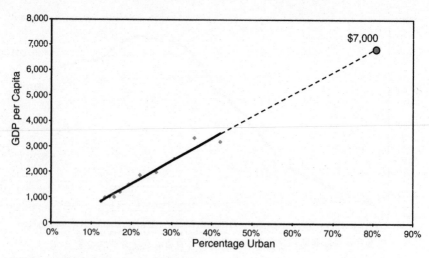

Data Source: **United Nations, Angus Maddison**

ing country that has a more democratic government but still relies on a largely agricultural, export-based economy and has not fully entered the industrial age, as have Japan and South Korea. Indonesia's projected GDP per capita is around $7,000, which is typical for a maturing emerging country and is slightly better than for most of Latin America. Indonesia represents the next-largest population in Asia after China and India, and its growth is limited mainly to continued workforce growth into around 2040.

At the other extreme is the Philippines (**Chart 8-13**), presently near 70% urbanization and with a projected GDP per capita of only $2,900 over the next decade or so. These factors explain why so many Filipino workers are migrating to Hawaii and the rest of the United States, Africa, and the Middle East. Many Sub-Saharan African nations like Kenya are similar in incomes and projections. If these countries continue to have only basic skills in agriculture and construction and in some cases continue to be suppressed by dictators and corrupt, top-down governments, then they are not likely to join the global free market and Industrial/Information Revolution. Some countries will always be the producers of the materials and commodities that drive continued growth in the world economy, and

Chart 8-13: The Philippines, GDP per Capita vs. Urbanization

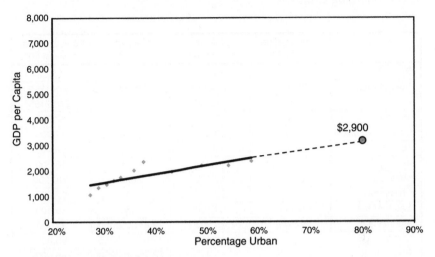

Data Source: **United Nations, Angus Maddison**

such countries will always be on the bottom of the economic ladder, even as they grow.

Chart 8-14 shows the summary from Chapter 6 in *The Great Depression Ahead* (from Figure 6.32) of our projections of GDP per capita for many countries around the world. As of 2000, urbanization was the lowest in Kenya, at 19.7%, with GDP per capita of $1,020. Brazil was at the top, with urbanization at 81.2% and GDP per capita of $5,556. Among the countries, we project that Mexico will reach 80% urbanization by 2020 at $7,800 per capita GDP, Turkey 80% by 2035 at $8,700, and South Africa 80% by 2050 at $6,400. Note that the United States was at $46,716 in 2005 near the top of the bubble boom.

Even with declining growth rates in the next decade, as we project, and with continued growth in emerging countries for decades to come, in no emerging countries, including China and India, are living standards likely to come even close to those of the United States. The economies of only China and India will approach the size of the economy of the United States or the economies of broader Europe in the next several decades, despite unprecedented progress. This estimate could change dramatically if living standards decline substantially in devel-

220   The Great Crash Ahead

Chart 8-14: Summary of GDP per Capita and Urbanization Projections, Select Emerging Countries

	Urbanization Rate in 2000	GDP per capita in 2000	Urbanization at 80%	Peak GDP per capita at 80%
Brazil	81.2%	$5,556	2000	$8,400*
South Korea	79.6%	$14,343	2000	$19,115*
U.S.	79.1%	$28,129	2005	$46,716*
Mexico	74.7%	$7,218	2020	$7,800
Czech Republic	74.0%	$8,630	2040	$9,700
Turkey	64.7%	$7,481	2035	$9,700
Iran	64.2%	$4,742	2035	$6,000
Malaysia	62.0%	$7,872	2025	$10,200
Philippines	58.5%	$2,385	2040	$2,900
South Africa	56.9%	$4,139	2050	$6,400
Indonesia	42.0%	$3,203	79.4% in 2050	$7,000
China	35.8%	$3,425	72.9% in 2050	$8,800
Pakistan	33.2%	$1,947	63.7% in 2050	$6,000
India	27.7%	$1,910	55.2% in 2050	$13,500
Vietnam	24.3%	$1,790	57.0% in 2050	$5,800
Kenya	19.7%	$1,020	48.1% in 2050	$2,800

*2008 GDP per capita from World Bank

Data Source: **United Nations, World Bank, and Angus Maddison**

oped nations, which is not likely in the United States, but is possible in Europe, Eastern Europe, and Russia.

We outlined our growth estimates for countries around the world, particularly China and India, to give you a sense of the obstacles faced by these countries. Many people are simply wishing away our problems at home and in developed nations by claiming that "China will save us through its own growth." Nothing could be further from the truth! While countries like China certainly will grow, they have severe imbalances today in terms of their infrastructure spending and their internal spending. Much of the emerging world exports to China, which is using the goods to fuel internal capital expenditures in an economy overrun with excess capacity and manufacturing of exports to the developed world, both trends that will slow in the years ahead. When the slowdown occurs in China, it will ripple through exporting emerging (and even some exporting developed) countries very quickly.

The current economic woes of the United States will not be corrected by reliance on some outside force for growth. We will have to curtail our spending and restructure our debt. This is going to cause major upheaval for people, businesses, and the government. In the chapters ahead we will outline how we can go about this process at each of these levels and how we can even use the years ahead not only to survive, but to thrive!

You can get free access to Harry's very popular webinar "Understanding the Economy and What Lies Ahead" by registering http://www.hsdent.com/webinar.

CHAPTER 9

How You Can Survive and Thrive: Strategies for Investments and Careers

We spent the first eight chapters of this book explaining in detail the obstacles that lay before us. The continuing change in the focus of the boomers, the massive debt that we carry in the private sector as well as the public sector, and the overall slack in the economy are combining to form a storm that happens only once in a generation. Now is the time to deal with excesses that we have allowed to pile up, not just in the past decade, but since our last generational storm in the 1930s. Entitlement programs, government-guaranteed mortgage programs, tax loopholes, bailed-out private companies, walking-dead banks, underwater mortgages—all of these and more must be dealt with in the years ahead. We can choose to tackle these programs on our own terms, or else the international markets will choose the time and place. Either way, this reckoning will happen. As discussed in Chapter 7, we face tremendous risks personally as this reckoning occurs.

It is not just our investments that are jeopardized, but also our standard of living and our long-term prospects. The US government as well as cities and states must take decisive, concrete steps to address the gaping fiscal holes in their budgets and our slack employment. At the same time, financial institutions will have to come to terms with the bad debt on their books. These things are going to affect us dramatically as taxpayers and consumers right when we are trying to address our own goals and needs (as the largest generation is saving for retirement). This turmoil and confusion is exactly what you would expect as the economic season changes.

We cannot overstate the change that we are going through. Moving from the economic Fall Season to the Winter Season has seemed gradual after early to mid-2009 up until now, but that is likely to change dramatically between late 2011/early 2012 and late 2014/early 2015. If you hold on to the activities and attitudes that served you well in the Fall Season, you will find yourself woefully unprepared and lacking as the Winter Season wears on in the years ahead. Simply building an asset allocation and holding on will doom your portfolio even though it may have worked well in the past three decades. Turning a blind eye to the tax consequences of the fiscal time bomb we face could rob you of your wealth every April 15 going forward. Holding real estate and hoping to be made whole by the markets is another way to tank your balance sheet. While all of these things worked before, they are attitudes and approaches best left behind. The key is to use the information that we have outlined in this book to discern the most likely path for consumers and the country, then identify the consequences or outcomes of the paths taken. Armed with that information, you can set a course not only to survive the Winter Season, but to thrive in the years ahead!

The Goals and Choices

So many times we have had to repeat our basic premise: you have to *pay attention to what people really want*. In America today, what people want is to find themselves in better economic health. They want their jobs to be more secure, their retirement plans to have bigger balances, their homes to have higher values and less debt attached, and their children to have bright futures (both in their personal lives and as citizens of this country) without being saddled with insurmountable debt. Nowhere did we list "and have a bigger TV," but we readily acknowledge that people will still buy stuff; they just will not do so on the same scale or go into the same amount of debt to do it. Of course, nowhere in there did we list "and stop eating out four times a week," either, but people already have begun to cut back.

The last piece—neither buying a bunch of new stuff nor giving up too much of what they have—refers to the goal of maintaining our current standard of living. That's an interesting phrase. To maintain your standard of living, you need to keep your purchasing power, which is your ability to buy stuff, at the same level in the future as you enjoy today. This is where things get tricky, because this list of goals is incompatible. The only way to achieve all of these things is to have someone come along and pay us more for what we produce, which would give us our current amount of income plus some more to use for paying down debt and saving for the future. In an economy marked by slack capacity and high unemployment, that's very unlikely. This is not the season in which to just grow ourselves out of our problems! This is the time to deflate bubbles, erase excesses, and purge our economy of the "fluff."

It *Is* Your Father's Economy

That old cliché about things in our time being unlike the experience of our parents is well known, but it is wrong when it comes to economics. In this arena, the old cliché of "nothing new under the sun" is more appropriate, because we see how our current mess mimics, but doesn't exactly match, the bubble bust of the 1930s in the United States or the 1990s in Japan, as well as the ending of many other speculative bubbles of the past brought about by a credit bubble. We are just four short years into a 12- to 15-year downward cycle in our economy that is driven by demographics and an extreme credit and real estate bubble, just as we saw in the Great Depression, and to a lesser extent experienced with an inflationary theme between 1968 and 1982. The overriding theme of this period will be deflation, as outlined in Chapter 5. We already have deflation, whether we call it that or not. Food and energy prices may be going up, but the cost of housing, our biggest purchase, is declining, as is the overall cost of living, which will decline even further in the next few years. When you look at housing or employment, we cannot get away from the fact that deflation is with us. Remember that deflation works on both sides of the coin, driving wages lower at the same time that it drives prices down. As we build a personal approach to this economic season, we always have to remember that the backdrop is deflation, not inflation, which means that growth assets, including those like gold and junk bonds, which are among the last bubbles, will try to lure us in but will eventually fail. The current commodities bubble will deflate, and our economic growth will stagnate or fall.

Debt Is the Grim Reaper

The act of taking on debt is something that most people never think about. They do it because "everyone else does," which our mothers all taught us was a bad reason to do something. (Would you jump off of a bridge just because everyone else does?) We take out loans for cars and houses, and many people use credit cards to add convenience or additional spending power to their lives. This is natural in our growing family cycle between the ages of 26 and 46 or so. To a reasonable degree we use debt to finance our family needs. In the last decade we went well beyond that, using massive amounts of debt even though our kids were set to leave the nest in the near future.

Shouldn't we think about debt before we incur it? As we pay back debt, are we using some of our future income so that we have to give up something else, like savings or like spending less on entertainment? Or are we expecting to get more income in the future so that the debt payments won't cut into our current standard of living? Beyond a cursory estimate of whether or not they can afford the monthly payments, we don't think most people go through this type of analysis, and we certainly don't think they get to the third question, "What if my monthly income goes down?" This is where debt really hurts, and it is what is devastating so many families in America today.

As deflation works its way through the economy, wages are remaining flat and, for those who are finding work after extended periods of unemployment, wages are falling. Thus, debt repayment is more expensive, as we described previously. So the very first thing that individuals should do is evaluate their current and future use of debt. The basic idea is, the less debt you have, the better! While this is an old piece of advice in terms of self-reliance, it has particular importance when it comes to inflation and deflation. In times of deflation with falling wages, debt payments can eat up an ever-larger part of your income, thereby seriously affecting your standard of living. In times of inflation, debt can be a very good thing, in that you use future, less-valuable dollars to buy hard assets that will appreciate.

This is a very hard lesson for most of us, as we have just been through over four decades in which debt was our friend! The rising tide of asset prices from the 1970s through the late 2000s made borrowing money an attractive, intelligent choice. Lending standards loosened, interest rates fell, and household income grew (through 1999) as we developed two-income families, all making reasonable amounts of debt not only afford-able, but smart. Things have changed. Now the best path is to take on as little new debt as possible, paying down old debt systematically. Without the growth possibility in equities or real estate, paying down interest-bearing debt is one of the better "investment" choices that a person or family can make. The higher the interest rate on the debt, the higher the "return" that a person gets from paying off the debt.

This brings up the opportunity associated with debt: if it is bad for a consumer to take on debt because of deflation, then it must be good for a lender to create debt for the same reasons, and that is exactly right. We look at lending money inside of a greater theme, which is creating streams of income.

Build Your Cash Flow

Whenever someone takes out a loan, it means that someone or some insti-tution made a loan. Mortgages, car loans, and credit cards are all examples of lending, of course, but so are bonds and notes. All of these financial instruments involve a borrower receiving cash or purchasing power today in exchange for a stream of payments—with interest—in the future. Bonds and notes include municipal bonds, Treasury bonds, Treasury notes, for-eign bonds, corporate bonds: they all work the same. In these financial instruments the bondholder or note holder is the lender. This person has agreed to give his or her money to the borrower in exchange for a stream of payments in the future. As we go through our deflationary period, these streams of payments will become more valuable, because the dol-lars received will buy more in the future as prices decline. This is already happening in locally priced goods and services. You can buy "much more house" today than you could with the same dollars four to six years ago, and you can get more in terms of services—anything from tailors to land-scaping to home renovations—than you could with the same amount of dollars as four years ago. This is deflation at work.

Obviously, due to this deflation we believe that bonds are a great idea. While all bonds are *not* created equal, they all do react to one thing:

changes in interest rates. In periods of deflation, interest rates are very low, as the government keeps short-term rates low to encourage borrowing and the lack of demand for loans keeps long-term interest rates low. We have been in this exact environment for over 3 years, with one big caveat. Since the spring of 2009, the Federal Reserve has been printing money out of thin air and buying bonds—first mortgage-backed bonds and then US Treasury bonds. The presence of this very large buyer with unlimited funds has worked to keep interest rates on maturities from 2 years to 30 years lower than they would have been.

Our view is that when the Fed stops buying bonds, we will see interest rates rise in the United States for a period of 3 to 5 months and then start to decline again as our economy goes back into its deflationary trajectory. This started to happen when the QE2 program of Fed bond buying expired at the end of June 2011, as the continued growth in the economy from the Fed's own stimulus argued that the Fed should not keep stimulating. The short-term boost in interest rates will be a reaction to the withdrawal of the Fed as well as a growing unease about the United States as a borrower with continued deficits of $1.5 trillion or so even in the recovery. With other countries raising short-term rates, the United States could find its currency under pressure near term as started to occur in the summer of 2011. With another round of credit crisis, this type of fear will dissipate and the United States will once again be the safe haven of international capital. The continued shrinkage of credit outstanding and the arrival of international capital will again cause rates to drop. We have anticipated longer-term interest rates spiking again into early 2012 or so, but then dropping again into 2015 and on and off for many years to follow. This higher interest rate environment will give investors an opportunity to lock in yields slightly above where they were in 2010 and early 2011, thereby creating greater cash flow. However, investors should be very discerning in the types of bonds they buy, as they will behave very differently in the years ahead.

The Fixed-Income Play: The Safest and Surest Way to Play Deflation

We expect that long-term bond rates are going to spike into early 2012 and then generally fall through the coming decade, especially between early

2012 and early 2015. If you can lock in higher yields when they spike, then you can benefit, both in higher yields and in higher capital appreciation for locking in those higher yields longer term.

Bonds rise in value when inflation or interest rates are falling. The great bond bull markets occur in times of disinflation or deflation, like 1932–1940, 1981–1986, onward into late 2008, and to come, likely 2012–2015 and beyond, into 2020 or so.

The general categories of bonds are Treasury bonds backed by the US government and then corporate, foreign, and municipal bonds, all three of which include the subsets of high quality and high yield (junk). Each classification of bond comes with its own set of risks and potential rewards. Municipal bonds typically yield the least due to their government status and tax benefits, but these days their yields are more like corporate bonds, adjusted for the tax savings, so many are higher due to the rising budget crises. Then come Treasuries with their government guarantee, and then higher-quality corporate, then foreign, then lower-quality corporate or "junk" bonds. The higher the risk and yields, the more money you stand to make in both yield and principal appreciation when deflation sets in and interest rates fall. But, of course, the higher-yield bonds have more volatility and downside risk if inflation persists.

The general logic for buying long-term bonds that most benefit in a deflationary crisis, as in the early 1930s, is:

1. **You buy the safer 10-year and 30-year Treasury bonds earlier in the crisis when they first spike in yield, as in late 1931, or likely in early to mid-2012.**
2. **You buy higher-quality corporate bonds next for more conservative to moderate investors, like in mid-1932, or likely in late 2013.**
3. **You buy higher-yield corporate or junk bonds and foreign bonds, for more aggressive investors next, like mid- to late 1932, or likely in late 2013.**
4. **You buy municipal bonds last, for more tax-sensitive buyers, as in early 1933 forward, or likely early 2014 forward.**

Treasury bonds are considered the safest bonds because they are backed by the US government, which until recently was seen as having an unlimited amount of borrowing capacity, given that the US dollar is the currency of reserve. This capacity allowed the government always to borrow more to pay back previous bonds, which made its bonds safe. Lately this ability to borrow unlimited amounts has been called into question, and the long-term fiscal health of the US government is also in question. Because of this, we believe that US Treasury bonds might dip some in value during 2011, but they will rally likely from the fall of 2011 through 2013, and likely on and off for most of the coming decade as the world looks for a safe place to wait out the economic upheaval. In addition, deflation in prices will continue to set in along with lower long-term inflationary expectations. We show a likely scenario for 10-year Treasury bond yields in **Chart 9-1**. Such Treasury bond yields have been declining in a predictable channel since 1989. They hit the bottom of that channel at yields near 2% in December of 2008 and have been rising since toward the top of the channel at closer to 4.2% in early 2012. If they break above this top channel line, then we will see a greater crisis in confidence in the US government's ability to meet its shorter- and longer-term debt that would curb any future stimulus plans even more, as occurred in Southern Europe in late April forward. But at a minimum such Treasury rates could peak closer to 4.2% and then decline for many years ahead back toward 1.5% or so, which would be very good for bonds.

Chart 9-1: 10–Year Treasury Bond Yield Channel and Projections, 1989–2024

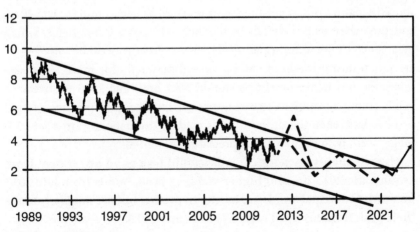

Data Source: Yahoo Finance

For individual investors who are risk-averse, do not need a high yield, and are most interested in the return of their principal, Treasuries are the place to be—especially from early to mid-2012 forward.

You can get free access to Harry's very popular webinar "Understanding the Economy and What Lies Ahead" by registering at http://www.hsdent.com/webinar.

Corporate bonds span the entire spectrum from the ultra safe (bonds issued by Microsoft and IBM) to the questionable at best, which are junk bonds (like bonds backed by casinos). The problem with all corporate bonds is that during 2009 and 2010 investors flocked to fixed income, driving prices through the roof, which drove down the yield that investors receive. At the end of 2010, long-term US Treasury bonds yielded about 4.7%, while high-quality corporate bonds yielded 5.7%, and junk bonds yielded 6.8%. The spread between these yields is very small, reflecting the strong demand for such investments. While we think interest rates will remain low over time, we do see economic disruptions, which should trigger a sell-off in corporate bonds, particularly in high-yield or junk bonds that will likely last much longer than the temporary sell-off in Treasury bonds into the late summer or early fall of 2011. We believe that this area of investing has reached very dangerous levels in terms of high prices and we recommend staying away for now. High-quality corporate bonds should see their prices fall and yields rise into as late as mid- to late 2013, and then they will likely fall further than Treasury bond yields, which means even higher appreciation. Higher-yield corporate or junk bonds are much more risky and will be a good play only for more aggressive investors. But in this area you should wait until late 2013 to invest, as yields could continue to rise to unprecedented heights, perhaps as high as 20% plus. Then the drop in yields cold be dramatic toward 4% or 5% longer term with very strong appreciation potential.

Higher-quality corporate bonds should be a good investment from around late 2013 on, and higher yield, or junk, bonds from late 2013 forward. Municipal bonds are harder to predict but are not likely to see their peak in yields until early 2014 or early 2015.

Again, in the 1930s deflation and depression, Treasury bonds first peaked in yields in late 1931 as the crisis worsened, but corporate bonds did not peak in yields until mid- to late 1932 as stocks bottomed at the worst of the crisis. Municipal bonds tended to peak in yields at the worst of the unemployment and the economy in early to mid-1933. Hence, there tends to be a succession of risk that causes these different bonds to spike and become attractive investment opportunities over time as deflation sets in and longer-term yields fall for many years to follow. We cover this phenomenon in more depth in Chapter 8 of *The Great Depression Ahead*.

Foreign bonds get very interesting. While the same metrics and analysis that apply to corporate bonds (too expensive currently, reactions to interest rates, and differences between high-quality and junk bonds) apply to these bonds, they also have the added component of currency risk. With the US dollar under pressure in 2009 and 2010, foreign investments went up simply because the dollar went down. This increased the returns that investors in foreign bonds received, because their interest payments were in a foreign currency and their bonds were priced in a foreign currency. The same will happen in reverse as the dollar strengthens in the next leg of the crisis and during the long deflation.

Remember, deflation makes the currency worth more because it shrinks available money supply by destroying massive amounts of private debt. The US created more of such debt and therefore will see a bit more deleveraging than Europe and much more than emerging countries like China or India. Hence, the US dollar will tend to rise and offset gains in foreign bonds.

In the United States, that would mean a rising dollar as credit contracts, which would make interest payments in foreign currencies worth less. One force that could overcome this situation would be a foreign bond that was shooting higher in value. This could happen in developing countries. However, you should wait until after the next leg of the credit crisis hits to buy such bonds so that these developing nations, which have run up dramatically since 2009, pull back to more reasonable valuations.

Municipal bonds offer the most interesting fixed-income play, as we hinted just above. Most municipal bonds are exempt from federal taxation, making them attractive for high-income or high-net-worth investors. As the United States goes about getting its fiscal house in order, we see much higher taxes ahead, especially in the next administration from 2013 forward. Any investment that shields you from taxes is worth a look.

Municipal bonds are usually backed by one of three sources: taxes (general-obligation bonds), identified revenue (revenue bonds), or special revenue (special-purpose bonds). Most people think that general-obligation or tax-backed bonds are the safest. We disagree! The current upheaval in city and state governments means the possibility of severe disruptions in the finances of these entities. While very few of them will actually go bankrupt, that does not mean that their general-obligation bonds will not miss a few interest payment dates, and that the valuations of these bonds will not fluctuate wildly. We see service-revenue bonds as much safer, because the monies used to pay the interest and principal are dedicated from a specific source, such as water and sewer or toll roads. Sewer and water are less subject to fluctuations than utilities than are toll roads and so on. Who is going to stop flushing their toilets? But people will cut back to a degree on electricity and the use of more expensive toll roads.

The last type of bond, a special-purpose issue, has the highest potential return and the highest risk. We say that because this type of bond also has the steepest "learning curve." Special-purpose bonds (also called economic development bonds, industrial revenue bonds, and many other names) require an investor to dig through the prospectus to see what entity actually is on the hook to pay the principal and interest; payment could be tax revenues from a small section of town, tax-free funding that a company received from a city or state to build a plant, or monies expected from a legal settlement (tobacco bonds). We understand that these bonds usually have higher coupon payments, but we strongly encourage investors to do their homework before buying them!

Currently a lot of turmoil is happening in "muni-land," because the typical role of a municipal bond in a portfolio, which was to deliver a small amount of tax-free income on a very boring and consistent basis, has been threatened due to a couple of factors. First, the fiscal mess of cities and states has called into question the ability of such government entities to repay; we have addressed this issue already. The second issue, which relates to the first, is the state of municipal bond insurance. As an added safeguard on an already boring, safe investment, many issuers of municipal debt purchased insurance, which made their debt AAA-rated, the highest rating from Standard & Poor's (S&P) and Moody's, the two widely recognized rating agencies. In the event of a default (missing an interest or principal payment), the insurance company would make up the difference. However, these are the same insurance companies that began insuring mortgage debt in the late 1990s and 2000s, so the paying ability of the insurance companies is very much in question. Additionally, the ratings of bonds backed by these insurance companies have fallen dramatically. Suddenly many investors who owned boring, quiet municipal bonds woke up to find that their investments were volatile. So they did what anyone would do—they sold them.

In the fall of 2010, municipal bond funds were seeing high outflows as investors fled the market. This pushed down prices on municipal bonds, which pushed up the yield. In many cases tax-free municipal bonds yielded more than US Treasuries! At the end of 2010 it was common to earn 5% on a AAA municipal bond. At a 30% tax rate, this equates to 7.1% taxable investment. Remember, high-yield corporate bonds were yielding 6.8%. So strong, good quality municipal bonds were yielding less than questionable, junky corporate bonds! The reason for this is the lack of information flow among investors. Aggressive investors who buy junk bonds are basically uneducated about municipal bonds, so when the safe investors fled municipals, no big group was around to buy these bonds. Because the bonds are tax-free, they do not show up on the radar of other tax-free investors such as pensions and endowments, which cuts out even more buyers. By the spring of 2011, hedge funds were beginning to buy municipals not because they are tax-free, but because their yield was simply too attractive to ignore, given their backing and their tax-exempt status.

In the area of municipal bonds, a great deal of uncertainty surrounds the combination of issuers and insurers, turmoil from the exodus of current investors, and the huge benefit of the tax-free status. This combination gives investors a great opportunity to buy municipal bonds at what should be the bargain prices of a lifetime. Keep in mind that the best bonds are those backed by revenues that are essential and cannot be diverted for general budgets. For researching specific municipal bonds, visit the website of the Municipal Securities Rulemaking Board (MSRB), set up to provide investors with a source for prospectuses and trade history (Electronic Municipal Market Access, or EMMA), http://emma.msrb.org.

Another, even less understood area of municipal bonds is taxable municipals. These bonds are exactly what they sound like—municipal bonds that are not tax-free; they are a small part of the bond market, so they often get overlooked. For those looking to generate cash flow instead of capital appreciation, taxable municipal bonds offer very attractive interest rates. Within this group is an even smaller subset: Build America Bonds, or BABs. Part of the 2009 stimulus program was an attempt by the US government to entice states to engage in infrastructure building. To that end, the US government offered to subsidize the interest payments of states that would issue bonds for building. Thus, a bond issued by California for building roads would be payable by California, but the US government would kick in 35% of the interest payment.

The hook was that the bonds would be taxable. To have this arrangement make sense, the portion of the interest on the bond that the state pays had to be less than what the state would pay if it issued a bond tax-free on its own. If California could issue tax-free bonds at 5.00%, then its portion of the interest on a BAB issue would have to be less than 5.00%, so the total interest on the BAB bond would have to be less than (5.00%/0.65), or 7.69%. The program was in force from March 2009 through 2010, and bonds were regularly priced over 7%. Remember this was at a time when corporate bonds were priced around 6%! It is still possible to buy BAB bonds, which are issued by states and have 35% of their interest subsidized by the US government, at higher yields than similar quality corporate bonds!

Annuities with insurance companies can also be an attractive option during deflationary times. The risk here is similar to bonds, in that you are trusting in the ability of the payer, or insurance company, to make good on its debt. Several insurance companies operating in the United States have been around for a century, including most surviving the Great Depression of the 1930s, so they have great track records for making their payments. In addition, with annuities you can create a payout on your money that matches your situation, such as a second-to-die policy or a period-certain policy. We suggest that if you are interested, please contact a financial advisor, as the world of insurance quickly can become hard to navigate.

If you think in terms of cash flow instead of just bonds or loans, then the possibilities for investing broaden dramatically. Anything that generates a recurring payment can be used as a stream of income. Rental properties are a prime example of this and can take several forms. The demographic wave of young workers entering the labor force is creating a need for multifamily housing as well as starter homes. We do not think that real estate has bottomed yet (as we will discuss below), but in terms of generating cash flow, the possibility certainly exists for buying quality properties at attractive rates today that will generate enough cash flow to more than offset future price declines. This specifically applies to smaller multifamily properties (not 800-unit condo buildings, which have association fees and other issues to worry about) and single-family homes.

The current backlash against homeownership is creating an even larger pool of renters than otherwise would exist, which is only exacerbated by those who lose their homes to foreclosure and are forced to rent, because they will be unable to get home loans for several years. The demographic trends that peak at age 26 for rental properties continue to favor multifamily demand into 2017 for the rising echo boom generation and, after a dip into around 2023, that trend continues up again modestly into 2033 to 2034. We cover the demographic trends in multifamily housing and other major sectors in Chapter 4 of *The Great Depression Ahead.*

If this is an area you are considering, then remember the rule of real estate, which is location, location, location! Just because a home can be bought for $5,000 in Detroit does not mean that it is a good deal! You have to look at population trends and employment opportunities. Keep in mind that the great baby boom wave of retirement has not happened yet. The bulk of the boomers born in 1957 to 1961 will not retire until 2022 to 2026. This wave, along with the continued move toward cheaper cost-of-living right-to-work states in the Southeast, will likely keep this area growing for over a decade. While Florida is the standout as a state that grew too much and is now modestly pulling back, the rest of the Southeast is still growing. No matter what area of the country you are considering, you should also determine what drives people to be in that area, which will give you information on how likely it is your rents will continue to rise. Is it a major employer? Is it proximity to a university, business center, or transit point? With deflation as the backdrop, determining the quality of the rent that is likely to be received on any investment property is paramount because you cannot rely on capital appreciation to carry you. It is entirely possible that you will buy a property in the current market and sell it for a value that is within 4% to 5% of that price in 7 to 10 years. Cash flow is everything.

Other rent-generating items include storage facilities, heavy equipment, and leasing agreements on things such as office equipment. In these areas it becomes a very specialized field of understanding the current and future needs of the local market, or simply investing in national organizations that are proven leaders in these fields. Many companies that are publicly traded deal in these areas. The goal would be to find companies that generate their income through such arrangements and have a proven track record of dividend payments and dividend growth. You will find that many of these companies operate as master limited partnerships (MLPs). Don't be scared off by that, but do have a conversation with your tax preparer before you get involved with these entities, as they require additional filings on your tax return.

Stocks: Be Out or Short Between Early 2012 and Late 2013, or Simply Look to Reinvest Selectively from Late 2013 Forward

First, understand that we do not agree with the old way of thinking, which is that equities always go up and the only variable is your age. If you are younger, you take more risk with potentially higher returns by holding more equity, and the older you get the less equity you hold. We think that approach is okay for much of the long-term economic cycle, but outrageous in the Winter Season! We don't care if you are 30 years old or 60 years old—you should position your portfolio for the best potential to make money with the lowest amount of risk, especially when most investments are falling, not rising.

Equities in general are a way to invest for long-term growth, but what if that growth is in question? Then what? Stocks in the United States did well from March 2009 through much of 2011, but they enjoyed an unprecedented $2.5 trillion tailwind in stimulus from the Federal Reserve that has never been seen before in history. What happens after that? Certainly some companies will continue to perform, but will they remain at their high valuations? History in Winter Seasons like the 1930s says otherwise. After the crash of 1929, it took 24 years, until 1953, before the Dow Jones Industrial Average (DJIA) went above its previous high. Similarly, it took until 1993, or 25 years, for the DJIA to go above its inflation-adjusted highs from 1968. Every generation, or 39 to 40 years, this happens, and yet most investors and economists do not see it coming.

After the next economic disruption, we should see equities fall by at

least 50% and possibly by as much as 75% to our best targets of 3,000 to 3,800 on the Dow. We believe that investors who are interested in US equities will be best served by purchasing those that have low volatility and pay strong dividends and those that have substantial revenue generated in developing countries, but even there, wait to buy them until at least late 2013, and possibly late 2014. For aggressive investors and traders, shorting US, European, and emerging country stocks could be very profitable, but with high volatility and risk. The play for foreign investors in US stocks could benefit even more from a rising US dollar.

In **Chart 9-2**, we give a very rough view of what we see as the most likely scenario for stocks over the next decade; obviously, don't expect it to go exactly like this. In this scenario the Dow would peak in late 2011 or early 2012. Then we would see a first crash back to the mid-2010 lows around 9,600 or so into mid-2012. Then after a milder bounce into the election, we would see the markets take a steeper drop into around late 2013. This scenario would be much like the 2-year 1973/74 crash that followed the 1970 crash as we showed in Chart 1-4 in the first chapter. The "Three Bubbles" chart from the Introduction (Chart I-2) repeated in **Chart 9-3** suggests an ultimate bottom around 3,300 on the Dow. Scenario 2 in **Chart 9-4** assumes the government is able to keep stimulating to a more substantial degree and they try to ward off the downturn for the

Chart 9-2: Scenario 1: Dow Jones Industrials, 2007–2024

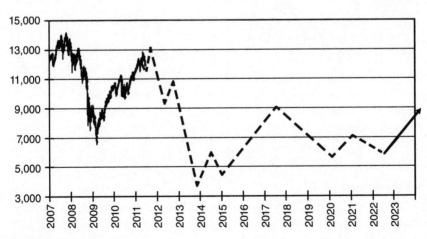

Data Source: Yahoo Finance

Chart 9-3: The Three Bubbles in Stocks, Dow Jones Industrials, 1985–2014

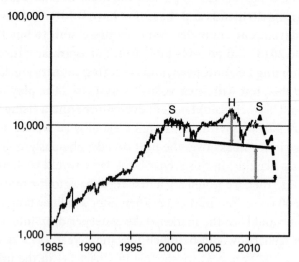

Data Source: Yahoo Finance

Chart 9-4: Scenario 2: Dow Jones Industrials, 2007–2024

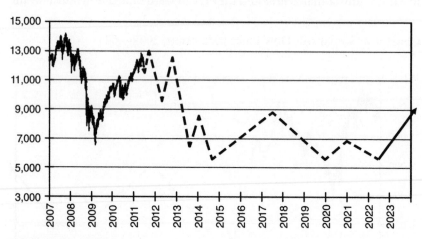

Data Source: Yahoo Finance

2012 election. In this scenario we would assume a similar top and crash to unfold into mid-2012, but a final strong stimulus program creates a bigger bounce into the election toward 12,000 or so on the Dow. Then the market sees a stronger crash into 2013 and 2014, but with ultimate lows perhaps not as extreme, more around 5,600 on the Dow. This scenario would be more like the near 3-year crash from early 2000 into late 2002 when the first bubble burst. In both scenarios we get a substantial rebound in stocks into around mid-2017 and then a less extreme downturn and crash into 2020–2022 before the next long-term bull market begins again.

The three bubble patterns with the highest bubble in the middle in 2007 are typical of many markets we see in the US and around the world, including the S&P 500, the ASX in Australia, the Hang Seng in Hong Kong, and many others. There is another three-bubble pattern, with each bubble peaking higher. This is called a rising wedge pattern, as we show in **Chart 9-5** with the Russell 2000, which represents small cap stocks. This chart says that this index could go as high as 1,000 before peaking in late 2011 or so. Many stock indices are following this pattern, including the Russell 400 (mid cap stocks), the Dow Transportation index, the TSX in Canada, and the emerging markets indices like EEM (ETF). If we hit the top trend line of these charts between late 2011 and early 2012, that would likely confirm a major long-term top in stocks. When we look at many

Chart 9-5: Rising Three-Bubble Pattern, Russell 2000, 1995–2014

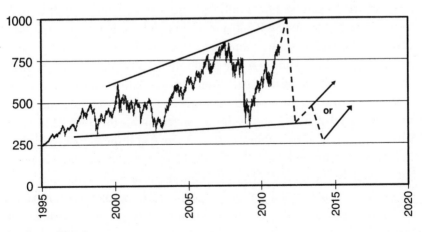

Data Source: Bloomberg

Chart 9-6: Rising Wedge Pattern, S&P 500, 3/09–12/11

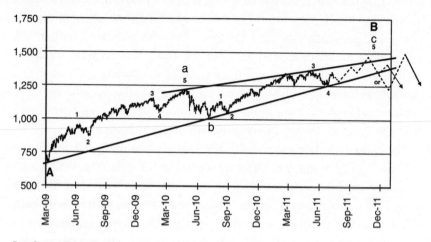

Data Source: Yahoo Finance

major stock indices around the world, we see patterns and projections that suggest crashes ranging from around 55% in India to near 80% in China and small cap stocks in the US.

We have been observing a "rising wedge" pattern (**Chart 9-6**) in the stock rally that started in March of 2009 with QE1. Stocks have risen in a narrowing channel that looks to come to a head between late 2011 and early 2012. Since this pattern is becoming more obvious the markets will likely try to fake like they are breaking above and below a few times. The first scenario would be a final rally into October or January of 2012 back to around 1,430 on the S&P 500 and a peak and crash to begin to follow. The second variation shown would be a clear break down out of this rising wedge later in 2011 and then one final rally to new highs before a peak. That final rally could peak in early January or as late as April of 2012.

If you are looking for protection in precious metals like gold and silver, look at **Chart 9-7**, which shows the last silver bubble that peaked in 1980. Silver went from $4 to $50 in less than 2 years, and then crashed back to $9 in just 4 months and back to $4 within 2 years. Gold was less dramatic, but ultimately crashed 72% from its 1980 highs of $880. Gold and silver are inflation hedges, not deflation hedges. Just the trend of lower inflation rates killed gold and silver in the 1980s and 1990s. In our newsletter we first told clients to sell silver near $50 in late April of 2011, then we look

Chart 9-7: Silver Prices, 1965–2002

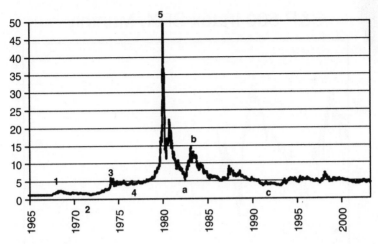

Data Source: **Bloomberg**

to give a final sell signal on in late 2011 or so. The crash in China and the emerging world slowdown will be the last nail in the coffin for gold, silver, oil and most commodities, as will be a long downturn in a near 30-year cycle we discuss just ahead. Food and agricultural commodities could be more the exception at times due to the planet's increasingly volatile climate, which limits supply, and the fact that in the growing emerging world, the last thing to be cut back in demand will be food.

We discuss the most important longer-term and intermediate cycles we use in Chapter 3 of *The Great Depression Ahead*, and we won't repeat that whole discussion here. But the most important longer-term cycle is a 500-year cycle that actually points upwards from the late 1800s into around the early 2100s—which would clearly revolve more around the demographic trends and middle-class evolution in the emerging world. Then there is the 39- to 40-year cycle in generations that is peaking around late 2007, as in late 1929 and late 1968, and points down into 2020-2023 before it turns up again. Then there is our broad Geopolitical Cycle that alternates between lower and higher risk in the world every 17 years or so with stronger stock valuations and then lower, beyond our demographic generational cycles. That cycle peaked in 2000–2001 and points down into 2018–2020. Then there is the 29- to 30-year Commodity Cycle that is peaking between mid-2008 and 2011 and also points down into 2020–2024 or so. Hence, the big

Chart 9-8: 24-Month, 40-Month and Decennial Cycle

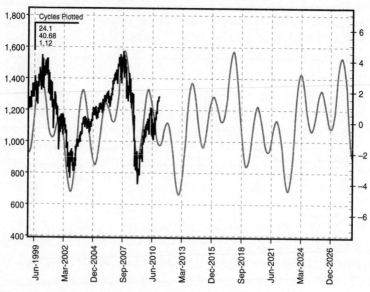

S&P 500 Index SPX, Monthly

Data Source: Richard Mogey, Foundation for the Study of Cycles, Inc.

picture is that all of our key longer-term cycles, except the 500-year, point down into the 2019–2023 time frame, and that there is a greater hierarchy of such cycles, with the 39- to 40-year Generation Cycle the most critical in the last century.

When we look at the most important intermediate cycles, we see a Decennial Cycle that shows high risk of stock crashes and economic downturns in the first 1 to 3 years of every new decade, and a 2- and 4-year political cycle that tends to bottom into midterm elections, like late 1982 or late 1990 or late 2002 and late 2010. Those cycles would have suggested the worst crash in stocks to come into late 2010 as we originally expected, but we saw only a minor correction into that cycle. The next such down cycles occur from late 2011 into late 2012 and late 2013 into late 2014. Richard Mogey, past research director of the Foundation for the Study of Cycles, has a composite cycle in **Chart 9-8** that we now think may be the best guide in the next few years. That composite sees a peak around the late summer of 2011 that then bottoms after a much bigger downturn in very late 2012, and then sees another down cycle between sometime in 2017 into late 2022.

Mogey's cycles have had the best correlation in recent years through all of this unprecedented turmoil and artificial market manipulation; hence, we are paying more attention to this cycle. This is also just a slight variation on our very reliable Decennial and 4-year cycles that have been best documented by Ned Davis. Even those cycles would suggest the next likely bottoms in late 2012 and mid- to late 2014.

When we look outside the United States we see even more risk, but also more reward. The risk is that emerging markets have again been pushed to dizzying heights in the past two years as the US dollar suffered and the Federal Reserve printed money with abandon. Investors flocked to markets that were based on commodities and those that trade heavily with China. As developed nations suffer through the next leg downward in our credit crisis, we believe the emerging nations will suffer just as they did in late 2008 and early 2009—with declines typically higher than in the US and Europe. However, we also believe that after the crash, many of these markets, like India, that are not as export- and commodity-dependent, will rebound the fastest.

In the years since 2008/2009, countries such as China have tried hard to change their reliance from exports to imports. China still relies on exports, but its own consumers are only slowly starting to spend more, as they still favor saving and investing in hard assets like real estate and gold. The Chinese have few of the social safety nets available to households in North America and Europe. We see these countries as great investments after the crash. Keep in mind that a strong US dollar will make overseas investments less attractive at first, which is why we see international bonds as a poor choice. Equities in developing nations should be able to generate returns that will make up for any deterioration in value caused by a rising dollar, and the US dollar is likely to see most of its gains in the next crash and downturn between early 2012 and late 2014. After that, emerging markets are not likely to be fighting the tailwinds of a rising dollar as much, if at all.

Among the developing nations, we like India the most. This country has 1.1 billion people, is growing more rapidly than China, and consumes most of what it creates. The reason is that India bypassed much of the heavy infrastructure phase that most countries go through. Instead, India jumped from agrarian to knowledge or services. Thus, although infrastructure is severely lacking in India, the country can move its workers quickly to a very high level of functionality in the economy. India does face some very high hurdles. The government is dysfunctional and bureaucratic, property rights are vague, and the education system in rural areas is weak, albeit improving. Additionally, the old caste system is still very much alive. From an investor's standpoint, the methods of investing in India are equally problematic. You are not allowed to own investments there unless you are a citizen. As a business you almost certainly need an Indian partner to effectively do business in the country and to deal with the bureaucracy. In the United States, you can purchase ETFs that follow the Indian stock exchange, but that is cold comfort. A more efficient way to approach this is to look for companies based in the United States or other major countries that do significant business in India, like General Electric—but again, after late 2012 or so.

Summary of Investment Ideas

1. Preserve capital into the next crash.
2. Start thinking in terms of streams of income.
3. Buy bonds, which are easy to get and are readily available; look to Treasury bonds starting in early 2012 and corporate bonds starting in late 2013.
4. Consider municipal bonds, especially taxable municipals, more like in early 2014 and beyond, including foreign bonds.
5. Look beyond just bonds to other income-producing assets, like rental real estate that you can buy cheap and refinance lower.
6. In equities, look to dividend-paying stocks; health care and emerging markets are best *after* the next drop in the US markets, likely from late 2013 forward, or possibly from late 2014 forward.
7. For aggressive investors and traders, shorting US, European, and emerging market stocks, between very early 2012 and late 2013 is the biggest short-term play.

What Not to Do: Buy Personal Real Estate Before Early 2014

We've spent several pages on what you can do; it is only right to warn you against what not to do. The very first thing is, don't be suckered into real estate just because it is cheap! We are in the midst of a major restructuring in the US economy, which includes a change in how we view real estate. For decades, owning a home was part of what every responsible family did; it was a show of seriousness, permanence, and credibility. Today that has ended. We look with envy on those who rent, as they have a level of mobility and control over their finances that homeowners can't touch. At the same time, lending standards have tightened dramatically, the amount of money available to lend on housing has declined, and the inventory of foreclosed homes is in the millions and rising. All of these things mean that more downside is likely on housing immediately ahead, and only modest appreciation is likely until 2020 or so, when the next generation starts pushing up its own real estate demand.

Without significant capital appreciation, why own real estate? Some reasons exist, including the ability to recapture some of the rent that you would have paid, control over the property itself (improvements, etc.), and control over your living arrangements (the landlord cannot kick you out). While these are good reasons and they will persuade many people to buy, we don't expect the go-go years of the past decade or so to return in the US any more than they have in Japan after more than 20 years of decline there. It is true that US demographics are better positioned than Japan's, but they are still not great, as most of the new demand from echo boomers will be offset by aging baby boomers, who will be moving into nursing homes and/or dying for decades to come. What we do expect is for real estate to continue to slide into at least early 2014, with that likely being a great opportunity to buy quality properties at great prices for those who want to do so. This particularly applies to starter homes for younger buyers and retirement homes for older buyers.

The demographic demand for starter homes is already rising again, but there is caution among the younger buyers that will only be exacerbated by the likely financial collapse and lower home prices into early 2014 to early 2015. But such starter homes are the best place to buy from early 2014 forward. The next and last round of vacation home buyers from the baby boom generation will hit from around early 2015

into 2026 or so. Hence, aging baby boomers should wait more until early 2015 to buy their dream vacation or retirement home. For trade-up homes, the best times to buy will likely be early 2015 and early 2020.

We cover the demographic trends and projections for real estate in different sectors in great depth in Chapter 4 of *The Great Depression Ahead*.

Buy Stuff Cheap

With all that we've said on real estate in this book and over the years, we still readily acknowledge that special circumstances can make some properties once-in-a-lifetime deals. Given that most property deals are local events, fire sales can happen at any time. We are not suggesting that you pass up these opportunities, but we are instead reminding you that you may have to hold these assets for some time before you can get your money out of them, or that you may get an even better deal if you wait until 2013 or later. The other key issue is whether you can buy the property cheap enough to generate strong cash flow over the coming years as the property potentially continues to drop in value. As long as you have the ability to hold for several years, then that's not a problem. Think of this as buying something and then socking it away, with no intention of messing with it for years. That is how you should approach assets that you are able to buy cheap, whether those assets are cars, homes, works of art, or collectible books. Deflation should affect them all, bringing them to prices that are very attractive. The key is to consider not only the price that you pay, but also how long you can hold the asset to get the most return on it.

Commercial Real Estate: The Last Sector to Recover

Commercial real estate is typically the last sector to fall and the last to recover, as it goes more with the general economy. However, commercial real estate is also driven by demographic forces (primarily workforce growth), just as are inflation trends, as we covered in Chapter 2. That is why commercial real estate had its best decade in the 1970s, even though broader demographic trends were slowing and mortgage rates rose to the highest levels in modern history. Workforce growth declines from 2010 into 2023 as baby boomers retire (on a 63-year lag), offsetting much of the echo boomers entering the workforce (20- to 21-year lag). Workforce trends and economic trends tend to rise more sustainably again from 2023 onward. Hence, commercial real estate will most closely follow the long-term deflationary trends and will not be a great investment again until 2023 forward. There will be pockets of opportunity from early 2013 on, and more so from early 2015 forward, with a likely midterm economic rebound into 2017 or so before the final slowdown occurs from 2017 into 2020–2023. The best time to buy commercial real estate is likely to be between early 2020 and early 2023.

Avoid the Government and Inevitable Rising Taxes

Is it just us, or has there been an increase in the number of speed traps on the road? Near our offices we have a nice residential neighborhood. The streets are wide. An elementary school sits alongside the main road, which has a tree-lined median. Seemingly at least two days a week a policeman with a radar gun is positioned at the school zone, and often a police car is sitting 400 yards past the school zone catching those who speed up as they exit! It sure looks like a revenue-generation scheme.

Maybe we are just hypersensitive to this, given that we have forecast busted public coffers for many years. Cities, counties, states, and certainly the federal government all desperately need more income. They have one way to get it: take it from constituents. While government entities cannot simply walk up and take your funds, they do have their ways. It doesn't matter if they call it a tax, a fee, a levy, or a fine—if it moves funds from your pocket to theirs, then it has served their purpose! We bring this up to remind you that one of the quickest ways to improve your cash flow is to stop sending it to other people. Shrinking your taxable footprint is a great way to do this.

Chart 9-9 shows what happens as an economy turns from boom to bust. Governments naturally lower taxes if possible in a boom when their tax revenues are rising and their social costs such as unemployment and defense tend to fall. When the economy turns down, their revenues decline and their costs only go up. US marginal tax rates came down from

Chart 9-9: Top Federal Individual Income Tax Rates, 1913 to Present

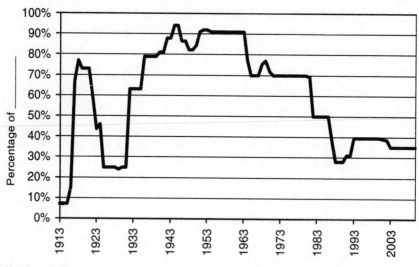

Data Source: IRS

78% to 25% in the Roaring '20s boom and then accelerated during the Great Depression and World War II to as high as 94% in 1944! Tax rates have come down in the last boom to marginal rates as low as 38% at the highest brackets and capital gains down to 15%. This won't last.

Marginal tax rates, capital gains rates, and municipal tax rates will only rise in the coming years; first on the highest-income taxpayers, and then well down into the middle class. Protect yourself now with maximum contributions to 401(k)s and tax-advantaged retirement accounts, personal foundations, tax-protected insurance annuities, and eventually in municipal bonds, before the government likely reverses many of those tax breaks and advantages in the years ahead. Another reason to minimize personal real estate investments is that the tax deduction will very likely continue to fade and even disappear.

It could be through investing in tax-free bonds or insurance products, successfully contesting the assessed valuation on property you own, or perhaps adjusting your inventory to avoid business tax. We are not suggesting that anyone attempt to evade taxes; that would earn you an orange jumpsuit and a small room. Instead, we are strongly suggesting that you think about the years ahead and what is likely to be a rising tax environment. If you can do things to minimize the taxes that you pay, then it is not only your right, but it is your responsibility to do it!

Work with Professionals

We strongly recommend that most people hire professionals to help them navigate the financial markets and tax arena, as especially the tax arena is more complex. In the financial markets, advisors are able to assist you with everything from a simple periodic review to a comprehensive plan, depending on how much or how little involvement you want to have. The key is to find a financial professional who has your view of the economic world and can bring to you investment ideas tailored to that view. If the advisor tells you to buy equities because they go up over the long haul, keep looking! Interview several financial professionals and ask questions about how they approach investing. A common approach is for an advisor to go on about the client's age, income, financial goals, etc. That's fine, but if he or she never mentions the economy, then you know they are probably a "set it and forget it" kind of shop. Keep looking. Talk to several and find one that matches you well.

On the tax side, you probably already have a person who prepares your tax return. When was the last time you had an in-depth discussion about how to lower your taxes? Chances are that you deal with your tax professional once a year, at the same time that everyone else is haranguing them. Set up an appointment outside of the tax season to discuss your current situation and what you want to do in the years ahead. Talk through some different ways of lowering your taxable footprint. If your tax preparer doesn't seem responsive, then it's probably time to look for a new one.

Employment

In a difficult economy, steady employment becomes even more important than it is in normal times. As we discussed previously, the ratio of those unemployed to jobs available is roughly 5 to 1, which means that competition among the unemployed is fierce. With over 100,000 new workers in the economy every month and very little increase in payrolls, the situation only becomes worse over time. When thinking about your own employment situation, consider two main areas: your current position and what you might do if you lost that position.

The easiest course of action is to keep your job. That might sound like an obvious statement, but it is worth making. Over the next several years we are likely to see unemployment remain high, with the worst unemployment rates in early 2013 or even early 2015, which means that employers have the upper hand not only in whom they hire but also in what they pay. Keeping your current position with your seniority, income, and benefits is another form of cash flow during difficult economic times. Employment consultants will tell you to find ways of making yourself indispensable to your company, be it through taking on new projects or excelling at your current tasks. Take a moment and imagine that you are going to start another company or department that does the same thing your current employer does. When you think through the positions and personnel needed, is your job or your name on the list? You definitely want to be on the short list of go-to players on your team. Look for ways either to make the company more revenue or to save the company money in its current operations, depending on whether your job is on the client side or the operations side. It doesn't matter if you are a high-powered salesperson or an administrative assistant, you can still look at your workflow or department with a critical eye toward improving the company's bottom line.

Of course, part of staying employed has nothing to do with you; it has to do with the well-being of the firm itself. Look for warning signs of trouble. An obvious example is layoffs, but a more subtle sign is a shrinking workforce through attrition. If your company is not replacing employees who leave voluntarily, management could be using attrition to trim payroll. If you believe that your department or specific position is in danger, career consultants suggest diplomatically approaching your manager about it to find out what they know. If you work at a public company, then you have a lot of information at your fingertips. Each publicly traded company is required to file quarterly statements of financial condition with the SEC, noting changes in its own financial health as well as changes in business conditions. This is a great resource that few employees actually use to investigate the health of their own employer.

The second facet is to consider what might happen if you lose your job. The two common choices are to find another one or to start your own business. If your position is such that working for another firm is best, then don't wait to fire up your networking activities and update your résumé. Think of the people you have heard from in the last two years who are looking for work. Long-lost acquaintances and friends from school have been working their extended networks, as they should. This is easier to do if you have kept up relations with people in the first place. Be especially attentive to professional groups that are immediately able to put you in touch with opportunities in your field. Keep in mind that it might be the case that your field is shrinking in the current environment and you need to position your résumé and skills for a growing industry like health care or engineering.

Self-Employment and Starting Your Own Business as a Near-Term and Long-Term Trend

Starting a business is hard, but obviously it is something that thousands of people do every year. The ability to do that will pay off even more in an economy with higher layoffs and slower growth. But there is a bigger trend emerging since the internet and the high-tech boom of the 1990s. New technologies clearly allow greater decentralization in business organization and decision making. We covered this topic in depth in *The Roaring 2000s* (1998) in "Part 3: The New Network Corporation." Internet and information technologies allow more information to be put directly into the hands of frontline workers and the end consumers. With evermore rapid changes in business as well as more customized consumer and customer tastes and needs, companies can only react and keep costs affordable by radically decentralizing. This will involve breaking complex corporations into internal "frontline browsers" and "backline servers" that are coordinated by a network management system.

In other words, companies have to operate from the bottom up, not the top down, just as the internet and Wikipedia operate, or even Wikileaks in the extreme. In the new world, "management is the problem, not the solution." Management needs to design corporations to run as close to real time as possible, and bottom-up like the New York Stock Exchange. Where is the management of the NYSE? Someone rings the bell at 9:30 a.m. and all hell breaks loose, then someone rings the bell to end the session at 4:00 p.m. All trades are made with no top-down control, and all accounts are settled by day's end. This can already happen in a near pure information industry. Management strives for real-time feedback systems and accountability for performance and profits at all levels, especially on the front line working with clients. This trend will increasingly spread to all companies and industries as the new, more decentralized product management model from Alfred Sloan did from the 1920s forward. That was GM's ultimate secret for beating Ford in the end, despite Ford's early lead in product (Model T) and production technology (assembly line).

The biggest impact in the decades ahead from information technologies will simply be that "everyone becomes a business, and every customer becomes a market." Frontline individuals and small teams will focus on small segments of customers and serve them like a responsive small business but will be backed by powerful backline servers and larger networks that provide economies of scale, lower costs, and specialization where necessary. The line between working for a corporation and running your own business will increasingly blur, with companies of all sizes outsourcing specialized functions to individuals and smaller businesses.

To summarize: the coming decades and century will be seen as the age of the individual and the entrepreneur. Everyone should be thinking about how to make what you naturally do and know into a business—inside a company or outside of established companies.

Now, back to near-term practicalities while you reconsider your entrepreneurial role in life. If you lose your job and another one is not readily available, self-employment could be the best path to take. Thousands of publications are available on how to do this, many of which take you through a step-by-step process that is meant to help you focus on what you have to offer, what type of capital it will take, and how competitive the industry is. Even if you are currently employed, you should still go through the exercise of mapping out how you would go about starting a new company, from the tools you would need to the services or products offered. The reason to do this is to determine whether you have an opportunity to increase your cash flow immediately.

One of the best ways to start your own business is to simply take what you already do for your present employer and begin functioning as an outside vendor. If your job description calls for individual professional or clerical work, you could provide that same function for your present employer as well as other similar companies from your home office at a lower cost. Companies can lower their costs by using your services in this way without losing your function altogether. If you can do this for many companies even at lower costs per company, your revenues could increase substantially instead of decreasing. Think win/win solutions!

The second opportunity comes from looking at the changes in your industry or field of expertise and identifying market segments, customers, or services that companies are exiting as they cut costs in an effort to survive. It is possible that with lower costs, you could profitably provide such products or services through partnering with suppliers and operating with very low overhead. The strategy could be to start a new business providing such products at lower costs or higher quality.

Finally, every major downturn sees new technologies and products emerge as older technologies and products mature and decline. Think washing machines and dryers in the 1930s onward after sales of refrigerators were slowing. Think biotech, nanotech, and robotics as the internet and smartphones mature. Working in such higher-tech industries is beyond most of us. Simply look at the new products and services that leading-edge and affluent consumers are starting to adopt as products are maturing in your industry or profession. These are what we call new "S-curves," which we cover more in Chapter 2 of *The Great Depression Ahead* and all of our past books. In such early-stage new business sectors, the key is experimenting at first with minimal capital and investment until you clearly prove your new product or service in early adopter or "niche" markets. Only then should you look to bring in outside investment, and on a lag outside management and expertise, otherwise your chances of failing longer term are high.

In Chapter 10 we will look at how your business can see this deflationary crisis coming and adapt ahead of your competitors to survive this "survival of the fittest challenge" that follows the greatest innovation and Fall Season boom in history. The advantages to businesses that cut back and restrategize earlier will pay off for decades to come, not merely years—as occurred in the bigger picture with companies like General Motors and GE from the early 1930s forward. How do you either sell your business at the near top here or reposition it to dominate its markets and to hand it down to your children?

CHAPTER 10

Expanding Your Business's Dominance in a Time of Slower Growth: The Ultimate Long-Term Strategy

The basic principle of deflation is a contraction in both money supply and economic growth brought about by a reduction in credit. The previous chapters outlined in great detail why we see shrinking credit in the years ahead, so the question at this point should not be, "Is it going to happen?" but instead, "What will it do to my business, and how can I use this to my advantage?" The first thing to understand is that deflation is not an equal-opportunity destroyer. It comes once in a lifetime in the longer-term business cycle, and it determines which businesses are going to survive and grow again. Deflation sweeps in after the most expansive times of innovation and new business models—like after the Roaring '20s, or now after the Roaring 2000s. For a business, the greatest challenges and the most rewarding benefits of the entire 80-year Economic Cycle come from recognizing and then surviving the inevitable Winter Season. This is the opposite of how most business owners view the current environment. Instead of seeing the opportunity to dominate in the years after deflation, they think, "The economy is bad; how can I just survive?"

You have two choices in your business: you can sell your business, cashing out before things get much worse in the next few years, or you can hunker down, working to increase your dominance and market share during this Winter Season, recognizing that it will pay off for decades to come with much less competition after the smoke clears!

We always tell the classic story of Ford vs. General Motors in the early 1900s and 1930s, the last time new technologies and business models were emerging. Ford was the clear innovator in automobiles early on with the Model T in 1907, followed by the assembly line in 1914. Ford dominated the car market through the early 1920s but then slowly lost market share to General Motors. As the 1920s boom continued, GM innovated both in the basic corporate business model of organization through the genius of Alfred Sloan, as well as recognized the desires of an aging and prosperous generation. GM created a tiered upgrade system that took buyers from Chevrolet to Pontiac to Oldsmobile to Buick to Cadillac, whereas Ford kept churning out Model Ts for the everyday market. GM also had decentralized, faster-responding management as well as modernized financial controls, which helped immensely when the downturn hit in the early 1930s. GM started the 1920s well behind Ford in market share—12% versus 60%, respectively—after the great recession of 1920–1922. By the close of the decade, even with all of its advances, GM had not quite caught up to Ford, but was close. As the Great Depression took hold in the early 1930s, GM catapulted ahead of Ford in market share and dominated the auto industry for decades.

The leaders of the emerging industries of the early 1900s were determined not as much in the Roaring Twenties boom, but in "the survival of the fittest" Great Depression that followed in the early 1930s. The next several years will determine the leaders in your business and all industries for decades ahead. That is "the diamond in the rough" for you to focus on.

There is a "survival of the fittest" challenge ahead that will determine the winners and losers for the foreseeable future. Are you a visionary? Are you fit? Are you determined to transcend the challenges that the worst economy in your lifetime will bring in the next few years and over the next decade? Are you willing to exit your job slowly and create your own business out of your unique skills? Do you want to hand down your business to your heirs in the decades ahead? If not, then sell your business now and retire early and/or start a new business that will benefit from the Winter Season and the failures of many businesses! If you don't want to sell your business soon, listen to us and we will tell you how to turn lemons into lemonade!

Because the method of spreading the pain is through the contraction of money and credit, all entities and people who use money will be severely challenged. This means that businesses, the lifeblood of the economy, are in the crosshairs because they are where the economic forces of government, consumers, and credit meet. Again, the strategy is to see this as an opportunity, not as an overwhelming challenge, which it will seem to be otherwise.

1. **Position your business such that you do not need credit from the deleveraging financial system. You need to maximize cash, cash flow, and credit quality. You need to be preparing now to cut your costs, especially fixed costs and overhead expenses that don't contribute directly to your growth and survival.**
2. **Focus on the segments of your business that you dominate now and/ or can continue to dominate in the future.**
3. **Shed or sell assets and the segments of your business where you are weaker, or where you can't sustain yourself in hard times amid tougher competition. This will create more cash and capital outside the banking system.**
4. **Invest short-term only in marketing and promotional efforts to grow your cash flow, and/or in software and technology measures to cut costs.**
5. **Defer major capital investments like new stores, production, and distribution facilities, as well as major information system upgrades until later in the cycle, when you can acquire them much more cheaply, likely from your bankrupt competitors.**
6. **Your reward, even if your sales and profits decline, will be greater competitiveness vs. your failing competitors, and the dividend of that reward will last for decades, not years. If you simply survive and grow your market share, especially between 2012 and 2015, you can be an industry leader for a generation!**

As any business owner knows, running a company is not a simple process of identifying clients and providing a service. There is financing to be secured, taxes to be paid, employees to be compensated, capital equipment and real estate to manage, and vendors with whom to negotiate. While the basic premise of selling goods and services in exchange for money is the base on which all else is built, it is far from the only concern. When considered in light of the deflationary background in which companies will be operating, each area offers its own threat/opportunity trade-off.

Our discussion is focused on businesses that deal directly with consumers. However, the same principles apply to all businesses because, except for defense contractors and a few other special cases, most every wholesale business can look through its clients to the consumer, who is the end user.

Understanding Buyers

Let's get one thing straight: consumers are not dead! Our point has never been that consumption would fall to zero, or that there would be a devastating cutback in expenditures that would lead to a gnashing of teeth or tearing of garments. What demographic trends foretell is a long, gradual shift to lower and slower consumption that is a hallmark of the economic Winter Season. Our gut-wrenching drop in late 2008 and 2009 was a reaction to the banking crisis that moved forward the start of the falling consumption trend. As we move through the Winter Season, retailers will try everything to entice buyers back into stores or back onto websites—and consumers will respond, but always with a little less enthusiasm. Part of this is because consumers in general have less money themselves as they deal with deflation in their paychecks. Part of this is because consumers, specifically the boomers, are starting to devote less of their income to consumption and more toward debt reduction and savings, which is a very slow and extended process. A third factor is less access to credit (credit cards, HELOCs, etc.), which consumers relied on heavily to fund spending during the mid-2000s. When these factors are combined, it is obvious that consumption is on a downward trajectory or a flat trajectory at best due to a growing population. Either way, business owners cannot look to growing spending patterns to raise their overall sales. However, there are some steps that businesses can take.

Baby boomers will spend less overall but will spend more in areas like health care and wellness, nursing homes and assisted-living facilities, and in conveniences like lawn and gardening care. The up and coming (albeit slightly smaller) echo boom generation will spend more on the basics as they form new families in the next decade, on things like apartments, starter homes, smaller cars, basic furnishings, basic cosmetics, and etc.

Is Your Product or Service on a Path for Growth?

In Chapter 2 we walked through our basic research, which combines predictable consumer spending patterns with population trends. The main
point was that spending peaks at around age 46, so if you measure the
current and expected number of 46-year-olds in your economy, you can
determine if growth or contraction lies ahead. From this we derived
the Spending Wave, originally shown as **Chart 2-2**, and repeated here,
Chart 10-1.

The Spending Wave is simply the Immigration-Adjusted Birth Index
moved forward by the peak year of spending, 46, as we described in Chapters 1 and 2. The Immigration-Adjusted Birth Index is repeated here for
reference, **Chart 10-2**.

To estimate when those born in 1961 will spend the most, we move
them to their peak spending year, which is the year of birth (1961) plus
the peak spending age, 46: 1961 becomes 2007. The peak in spending at

Chart 10-1: The Spending Wave, Births Lagged for Peak in Spending

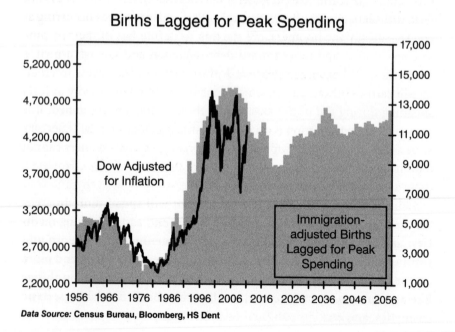

Births Lagged for Peak Spending

Data Source: Census Bureau, Bloomberg, HS Dent

Chart 10-2: Immigration-Adjusted Birth Index

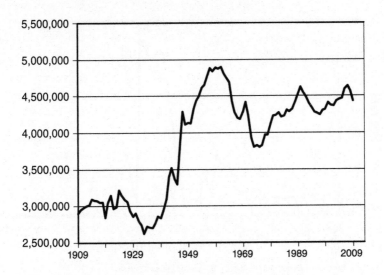

approximately age 46 is information we get from the Consumer Expenditure Survey, an annual survey that has been conducted by the US government since 1984, and that peak has generally been more or less consistent for many years. Back in the 1950s and 1960s, with marriages occurring at younger ages, the peak spending age was more like 44. The survey consists of questionnaires and interviews that record not only what people buy, but also demographic information about the people themselves, such as age, income, education, marital status, etc. This treasure trove reveals much more than just aggregate spending by age. We are able to tease out demand curves by age for hundreds of individual products and services. A common chart we use to illustrate this point is the spending by age for motorcycles, shown in **Chart 10-3.**

As you can see, spending on motorcycles pops a little in the mid-'20s but the real spending is in the 45- to 49-year-old age range. Our theory is that as consumers reach their mid-40s, they have the income to spend on a Harley-type big bike, they are trying to recapture some of their youth, and their children are finally leaving the nest, freeing up time and money for what they really want to do in life. Spending on motorcycles drops dramatically after age 50. What does this mean? Not much, until you combine it with the Immigration-Adjusted Birth Index above.

Chart 10-3: Motorcycle Sales by Age

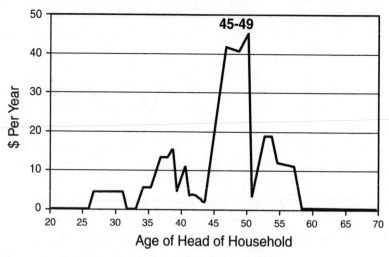

Data Source: **Consumer Expenditures Survey, Bureau of Labor Statistics**

Chart 10-4: Past and Future Motorcycle Demand

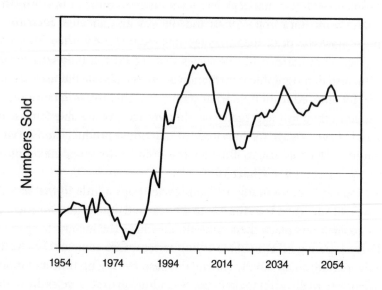

Just as we do to create the Spending Wave, we can move forward the Immigration-Adjusted Birth Index by 45 years to estimate the peak in motorcycle spending, which we have done in **Chart 10-4**.

Starting in the early 1990s, using this simple approach, we forecast that motorcycle demand would accelerate as the boomers aged until 2006, which is the peak year of births (1961) plus the peak age of spending on motorcycles (2006). This corresponds to what has happened at Harley-Davidson, which is now fighting contracting demand. An article in *Forbes* in late 2010 put it best: ". . . it is struggling against a foe that not even cost-cutting nor brand loyalty can overcome: demographics. Its current owners are getting old, and not enough younger ones are coming up behind them." *

You will recognize this problem—not enough people in the rising generation to keep demand high—as our constant theme and the reason behind the economic Winter Season. This plays out over and over, on stages large and small. In your business you can take the same information and use it to your advantage. By estimating when your product or service is in the most demand by age, you can develop your own demand curve. This is where target marketing and economics meet!

Business owners typically know, or definitely should know, who is their best client: meaning the type of person—by age, income, location, or situation—who is most likely to buy their product or service. This is the genesis of building a demand curve. The next step is to determine your potential audience. Is it the entire US? The world? Your neighborhood? We use charts about the US, but we recognize that many businesses reach beyond our shores, and some go no further than down the street. Once you identify your potential market, you can use any number of sources to estimate the population in that market. For demographic information on the world, there is the UN, IMF, and the CIA World Factbook. We have a database on our website that consolidates much of this information and makes economic projections by regions and countries for decades forward, as we discussed in Chapter 8.

For the US nationally there is the US Census Bureau, and for subsets (states, counties, zip codes) there is the American FactFinder (part of the Census Bureau). For those who want to be more methodical, ESRI

---

* A. Taylor, "Harley Davidson's Aging Biker Problem," *Fortune*, September 17, 2010.

(Environmental Systems Research Institute) offers a wealth of information in premium reports. We have used ESRI for years and highly recommend it. All of these groups can be found on the web by simply searching their name. Once you know your best client and the age distribution of your potential market, you have the pieces necessary to build your own demand curve. The questions to answer: Is the number of people in your business sweet spot growing or contracting? Is there a large number of people in your target market that are younger than your peak demand age so that you can expect rising sales, or has the peak of potential buyers passed?

This analysis should be done on each business line or product that a company has. The reason is that companies will have to make choices during deflationary times: Do they keep trying to support all business lines? Do they narrow their existing offerings? Or do they change products altogether? This demand curve and potential market forecast will make the answers to those questions clearer.

At HS Dent we have built demand curves for decades. We estimate the change in demand according to age on a wide variety of products and services, including breakfast cereal, camping equipment, automobiles, home purchases, and women's beauty products. We are offering access to our database of age-based product demand curves for *free*. Simply visit our website at www.hsdent.com/demandcurves, register, and you will immediately be able to peruse our database.

Recognize the Change in Perception

Over the last three years consumers have changed not just their behavior, but also their outlook. The words *conspicuous consumption* are gone, except when used to speak badly about someone. Only the more upscale markets have held up better due to the Fed quantitative easing programs that have directly fed the artificial rise and "third bubble in stocks," which greatly benefits these higher-net-worth consumers. Even though the equity markets rebounded, the average consumer is still worse off than he was in 2007. Bargain hunting, which was out of vogue for many years, is back to the fore. Consumers are quicker to switch brands and stores, seeking out the deal that will give them the most for the least amount of money. Retail store margins were squeezed a little bit at the end of 2010 as companies realized they could not pass on price increases due to supplier costs to the end consumer. As 2011 has evolved, higher food, energy, and apparel costs all began working through the system. As of this writing, retailers were lowering their forecasts in response.

Business owners have a great opportunity to position their brand, service, product, or store as being on the same side as the consumer, working to increase what the consumer receives in exchange for his money. This is not meant to commoditize a product or service, unless a business is already in a market that competes mostly on price. Instead, this is meant to alert business owners that the presentation of how a product or service will bring much more to the client than the cost will resonate for years to come. Approaching product placement in this way is not new, but it should become the dominant theme during the deflationary years. Illustrating how consumers can maintain their current standard of living while spending less is part of the presentation.

Note that this is for the average consumer, not the luxury consumer, as mentioned above! After the initial drop, many of those who deal in luxury goods and services have been spared the pain of our current economic woes—but even that will not last. Ask the investors who bought condos and houses in the Turks and Caicos Islands, the ultimate high-end retreat, before prices and developments there collapsed from 2009 forward. As the income inequality grew in our nation, a small but very affluent group of consumers was created. So far, they have been somewhat insulated from the continuing effects of the credit deflation, fall in housing, and unemployment. However, this will not be the case as the great fall in asset and investment values, which expanded in the 1990s and 2000s, continues to deflate.

While average-income and above-average-income households are still struggling with issues like employment, the value of their house, and a diminished retirement account, it is actually the new rich, or top 1% to 10%, that benefited so much in the bubble boom, who will be hit the hardest by deflation in asset and investment values. Why? Because they had so much more invested in the bubble, and the newly

formulated government and tax policies will penalize them more in the decades ahead. History shows that the Winter Season and following Spring Season increasingly favor the everyday household and worker, as occurred in the greatest mass prosperity boom in history, from 1942 to 1968, and even to a lesser degree in the early 1970s.

In the financial world, investment firms and banks will have to reach down, bringing mass investment and financial services to the upper-middle-class and middle-class households rather than focusing merely on the highest-net-worth households in order to continue growing in the decades ahead. This change will require more automated, lower-cost models for investment advice, financial decisions, money transactions. I (Harry Dent) invested in a number of firms, including SaveDaily (one of the few that survived), that allow everyday households to make invest-ments in smaller accounts and HSAs without punitive transaction and financial fees, as I saw this trend coming many years ago.

Elusive Lending

As 2008 wore on, businesses were in a panic. They were seeing sales and revenue drop, which was bad, but they were also getting calls from their bankers, who wanted to chop down existing lines of credit. The squeeze was on. As the credit crisis got into full swing, banks were shutting down any existing piece of credit they could find, including letters of credit, lines of credit, home equity loans, and business credit cards. Company owners who had relied on such financing options were suddenly faced with a cash crunch on two fronts—sales and lending. The outcome was foreseeable: many businesses failed. This was a problem not just for small businesses, but for businesses of all different sizes. It was not bad assets that killed Lehman Brothers; it was its failure to obtain what had been its lifeblood for years—short-term lending. Since the dark days of the first leg of this crisis in 2008–2009, some access to credit for businesses has been restored; however, there were lessons learned in those days that should not be for-gotten, as we see another credit crunch on the horizon. The next one will not be short-lived, as the US government will lack the means and the will to attack it with the same force (bailouts and stimulus) as it did before.

Big businesses answered the events of 2008–2009 in a very sensible way.

They became their own banks. Microsoft raised $4.75 billion, setting a corporate record for the lowest interest ever on 3-year notes, 0.87%. This eclipsed IBM, which had just sold $1.5 billion of 3-year notes for an interest cost of 1.00%. Both of these low-cost loans were eclipsed by Walmart, which borrowed billions for 3 years at 0.75% interest. These issuers were joined by the likes of General Electric and Harvard University, which along with many others issued corporate debt in 2010. The point is to understand that large companies have looked across the economic landscape and determined that now is the time to borrow as much as they can so that when the next crisis erupts they will not be subject to the vagaries of bankers who must slash credit to save their own skin. Small businesses need to take a page from this playbook by arranging today any credit or financing they might need over the next several years.

You don't want to be caught flat-footed by banks and lending institutions again! Build a war chest so that you can act as your own bank during the turbulent times ahead. As credit continues to shrink, banks will be looking for the areas where they can cut. You can rest assured that if you are a small business, they will be looking at you.

Since late 2010, longer-term interest rates have moved higher and, as we anticipated, they are rising even more in late 2011. We expect they will likely retrace as the economy slows in 2012 and beyond. The Fed's policy of stimulating the economy to unprecedented extremes is backlashing with rising long-term bond rates and higher mortgage rates that have only made the housing market fall more. Unfortunately, the same thing that brings interest rates down will most likely curtail lending to businesses for years to come.

Businesses that need financing in the coming years should now only refinance at lower short-term rates and wait for lower longer-term rates to fall before securing longer-term rates between early 2013 and early 2015.

Less Credit Applies to All

Deflation is pervasive; it hits everyone. It is not a business phenomenon or a consumer or government issue. It is universal in an economy. This means that while businesses are dealing with less credit, so are their clients and their suppliers. This has caused clients to slow pay businesses while vendors demand faster payment. Part of the process of dealing with this is setting parameters early for client payments that stretch out over time by charging interest on late payments, as well as negotiating concessions from vendors for early payment. What a business does not want is to end up with a working capital deficiency where receivables are high and payables are low, which means that the company itself is carrying more risk by investing more short-term capital. This just highlights an even greater need to secure financing and build a cash cushion before the next downturn.

The Falling Value of Land and Equipment

One of the reasons that deflation hurts so much is because the things we own lose value. This applies to cars, houses, equipment, land, buildings, inventory—you name it. If it's a hard asset, it will most likely drop in price. This fall in price is due to the fact that people have less and less money to use to pay for things, so prices must drop to keep commerce going. The one thing that goes up in value is cash, because as credit and money supply shrink, the dollars that are still in circulation rise in purchasing power. That is precisely why we expect the US dollar to rise more than fall in the years ahead! When you apply this to your business, you can see how having excess inventory, unused capital equipment, and too much office or warehouse space can cost you twice. Not only would you expect such items to fall in value while you hold them, but the money you could have amassed by either not buying inventory or selling excess equipment would have risen in purchasing power!

The insight with equipment, land, buildings, and other assets is not to be enticed into buying or holding on to things just because they are cheap. Deflation will make them cheaper, which is the same as making the dollars in your bank account more powerful! Keep your powder dry until you absolutely need to purchase something. Wait at least until early 2014 to consider buying new assets and capital equipment, and perhaps much later in areas like commercial real estate and office properties. It is likely better to rent or lease than buy until at least 2013, and more so until 2020–2023.

The 800-Pound Gorilla: Employment

Most businesses did what they had to do in 2008–2009: they got lean. There was a mad rush to trim payrolls as quickly as possible and as much as possible. The reason is simple. For most businesses, the greatest cost is employee compensation (including payroll and benefits). As revenue fell off, it was only natural to cut expenses commensurately. Now we have the government trying to prod businesses to hire under some sort of "build it and they will come" theory. We don't agree. As deflation continues, the pressures of falling credit, falling money supply, and diminishing wages will keep weighing on consumption. Hiring more people will not lead any business to increased revenue, only increased expense. Our view is that you should do your best to find ways for technology to replace people or to only add people who directly contribute to growing revenues and cost cutting—like in internet and direct marketing, etc. In a world of falling prices, if there is a computing application that can help you trim payroll, then it will probably help you survive the next several years.

In this area we cannot go without mentioning benefit programs, specifically the US government's health care initiative. We do not take political sides about whether the Obama administration's health care program is right or wrong, we are just pointing out that this drive to enroll everyone in a health care plan will have dramatic consequences, not least of which is an anticipated increase in health care premiums for employer-sponsored health care. Higher benefit costs make employing people even more expensive. This is part of the issue of businesses being the intermediary between employees and the government.

With all of that said, there is no substitute for quality workers. They boost productivity, morale, and client retention through superior work and work ethic. This environment of high unemployment and low opportunity is a business owner's dream when it comes to finding the best people at competitive wages. A famous investor quipped in 2008 that he had just hired his "last employee with no experience," meaning that in the coming years he would have his pick of job applicants with experience who were hungry for work at competitive salaries. For those that rely on younger staff, keep in mind that unemployment for those in the 18–24 age range is close to 20%. The US government does not break out numbers for recent college graduates, but there is no doubt that jobs are hard to come by.

All of this adds up to the fact that employees are still very expensive, and if you can use technology to cut payroll, then you should seriously consider it. However, if and when you do hire, keep an open mind about the type of applicant you want (experienced, trainable, etc.) and be very choosy in whom you hire. You are in the driver's seat, which hasn't happened in almost two decades!

If you stay lean and mean in the coming years of the deflationary downturn, you will be able to hire the most promising new recruits and the best laid-off employees from your competitors. Cut excessive employment costs now and look to hire the best candidates in the years to come, likely with the added bonus of government incentives thrown in!

Shop Your Competition

Hard economic times reveal people and businesses that are operating at the margin, which spells opportunity for others. As a business owner, you should take stock of your industry, meaning identifying and ranking those in your business. Include your own business in the analysis. What are the strengths of each one? Do they have locations, equipment, clientele, expertise, or staff that make their company valuable? Are they the largest player or near the bottom? Are they well capitalized or have they always struggled? The reason to do this is to estimate how your industry might consolidate in the years ahead and what the position of your company might be. With most business contracting and with credit harder to obtain, there will definitely be business casualties. The goal is to identify ahead of time which are the likely winners and which are the potential losers. Once this is done, you can determine strategic moves for your own company, like partnering with or selling to the strongest player, or perhaps combining forces with or simply purchasing a weaker link. The goal is to ensure your own survival during the Winter Season, because whoever lives through this period will be set to profit handsomely as the next Spring Season emerges!

Gaining market share from weak competitors during the downturn, especially those who overexpanded through increased capacity or

inventory, is a great way to grow your business even though the overall market might be shrinking.

In Chapter 9 we discussed what individuals can do to avoid harm and even prosper in the years ahead, and in this chapter we addressed what steps businesses can take. That leaves the biggest challenge for last: what the US government should do, and more important, what it should not do! In Chapter 11 we will outline several steps our government could take, starting today, to put our country on a sustainable path.

Government Needs a New Approach: Focusing on the Causes, Not the Symptoms

Matching Policy to Incentives

In the late 1700s and early 1800s, England had a problem beyond just the pesky colonies. Specifically, it had a criminal problem. As the nation industrialized, people were flocking from the rural areas into the cities seeking employment. With the influx of population came waves of crime, from the petty (stealing bread) to the heinous (murder, rape, etc.). The prisons soon were overflowing. In response to the crowded prisons, the government started housing prisoners on idle ships in harbors, much as the characters Abel Magwitch and Compeyson were housed in Charles Dickens's novel *Great Expectations*. Soon, these ships also were full.

In years past, the British parliament had addressed this problem of too many convicts through the process of "transport," meaning that anyone who committed a felony was subject to being transported to penal colonies abroad to serve their sentence. After the American Revolution, no more prisoners could be exiled to penal colonies there, as the newly formed US government would not accept the worst of British society as immigrants. The Crown went looking for another solution. They found one: Australia.

The island nation was particularly barren, with the hard-pack clay giving way to very little in terms of vegetation and (aboveground) natural resources. It was the perfect place to set up penal colonies. Given the lack of evidence of any cultivation of crops, it was assumed that the indigenous population was uncivilized and therefore it was not necessary to consult with them before commencing the transportation and relocation of thousands of prisoners to the new land.

Over the course of eighty years, from 1787 to 1868, the British made 825 shipments of prisoners to Australia, at an average rate of 200 prisoners per load. Government boats comprised the first fleet to sail; private contractors made subsequent shipments. In all, more than 160,000 prisoners were sent to the desolate island. Unfortunately, in the early years, many of those put on the ships for transport ended up dying before they arrived. The conditions on the ships were horrid, and the rations were far from adequate. The second fleet of prisoner ships sailed in 1790. The trip took over 250 days. When the fleet finally arrived in Australia, more than 260 of the 1,006 prisoners had died. Once on shore, another 150 soon perished. The death rate was over 35%, and that's before the prisoners truly began living in the new land. Given that the government had undertaken transport as an alternative to more drastic punishment at home (like hanging), to have that many prisoners perish was a problem.

In the early years of transport to Australia, the shippers were private contractors compensated based on the number of prisoners transported. This means that every shilling spent on things like food or medical care for the prisoners was just another cost that ate into profit. The contractors were not motivated to care about the well-being of their cargo. In the early 1800s, the English government changed the compensation structure from one based on the number of prisoners transported to a system based on the number of prisoners who arrived in Australia alive. There was an immediate boost in the health and general well-being of prisoners transported to Australia! The point is simple: incentives matter. However, incentives cannot stand alone; they must be aligned with the goals of the people who are making the choices of how to behave. In this case, the private contractors chose to treat prisoners better in terms of attending to their health needs because the new incentive structure rewarded the contractors for such actions with more of what they wanted, namely profit. Current-day governments could learn a lot from this story.

We are at the point that the largest group in our economy is moving toward spending less and saving more, with little regard for government policy. The boomers rationally are fending for themselves as they pay down debt and prepare for retirement. No government policy will change this! Short of confiscation, we cannot force people to

spend their dollars. Our best path is to create programs with proper incentives that deal with our massive debt and unemployment as we transition into this economic Winter Season. Deflation will always be painful, but our current programs, which are based on the delusion of returning to the economy of yesterday, are only making things worse!

First Things First: Stop the Madness of the Fed!

The Federal Reserve definitely has an impact, although it is often not the impact that was intended. This quasi-government entity is lousy at attaining its mandates of low inflation, moderate interest rates, and maximum employment, but it is fabulous at creating false incentives and artificial bubbles. The first question should be, "Why do we assign these tasks to anyone?" These mandates go back to the idea that the business cycle can be "tamed." The problem is that out in the real world, the notions of price movement, risk, and consumer demand change constantly based on a multitude of factors. The business cycle is not a nice, even flow of inputs that can be smoothed through monetary manipulations. The Fed printed money out of thin air, taxing all existing holders of dollars, and spent it to buy troubled mortgage securities and then US bonds. What did that achieve? The Fed moved bad assets from banks to the books of taxpayers and then artificially lowered long-term interest rates to try to goose the housing market. It didn't work. The Fed should stop immediately! Then we can address the real problem at the Fed: it is tasked with a job that cannot be done and should not be done. Its mandate should be simplified to only one job.

The Fed should have its mandate changed to keeping inflation in normal times under a certain amount, say 2.5%. That's it. Notice that we did not say "0% to 2.5%," meaning that we do not believe the Fed should be fighting against deflation. As we have discussed, deflation is the process by which asset bubbles are corrected. Fighting against this correction puts the Fed in the odd place of defending the misallocation of capital. Should we really be trying to prop up valuations of assets that became artificially too high? No! Instead, we should be assisting the markets in identifying what are the new "market-clearing prices," meaning the fair-market value of assets based on today's economic environment. This is not a monetary

(Fed-based) issue, it is a fiscal and legal issue, which is the proper provenance of the elected Congress. But on the flip side, maybe the Fed should have a similar target of keeping deflation to 2.5% to ease the transition.

With its new, narrowly defined mandate, the Fed would stop printing new dollars and stop buying US Treasury bonds and would allow Fed funds to float. Interest rates would gravitate toward their natural levels. What levels are natural? That depends on the amount of capital available in our economy and the outlook of consumers, investors, and business owners. Right now, it is possible that short-term rates would remain quite low, reflecting the huge amount of liquidity in our system. However, long rates probably would climb in the short term, because the Fed is no longer buying bonds and market participants are unsure of the future. This would allow savers to earn more and it would charge long-term borrowers a higher price. Those investing in long-term fixed-income assets immediately would start earning a reasonable rate of return, which would assist in meeting goals such as saving for retirement, college education, etc. In addition, those who run pension funds would also get a boost, because their new fixed-income purchases would be better able to meet their long-term liabilities of pension payments. While this might slow economic activity (borrowing costs would increase), it would more correctly assign capital to the right projects, meaning that money would not be borrowed for a home, an equipment purchase, or some other reason unless the borrower was able to pay a higher interest rate, which, with hope, would reflect a better ability to repay the loan or a stronger conviction on the part of a business owner that his venture would succeed.

THE FED: JUST FACILITATE TRANSACTIONS AND TRADE

The Fed is still necessary to defend our economy against the currency decisions of other nations. Also, having a lender of last resort can restore order in times of calamity, as happened in the fall of 2008. A long discussion can be had about the merits (or lack thereof) of paper money not backed by gold or any other internationally recognized storehouse of value. Many people see our current money system as nothing more than a sham and believe that we should return to a gold-based system. We simply do not see gold as having the capacity to expand with changes in economic growth and monetary transactions. The Fed should simply provide for enough credit to meet transaction and growth needs without extremes in prices or speculation.

In a nutshell, here is our summary proposal for the Fed:

- Stop printing money to artificially support the economy.
- Stop loan guarantee programs.
- Reduce mandates to one: maintain inflation below 2.5% and deflation below 2.5%.
- Remain as the lender of last resort, following the advice of lending freely but charging dearly in times of trouble (this part is borrowed from Bagehot).

With our proposal to get the Fed out of the long-term-interest-rate-setting game so that risks are clearly priced by lenders and borrowers, we can move on to the big holdup in the economy: existing debt and our addiction to new debt. This is basically a conversation about living within our means both personally and publicly. The problem, of course, is that suddenly changing to a lifestyle and budget within one's means after years of supplementing spending with debt is painful! Nobody wants to do it. This is hard for individuals, who have to suffer their own consequences, but it seems impossible for the elected officials at almost every level who preside over our tax dollars. However, it is necessary, and if we do not take on the discipline ourselves, we will suffer even more when the choice is forced on us in the future. If we put off these choices today, we will be limited in the years ahead by the stark choice of forever printing more dollars, which is inflationary, or paying higher rates of interest to sell government debt. Either way, it erodes our standard of living and limits the possibilities that our children will have. This is something that we should have been doing all along, of course. At the least, we should have taken steps toward fiscal responsibility during the economic Fall Season when revenues were plentiful. We didn't. We are left with tough choices in a difficult economic climate. We must start making changes today, personally, and we will have to make changes at the state and national levels as well. Here are some ideas as to how.

Personal Debt: Mortgages Are the Issue

Revolving (credit card) debt has been on the slide for years now. Those who issue credit cards are more cautious, as are those who use them. The overwhelming issue in the private sector is existing mortgage debt. The mortgage mess needs no introduction. We need to address the incredible mismatch between the values of homes and the mortgages owed on them, what is commonly called negative equity (the amount by which the mortgage exceeds the home equity). So far, the US government has created many initiatives to prop up housing prices and rearrange mortgages so that people could keep their homes. Loan modifications have been made to lower payments for a period of years, stretch out mortgages over more years, or reduce the interest on the mortgage, effectively lowering the payments. All of these programs attack the ability of the borrower to pay, which, while obviously a problem, is not what got us here. What caused our issue was wildly overinflated valuations on homes! Lenders developed ever more creative ways to get buyers into homes but were not banking on the ability of the borrower to repay. If so, then the lenders would have stuck with much more restrictive lending standards and with "plain vanilla" loans. The NINJA loans and "no document verification" loans were bets by lenders that the value of the real estate would cover any and all potential problems. They were wrong. The housing asset bubble caused a mortgage debt bubble. We have seen housing drop by over 40% in the worst-hit areas, and yet mortgages remain mostly intact. It's time to pay the piper. We need to attack the mortgage bubble through a write-down program that recognizes the true value of housing, assigns losses to the parties that created the mess, and relies as little as possible on the US government.

According to CoreLogic, at the end of 2010, 22.5% of the mortgages on homes in the US (representing more than 15 million homes) were underwater, and 10% of all home mortgages (representing more than 7 million homes) were underwater by 25% or more. The total amount of negative equity was $770 billion. We know the parties involved: (1) homeowners, who owe more than their homes are worth; (2) lenders (banks, mortgage-backed bond investors, etc.), who are owed principal and interest but for whom the security on their loans (the homes) is not worth as much as the loans; and (3) servicers, those companies that act on behalf of lenders by receiving in mortgage payments and distributing funds where they are supposed to go and that get paid the most by receiving extra fees when loans become delinquent and go through foreclosure. A separate but important group is composed of several US government entities (FNMA, FHLMC, and GNMA, Government National Mortgage Association, aka Ginnie Mae) that guarantee roughly half of all mortgages, some of which are underwater. Each of these groups has different goals that need to be addressed, and we will go through this in several steps. We're going to work backward, starting with the asset.

Step 1. It's All About the House

You wanted the house? You got the house! That should be the attitude of the US government and state governments. Currently most states have judicial foreclosure, meaning that to discharge a mortgage, you must go through a court. This is sort of a fancy way of saying that the lender can sue you for whatever losses are incurred when the foreclosed home eventually is sold. This is different from states like Arizona, where the only thing a lender can go after is the property itself. We should immediately move to nonjudicial foreclosure in all jurisdictions, which would sever the link between the homeowner and the loan, leaving the loan backed by the asset itself. This would give the borrower more power. If the borrower cannot be sued for the loss, then he or she is less motivated to go bankrupt to pay for the asset. Lenders would immediately see a spike in delinquencies as borrowers determined it is not worth it to keep paying, unless of course the lenders quickly began working toward an equitable solution.

Step 2. Speed Up the Resolution

In many states there is a long lag between delinquency and foreclosure. In the state of Florida, a homeowner can stop making payments and remain in the residence for almost two years before being forced to leave. This is outrageous! This motivates people who are considering defaulting to do exactly that. If you can't pay for the home anyway, why not live rent-free for years! Florida has set up foreclosure courts to address its backlog of cases. This is a great step and should be expanded in Florida, replicated elsewhere, and funded by the US government. It is in all of our interests to have this play out quickly. The length of time for a property to move from 90 days delinquent to foreclosure should be no more than 120 days, which would be roughly 7 months of a homeowner not making payments.

Unfortunately, some of these proceedings have become the playground of trial lawyers who are bent on attacking the lenders for lack of proper documentation. While this lack of documentation certainly has happened, and even potentially has happened on a grand scale, the fact remains that the homeowners took out the mortgages and bought the homes. To claim that a technicality obviates their repayment obligation is idiotic. If a lender is found to be deficient in his claim of ownership of the loan, then the homeowner's obligation should become the property of a pool set up for this purpose at FNMA. It should not be a ticket for a free ride.

Step 3. Figure Out Who Speaks for Lenders and Who Has Priority

Currently too many parties have claims on a given home. If the home has no equity, then it becomes the mortgage holder that has the claim. The mortgage holder could be a single bank, but the loan could have been sliced into a thousand pieces and now have thousands of owners. If the mortgage holder is one bank, then working through the problem is relatively simple. However, if the loan has been sliced up, then things get complicated; who has the right to agree to any modifications or changes? We need a change of law that allows for the appointment of a person who has the authority to negotiate on behalf of the pool of owners. If 25% of the pool is held by fewer than 50 investors, then they can elect one of the top 50 as the point person or entity through a simple plurality of votes. If the holdings are more widely disbursed than that, then the originator of the pool could appoint the lead person. Note that this person should not be connected to the loan servicers! This group has an inherent conflict of interest with the lenders, as servicers earn more through fees when mortgages go bad.

Many times, the property has more than one loan on it (second mortgages, HELOCs, etc.). A common practice at the height of the real estate boom was to get a borrower to take out a first mortgage for 80% of the loan and then a second mortgage for 20% of the loan, effectively buying the home for nothing down. This also allowed the borrower to escape the necessity of mortgage insurance, which is usually required on mortgages written for more than 80% of the value of the home. Second mortgage holders by definition are at the end of the food chain, in that they get nothing if a home goes through foreclosure and there is not enough to satisfy the primary mortgage. Instead of this all-or-nothing approach, second mortgage holders should participate at 150% of the rate of any primary mortgage alteration.

For example, if a home has a $150,000 mortgage and a $30,000 second mortgage, and the primary lender agrees to a 20% reduction, then the second lender would be forced to take a 30% reduction. The new amounts would be a $120,000 first mortgage and a $21,000 second mortgage. Lenders that hold second mortgages won't like it. Tough! They lent money in a very speculative, risky manner. This is what happens when things go bad. Losses will be had. Keep in mind, as pointed out in Chapter 7, over $500 billion in HELOCs is outstanding, so this is a big market.

Step 4. Offer Another Choice

If a homeowner cannot afford his mortgage or if a home mortgage is significantly underwater with little chance of recovering soon, there are few options. The homeowner can attempt a short sale, in which he sells the property for less than the mortgage and he shares the loss with the lender, or the homeowner can default and go through foreclosure. Loan modification programs for the most part have been ineffectual because they did not address the underlying problem of a gross mismatch between the asset value and the loan. We should offer another alternative: the possibility of cutting the mortgage into pieces.

William Wheaton, a professor at MIT, has proposed a solution that has made the rounds over the last two years: take mortgages that are underwater and divide them into two pieces. The first piece will be a new mortgage for the current value of the home. This new, lower mortgage will replace the first mortgage that currently exists. The other piece, the remainder of the old first mortgage which is the part that represents the negative equity, would become a security owned by the lender that entitles him to a percentage of the gains realized when the home is sold. An example makes this easier to see.

EXISTING SITUATION	
Current loan	$150,000
Current home value	$95,000
Amount underwater (negative equity)	$55,000
NEW STRUCTURE	
New loan	$95,000
New security	$65,000 (owned by bank)

The new security is a nonrecourse lien against the home that is secured by a percentage of the gains realized when the home is sold (for example, 50%). If the home is sold in two years for $115,000, then the new loan of $95,000 is paid off, 50% of the remaining $20,000 goes to the bank for the new security, and the rest goes to the homeowner:

SALE OF HOME FOR $115,000 IN TWO YEARS	
Loans	
New loan	$95,000 (paid in full)
New security	$10,000 (50% of $20,000 gain)
	−$55,000 (loss incurred by bank, $65,000 to $10,000)
Homeowner	$10,000 (50% of $20,000 gain)

If the homeowner chooses to sell immediately after the arrangement is struck, then the bank incurs 100% of the loss. This certainly might motivate some homeowners to sell immediately; however, they would have to go somewhere. If their new mortgage is set at a market rate for the area, then it would not make sense to move for a comparable rent payment; the rental would have no upside. Also, it is very likely that the homeowner would not be able to buy another property immediately due to lack of a down payment. In most cases, the homeowner probably would not pick up and leave except to move for a job or some other compelling reason.

The impact of such an approach would be felt in all areas. Homeowners would be able move if necessary for employment or other reasons. The housing market would quickly move to market-clearing prices in those areas that are the hardest hit. Banks and other lenders, such as bondholders of mortgage-backed securities, would see an immediate reduction in their payment stream and would have to recognize these losses on their books, which brings up the next point: tagging lenders with losses.

Step 5. Force Lenders to Return from Fantasy Island

Currently lenders are holding hundreds of billions, if not trillions, of dollars in bad loans on their books. We do not know what the numbers are because the lenders are not forced to disclose them. In the spring of 2009, the Financial Accounting Standards Board (FASB) relaxed its rule requiring companies (including banks) to value their assets at current market prices. This system is called mark-to-market. Lenders argued that when the credit market froze, this requirement caused their balance sheets to be severely impaired (because the mortgages were valued so low), even though the cash flow they were receiving (timely payment of principal and interest) had not changed. This is a fair and reasoned argument, but the outcome was not. What lenders did in response to the lifting of this restriction was to value most loans at 100%, which implied that no losses had been incurred and none were expected. In the financial industry this approach is called "mark-to-make-believe." With record foreclosures in 2008, 2009, and 2010 (2.3 million, 2.8 million, and 2.9 million, respectively), it's hard to see where this expectation of full repayment comes from, especially with regard to HELOCs.

Instead of moving from "many mortgages are worth very little" to "almost all mortgages are worth 100%," we should adjust the valuations of mortgages to reflect the experience of similar mortgage pools, plus some external factors. If a lender holds thousands of mortgages that are subprime loans in Southern California, then these mortgages would be valued at a lower percentage than the same type of pool in, say, Texas. The adjustment would be based on the decline in valuations in the area, the unemployment in the area, the percentage of homes underwater in the area, and the current experience of similar quality loans in the area.

We should enlist mortgage analysts from the private sector to make such judgments and then publish their estimates of value (expressed as a percentage) for all to see and use as a guide.

This approach would immediately put many lending institutions at risk of insolvency on paper, as the value of their assets would fall below their liabilities and certainly below their capital requirements. If the assets are sitting on their books today, aren't they already insolvent? Banks are already in this position but are hiding it through their ability to value the worst of their holdings at whatever they want. It is this black hole of assets that has created the facade of banking that exists today. With such legacy assets on their books, many banks are basically the "walking dead": they have not written down their assets to recognize losses, so they seem to be alive, but they know the losses are there, so they refrain from any substantial new lending. This is one of the reasons that banks keep such high amounts in their excess reserve accounts at the Fed. They know that they will need the money.

If by forcing such asset value recognition we consequently could force many banks into insolvency, then we would be well on our way to cleaning up the mess we are in instead of merely wishing it away, hoping that somehow future economic growth will bail us out. We could then go about breaking up these failed institutions and restructuring the banking industry, rebuilding the wall between investments and lending (bringing back Glass-Steagall) and ending the practice of rewarding the exact group that helped to create this mess in the first place.

This is where backing by the US Treasury in some sort of shared write-off plan could have the most effect, just as we mentioned at the beginning of this book. Much of the stimulus so far has been funneled into programs that simply maintained the status quo. What if we used the funds instead to erase the anchor of debt that is holding us down? Providing an incentive for lenders to write down or write off debt through the changes above and then pairing that with a monetary inducement from the government could be the way to break the current stalemate between borrowers and lenders.

Step 6. Remember That We as Taxpayers Will Pay

The US government and we as taxpayers do not get a free pass. Through our entities FNMA, FHLMC, GNMA, and FHA, we are guarantors of mortgages. Fortunately, most of the loans these entities insure are prime loans, meaning that they are to prime borrowers and therefore have a lower chance of default. The exception is FHA, which requires a lower percentage down payment. Although the loans backed by these entities have lower default rates, they still go into default. Through 2010, the US government had $130 billion in losses in these programs, with estimates of total losses ranging between $250 billion and $400 billion. We should approach homeowners with loans backed by these entities with the same modification program that is discussed above for private lenders.

Summary of Housing Recommendation

If we did all of the above, we would have moved mountains! We would have created a laser-like focus on the problem, which is a massive mismatch between the credit extended to buy homes and the current valuations of the homes. We would have given lenders a reason to work with borrowers (less claim on the borrower, therefore a need to be flexible) and better tools to work with (a point person, an expedited process, and a choice as to how to work with the borrower: foreclosure, short sale, or modification). Along the way we would have ripped the bandage off of the sore, acknowledging that our housing issues will not heal without massive, corrective action. This approach would lay bare the true state of health of lending institutions, giving investors and regulators a clear understanding of what each company is worth.

Steps to Fix the Housing Market
1. Change the law to reflect that the only backing of homes is the asset.
2. Change the law to speed up the foreclosure process, including foreclosure courts.
3. Allow appointment of a person to negotiate on behalf of widely dispersed owners.
4. Allow modification of loans into two separate pieces.

5. Force lenders to recognize valuations of loans according to an independent scale and offer a government-funded monetary incentive for each dollar of debt written down.
6. Recognize that taxpayers will still be stuck with government entity losses, but with the option to use the modification program in step 4.

The ensuing write-down of assets would create a swift reduction in credit outstanding, which would cause the forces of deflation to move faster. We should welcome this response, because it would reward savers with more value for their dollars (deflation makes current dollars worth more) and would bring asset prices and the debt outstanding on those assets in line more quickly than the long, slow bleeding process that we are experiencing today. The quicker that we get debt and prices in line with realistic valuations, the quicker we can get our housing market restarted, giving homeowners the liquidity they need in order to move for reasons like job opportunities.

Nothing in this approach is a magic bullet or a giveaway. If a homeowner who is now liberated from the personal guarantee on his home decides to default, he must still deal with the credit impairment, and the new speed of foreclosure would mean that he cannot simply sit "rent-free" in the home for years. If a lender chooses to ignore the new modification program, he can certainly force nonpaying borrowers into foreclosure, but then the lender is stuck with more housing inventory in an oversupplied market. Finally, forcing holders of this debt to recognize it at market value based on an independent scale is shedding light on an existing problem, not creating a new one. The depth of the credit crisis was over two years ago. The fact that the valuations on these securities have not come back doesn't reflect a credit crisis; it reflects the fact that these now are assets that nobody wants, which is now normal.

States and Some Cities

State budget woes were discussed at length in Chapter 4. The problem is both current expenditures (reflected in annual deficits) and unfunded liabilities. These problems are woven together in that states have taken on paying for much more than they can afford, so as the unfunded liabilities become current expenses (people retire and have to be paid benefits), the states face insolvency. Because large parts of their budgets are mandated or legally contracted obligations, states have backed themselves into a corner when it comes to adjusting what they spend.

With the unionization of public employees, cities and states have lost much of the right to reduce salaries and benefits unilaterally. They are locked into contracts. So when states need to reduce staff spending and cannot make pay cuts across the board, they begin taking what steps they can, such as furloughs for thousands of employees at a time (as happened in California), and even the dismissal of employees so that others can keep their current pay. In January 2011, Camden, New Jersey, a city that has suffered blight and crime for many years, laid off half of its police force. The city could not afford the payroll, but the police union would not budge on their salaries. Who loses? The citizens of Camden, of course. The citizens are being told that if their house is robbed, a policeman will not be sent over. If you smash your car to bits but no one is hurt, a policeman will not show up. In the world of public safety, this makes no sense. This situation, albeit in less drastic form, is playing out all over the nation at the city and state level.

When will we recognize that President Franklin D. Roosevelt, who refused to allow public employees to unionize, was right and that President John F. Kennedy, who signed Presidential Order #10988 allowing for such unionization, was wrong? As we discussed in Chapter 4, these entities are not businesses in the typical sense. There is no sharing of profits with the workers who labored to create the business. This is the distribution of taxes collected from citizens for the purpose of providing services. When the union contract of a private company becomes a burden, there are choices, including the end of operations of the company. Cities and states cannot take this approach in the extreme; they can't just cease to operate. This means that in a way the union contracts of public employees have an unfair advantage; the unions know that their bargaining counterpart must continue operations. The threat of dooming a city or state through overly generous contracts is met with a yawn. "They can always raise taxes!" is the reply to this line of thinking, and it is true. However, it is also true that rising taxes will drive out property owners and businesses.

When one section of the spending by states and cities is locked out of the budget discussion, it pressures all other parts of the budget. What should be cut first, the disbursements from states to health providers that care for the mentally ill, the pay for safety officers and firemen, the pay for teachers, or unemployment benefits? The choice is not easy, nor is it up to anyone but the constituents. What we as a nation should be providing is the ability for individual states and cities to make these choices as they see fit, free of federal government intervention. Removing contract labor and benefit agreements would go a long way toward this end. The idea of benefits brings up another issue: federally mandated or matched spending.

Health care is a touchy subject at every level. States pay for health care not only for workers and retirees, but also for Medicaid recipients. While Medicaid is not required by the federal government, if a state chooses to participate (which all states have), then the US government will match whatever dollars the state spends, but it also mandates how the program must be run. This is a catch-22. The State of Washington spends $6 billion on Medicaid, almost 20% of its annual budget. The state receives an equal amount from the US government for the program. If Washington opts out of Medicaid, which it has the right to do, then the state will lose $6 billion in funding for the medical care of the poorest and most vulnerable in society. Even if the state institutes more efficient rules about the provision of care, it would not come close to making up the loss of $6 billion. The federal government must change how Medicaid is run to allow states the latitude to change their methods of implementation to fit their own needs. This can be done by matching state spending with block grants instead of through the current Medicaid funding, which comes with so many regulations and strings.

As for current workers, cities and states should implement an orderly wind-down of employer-provided (by the state) insurance benefits over a 7-year period. Public employees would have their pay increased to compensate for the loss of benefits and then would have to buy insurance on their own. This would get states out of the business of dealing with everescalating health care costs as well as make workers more sensitive to the costs incurred. If this approach is taken, it would cause quite an uproar, but the alternative is to keep hiding the runaway cost of health care inside of the budgets of public entities. We must keep in mind that these are not businesses that can pass along costs to customers! The goal should be to offload any and all costs that are not the direct provenance of the government entity, period.

Each city and state has its sacred cows and pet programs, all of which should be on the chopping block to take governments back to their original purpose of essential service provision, not the distribution of favors in the form of tax dollars. The recent turnover of so many governorships in the election of 2010 will, with hope, usher in exactly such changes.

On the unfunded liabilities side, the situation is both easier and harder. Health care benefits, which are a smaller liability than pensions but have less funding, should also be put on a 7-year phaseout plan just like public employee health insurance. These benefits are costly and well beyond the purview of any state to guarantee, as the continued inflation in health care makes the liability theoretically limitless. The phaseout of these benefits would allow states to focus more clearly on the other liability they carry: pensions. While there is no way to adjust pension payments for current retirees, states can certainly adjust the cost-of-living adjustments, guaranteed increases, and bonus structures that many of these plans added on in the growth years. As for current workers, there must be increases in what current employees pay in terms of their pension contributions and changes in the requirements for retirement (for example, retirement should no longer be allowed at 90% of pay after only 20 years, as some plans now allow), as well as an end to gaming the system. Many public pensions are based on an employee's last year of income. In some instances, employees "spike" their pensions by working tremendous amounts of overtime in the last year or by taking a distribution of their acquired sick days or holiday pay. As this practice has come to light, there have been steps to quash it; however, current employment contracts bar many changes. All of the shenanigans should end immediately, along with unionized public employment.

Once sweeping changes like those mentioned above have been implemented, cities and states will have a clear sense of where they stand in terms of revenue and expenses. It might be that in order to fund what their constituents believe to be necessary and proper programs, they will have to raise taxes. With our economy still operating at a low level and expected to for years, it is likely that the services offered by states in particular will see heightened demand for the next decade. Taxes in and of themselves are not bad or wrong, as long as they are determined by the constituents.

The spending changes discussed above will not completely bring cities and states back in line, but they will go a long way toward addressing the most out-of-balance problems that they face and will bring control over their budgets back to their own constituents. Just as with housing, there is no magic bullet in any of this, and there is a lot of pain to go around. Solving these fiscal woes most likely will require a combination of taxes and spending cuts. No matter how it is done, it should be done immediately. The current head-in-the-sand approach does not preserve the status quo, it moves us backward—because those who do business with insolvent cities and states, such as investors who buy their bonds and vendors who provide services, don't know what to expect. With big fiscal questions left unanswered, people start building in provisions for the worst case. This means that investors require a higher interest rate or vendors require quicker payment. Actions such as this make it even harder to operate. It's like giving a loan to someone who is financially questionable. You might make the loan, but you'd have a high rate of interest and a short time frame in which you wanted your money back. For someone who is financially shaky, just the terms of the loan make them even more fragile.

The Biggest Deadbeat of All: The US Government

As we outlined extensively, the federal government has two main debt problems, just like states: what it owes today (deficits and debt) and what it owes tomorrow (the incomprehensibly large unfunded liabilities of Social Security and Medicare).

Any conversation about deficits and debt that leave off defense, entitlements, and tax increases borders on intellectually dishonest. We acknowledge that there are ways of bringing our deficits immediately into balance and attacking the national debt, but these ways rely on a very strict adherence to the libertarian point of view and stand no chance at all of being adopted. Let's stick with the possible (or at least what we hope is possible!). We are going to cut defense spending and entitlements, as they are two of the biggest budget items, and of course we are going to raise taxes. The question is not if but when. Let's get it done right now.

We start with the Department of Defense (DOD), because it is the shortest conversation. We are not DOD experts and would not presume to tell the Joint Chiefs of Staff or Secretary of Defense exactly what cuts need to be made. Instead, we will recognize that the budget of the DOD represents 14% of the US budget, or roughly $714 billion. Per Wikipedia, US military spending in 2009 did not just represent the highest level of military spending of any country in the world; ours was more than the next 15 highest expenditures *combined!* We recognize that over $150 billion of this is for the wars in Afghanistan and Iraq, but still, roughly $550 billion is a lot of money, when the next highest level spending after us was China, at roughly $100 billion. As was already begun in early 2011, we should set a path for reducing this budget (the core, not the extra $150 billion, as the two war initiatives already have wind-down schedules) by 25% over 5 years and allow the department secretary to determine how the goal is met. We do have one suggestion: close some of the more than 1,000 military bases that the US maintains outside of the United States. According to Hugh Gusterson of George Mason University, US military bases abroad account for 95% of all military bases held on foreign soil (meaning that a country maintains the base outside of its own borders). This is a distinction that we could live without. Closing a fraction of them could save us tens of billions of dollars.*

Entitlement spending is going nowhere but up. When Social Security and Medicare were first introduced, they were pledged to be "off-budget," meaning that their surplus trust funds were never to be used for general government spending. That is a sham. The so-called trust funds purchased only one thing: US government bonds, so these trust funds are nothing but shell entities that collect money and hand it to the US government to spend any way it wants. That sure sounds like general government spending to us! Neither program is a savings arrangement by which those who pay in receive back their own money. Both programs are pay-as-you-go, meaning that current tax revenue is used to pay for current recipients. We have all hoped that in the future enough taxes would be paid in to pay for what will then be the current level of recipients. Not only will this not be true in the future, but it is not true today. Medicare began running a deficit in 2005, and Social Security fell to a deficit in 2010.

These programs now take in less money than they spend. They approach

---

* H. Gusterson, "Empire of Bases," *Bulletin of the Atomic Scientists,* March 10, 2009. Available at: http://www.thebulletin.org/web-edition/columnists/hugh-gusterson/empire -of-bases.

the US government to redeem their bond holdings in order to make all of their required distributions. Of course, the government has no money, so it simply issues even more bonds to other people to cover the redemption. This is all a shell game inside of the government. We must have a straightforward conversation about these programs, including what they are, who receives benefits, and how they are funded, so that we can address their drain on the current budget as well as their unfunded status in the years to come. We should immediately put these programs on the US budget, removing the accounting charade of keeping them separate. This action would cancel out over $3 trillion in US debt that is currently held by the trust funds for these entities. The US government owes the money, no matter what. Why keep the pretense going that this money is separate? This change would not do anything to affect the funding status of these programs; it would just more clearly identify who is receiving and paying out the funds (the US government). There is no savings, and there is no longer any surplus, which brings up the part that is hard to reconcile: there never was any savings, or at least there has not been for the last fifty years, because Social Security is not a retirement program at all.

Instead of having the psychology that "I've paid into it, so I deserve my part back out of it," let's look at the facts about this program. Social Security is an involuntary tax that is levied on wage earners. The benefits are not determined nor influenced by the desires of the recipients, and the investment of the trust fund dollars is not controlled by the recipients, and the returns on such investment are very minimal. We as taxpayers do not "own" the funds that we pay into the program, as a portion of the payments was always used to pay current recipients. There is nothing about this program that works like a retirement system except that we can begin drawing payments from it after a certain age, and even this can change without our consent. The Supreme Court found that Social Security benefits do not have to be granted and can be changed at any time at the whim of Congress. Does that sound like any retirement program that you would willingly sign up for? Anyone who believes this to be a retirement program is sadly mistaken. In the years that the program ran a surplus, our government used the excess as its own piggy bank to spend beyond even its already excessive deficit spending, and now those days are over.

There is no surplus, and workers do not own the program. Social Security is a wealth distribution program that takes funds from current workers and distributes them to retirees. That is it. All of the rest of the discussions around Social Security are merely semantics.

Once we come to grips with the true workings of Social Security, it becomes easier to discuss possible solutions to its funding status. Currently Social Security brings in enough to pay for itself, or very close to it. In the years ahead this will change. We will have workers retiring in very large numbers over the next 15 years who will swell the ranks of the program for the next four decades. Is this what we want? The very first question in deriving a solution is to ask if the program is in our national interest at all. With so many Americans dependent on these payments, we think that some form of Social Security should remain; however, we should critically evaluate how the program is operated.

Once we have acknowledged that Social Security is a welfare program rather than a retirement program, we should immediately change the eligibility requirements. We need gradually to phase out people who meet certain income and asset thresholds (and thus not send Social Security to those who are wealthy) and to stretch out the age range as to when benefits can be drawn. Right now recipients can draw their benefits at the ages and percentages listed below:

70% of full benefit at age 62
75% at age 63
80% at age 64
85% at age 65
93% at age 66
100% at age 67

There is no mathematical or biological explanation as to why these ages were chosen, we simply got stuck on age 65 at the end of the nineteenth century, and that has become the anchor for retirement age. If we change the full benefit age to 73, raise the minimum to at least 65, and lower the percentages for those at ages 65 to 72, starting with more like 50%, we will dramatically decrease the funding requirements of the program.

Between these two adjustments, the reduction or elimination of payments to those who hold wealth and the lower and later payments to recipients, we can cut trillions off of our enormous Social Security liability and reduce our current deficit as well.

On the revenue side, we could choose to tax all earned income (effectively removing the current cap of $106,800 that is taxed today), or we could forgo this tax altogether and roll it into the federal income tax code. This is a radical departure from what we do now, as this would immediately remove the poorest among us from paying anything into the program, placing the burden squarely on the shoulders of the top half of wage earners, as the bottom 50% pay almost nothing. The reason that we bring this up is to highlight what should be an honest conversation about Social Security, recognizing that it is a wealth transfer program from current workers to current retirees that the US government has skimmed money from for years. If the government wants to make a higher level of real retirement saving a national policy, then it could force a certain percentage of paychecks and self-employment income to go into personal retirement plans with a rising percentage over time. Such a plan could start at 1% and increase to 5% or higher by age 55. It is doubtful the American public would vote for that, even though this is exactly what has worked well in other countries, such as Australia.

Unfortunately Social Security, at a mere $16 trillion underfunded, is a "small" problem. Our larger issue is health care, specifically Medicaid and Medicare. We are not health care experts. We do not pretend to know all of the intricacies of the new health care law, Medicaid mandates, or the insurance regulations of the fifty states. Health care spending represents over 17% of GDP today and is rising rapidly, with its share of GDP expected to hit 20% in just a few years. The anticipated unfunded portion of Medicare is estimated to be $40 trillion, or almost three times our annual GDP, and we are certain this is a lowball number! Of course this won't work. We will ration care and we will refuse certain treatments and drugs. We must. But just like Social Security, we should recognize the nature of these (Medicaid and Medicare) programs: they are wealth transfer programs from current workers to retirees, the disabled, and the poor. These are not benefit programs! The government does not create health care, and it does not employ doctors (except for military doctors, of course). What we are providing is the economic ability to pay for health care. This is purely a transfer of paying ability, which is a transfer of wealth.

To get even close to adjusting these programs, we must address them just like Social Security. We can have benefits phase in over time, starting at age 65 and phasing in through age 72. We can also apply metrics for wealth and assets that phase in. The point is the same: to limit the wealth transfer to those who are truly in need. We also can immediately repeal the Medicare Part D program (prescription drug benefit) adopted under President George W. Bush. The point of this program was obvious: to assist seniors with the cost of prescriptions. But the execution did nothing but shift the cost to taxpayers in yet another wealth transfer program.

The 800-pound gorilla here is the hardest to address: at least half of health care costs come in the last 6 months of life. No one wants to see care options cut for relatives who are nearing death, but the trade-off is that younger families will not be able to afford adequate health care due to the rapidly rising costs of funding Medicare/Medicaid benefits as the baby boomers age rapidly in the next 3 decades. It simply doesn't make sense to pay $100,000 to $500,000 for transplants and operations that will keep people alive only another several months or less. These sorts of procedures have only emerged in recent years and decades due to the continued progress and innovation in health care. Just because such treatments and procedures exist does not mean we can afford to provide such luxuries never before known to mankind.

A certain level of health care may be deemed as a right—but providing unlimited health care absolutely cannot be done without bankrupting our government and robbing younger families of adequate and affordable health care.

As for how the programs are run, there is obviously much to be debated that is outside the scope of this book. However, we are very much more in favor of giving more flexibility to the states in terms of addressing the health care needs of their own constituents than a forced, top-down approach from the federal government. States like Arizona already have begun restricting what they will pay for in terms of health benefits. Such efforts will have to be expanded.

With 92 million baby boomers moving into retirement, we truly do not have the workforce necessary to pay for all of the benefits that have been promised. Our senior programs were designed for ever-increasing populations. That has not happened. Unless we want to bankrupt our country, we must make adjustments. The quicker we do this, the less painful these adjustments will be.

Considering Revenue: Taxes

The current financial crisis gives us the opportunity to address big problems. With such incredible dislocations in employment and personal finances now coupled with huge government deficits, people are open to change. We should take advantage of it. With radical adjustments presented on the expenditures or benefits side, we can turn our attention to the matter of taxes. We have been in a low-tax environment for two decades, which sounds great, except that the revenue was not enough to pay our bills even in the good years, so how can we expect this revenue to pay our bills in the lean years? It does not, and it will not. Some will point out that we had balanced budgets at the end of the 1990s, which is true, sort of. Those budgets did not take into account that we were spending the surpluses of Social Security and Medicare without counting it as deficit spending. Still, we are here in the 2010s, and we need more revenue. There are two things we can do immediately: attack the tax code and raise taxes. The more we do the former, the less we have to do the latter!

Our tax code is in shambles. It runs longer than 16,000 pages and is so difficult that according to the IRS, Americans spend 6.1 billion hours a year on tax compliance. Over 60% of Americans pay someone to prepare their taxes for them.* Why are taxes so complicated? Our elected officials have spent the last century (since federal income taxes were introduced in 1913) producing loopholes for special-interest groups as well as using the tax code to encourage or discourage certain behaviors. We get a break to have a mortgage. Our employer gets a break to provide us health care. We get a write-off when we have children and when we insulate our homes. The code contains thousands of items large and small that create a web of regulations that must be followed. To this end, tax avoidance has become a huge business. The final tally of all of those tax breaks is $1.1 trillion. Keep in mind, this is not the amount that is lawfully owed but not paid (which is estimated at over $100 billion annually); this is the amount that is legally *not owed* due to deductions and credits. If we moved to a simpler system, we could greatly reduce the effort required to file taxes and receive more revenue at the same time. Money would not be created out of thin

---

* *National Taxpayer Advocate Report to Congress,* January 5, 2011. Available at http://www.irs.gov/newsroom/article/0,,id=233959,00.html?portle t=7.

air, of course. If we simplify the system, then the real tax burden becomes evident to all, and then we can have a clear conversation about how much we as constituents of the United States believe should be sent to the federal government.

How would such a system work? The most plausible way seems to be a graduated tax scale. It could not be as simple as "send in 10% of what you make," which is a flat tax, because we are more progressive as a society. We give the least among us a break, and those who have more to shoulder the main burden. One possibility is to create a minimum income level below which no one pays taxes (except perhaps some level of Social Security or other retirement contribution), say $40,000. All income earned from $40,000 to $50,000 would be taxed at 10%, and all income from $50,000 to $60,000 would be taxed at 14%. After $60,000, all income would be taxed at 18%. After $100,000 it would rise to, say, 22%. This could be modified depending on the number of people in the household and with inflation and income gains over time. All income would be included, even unearned income, dividends, capital gains, and interest. There would be no more mortgage deduction, no child credit, no solar power rebate, no charitable giving deduction, or anything else. Corporate taxes could be set at 15%. No gimmicks, no subsidies, no carryovers or holdbacks, no deductions for insurance, no nothing. If you earn it, you pay your percentage.

This is not the only possibility. Another option is the fair tax, which taxes consumption. We do not believe that to be a workable plan because people can choose, and recently have chosen, to spend less. A third option is a true flat tax, and there are myriad other choices. Our point in bringing this up is to highlight a tremendous anchor on our system, the deduction-riddled tax code, which eats up so much in productivity and cost just to ensure compliance. There has got to be a better way.

In terms of raising taxes, simply put, we must. The extension of the current tax rates in December 2010 was fiscally irresponsible. The act created another $900 billion in deficits for the United States. In 2011 alone, our estimated deficit went from $1.1 trillion to $1.5 trillion during a stimulus-induced recovery that brought us back to near-normal levels of GDP growth! The underlying assumption is that if you raise taxes on consumers, then they will spend less. Because we want more spending, we should not tax them! While this is obviously true, it does not address the motivations of taxpayers. Because we have the large group of boomers moving to a point of saving more and spending less, keeping their taxes low is not going to spur higher spending. Consumers are not waiting to see their tax bill before they hit the malls. We can see this in the outcome of recent stimulus measures that put dollars in consumers' pockets. The consumers did not spend it all, not even close. While extraordinarily high tax increases definitely would impact spending and slow our economy even more, we are firmly convinced that returning to the tax levels that prevailed in the 1990s would not only be good for our fiscal health as a nation, but also would not be much of a blow to our consumers.

The fact that we took the opportunity in December 2010 to cut Social Security taxes in the name of stimulus just added insult to injury. The position of the White House was that this move did not change the long-term fiscal health of Social Security—and they were right! When you are underwater by $16 trillion, what's another $150 billion? The problem is that this is one more step in the wrong direction and does not address the right hot buttons for consumers. People do not want another 2% in their paycheck, although no one who got it would argue against it. What boomers in particular are going to want is long-term financial security with a guaranteed standard of living! That's not something that you can buy at Walmart.

In brief, we believe that in addition to all of the small programs and ear-marks that get so much attention in the papers, we will have to address the huge issues we face. These issues include the sacred cows of our national budget, items like defense, Social Security, and Medicare. The cuts will not be enough, and we will have to raise taxes. The question is not *if* we do these things, but how and when.

A Spending Plan We Need Right Now

We discussed above that we do not believe in forcing spending dramatically lower at this exact minute or raising taxes sky high. What we are in favor of is a series of planned, discrete steps to move us to a fiscally secure footing. Also, we pointed out repeatedly the utter failure of Keynesian economics, in that this approach of trying to stimulate demand through government spending absolutely does not work. It puts the government in debt and artificially increases prices in some areas. However, that does not mean that we are against government spending programs. In light of our current circumstances, there is one large area of our economy where we desperately need the intervention of an entity the size of the US government. We need to create jobs.

When we say this, we do it from the standpoint of recognizing that the jobs we are creating will not be for the benefit of any stimulus on the greater economy. The jobs we are discussing are solely for the purpose of allowing people who are currently out of work to earn a paycheck and to keep their employment skills sharp. We obviously would choose that the work to be done would be useful, so we as a nation should choose areas that have long-term benefits but high upfront costs, as those are the jobs that private industry would shy away from in today's economy. This approach would also lower the burden on unemployment compensation, which consumes tens of billions of dollars per year.

A jobs program could operate similar in nature to the Civilian Conservation Corps of 1939 or the Work Projects Administration. While we would not want to see the program get as big as a percentage of the workforce as either of those programs, we do believe that the government could employ an additional 3 million people, which is 2% of the labor force, in productive works. This could involve rebuilding our infrastructure, including aging roads, bridges, levees, and dams, as well doing as office work, such as digitizing health records. Have you applied for health or life insurance lately? It's always the same questions about doctors' visits from eight years ago. Who remembers that? VISA can pull up the record of a purchase at Lowe's 3 years ago, and yet our health records are still conveyed by fax and copy!

The US government passed an $800 billion stimulus in March 2009, and then another $900 billion stimulus (extension of tax cuts) in December 2010. These two programs equal $1.7 trillion and would have funded 3 million jobs at $566,000 apiece. We could pay 3 million workers $100,000 apiece for five and a half years! Obviously we could adjust the math and pay more workers a lower amount. This is what we should be doing, not as a stimulus plan, but as something of a placeholder until our economy begins to pick up again when the next generation, the children of the boomers, start pushing our economy higher.

Summary

The proposals we have outlined here are dramatic changes, but we have not made any outrageous claims of sudden recovery and growth. These changes are meant to recognize the limited ability of cities, states, and the federal government to pay benefits and to provide a path to fiscal balance. Through our research, we see flat or muted growth for years to come, leaving many government entities with no way to pay for the promises that they have made. If we begin to change our way of approaching and funding some of our biggest programs, we can at least ease some of the pain of the adjustment. It will take cuts to spending and increases in taxes, and even that will not be enough to get the economy back to full speed. We will have to develop some sort of plan for the millions of workers who are caught in this downturn and whose skills are becoming dull over time.

In this book we have outlined our situation today in terms of how we got here and what lies ahead. We have given you a framework for understanding the scope of our problems, the likely nature of the economy in the years ahead (deflationary), and even some ways of using the years ahead to your advantage. In the final chapter, I, Harry Dent, will broaden the picture, focusing on the long-term evolution of how we interface with each other through business, and how we are experiencing a revolution that is on par with the Democratic and Industrial Revolutions of the eighteenth century. We have an opportunity that is rarer than once in a lifetime—it is more like once in 250 or even 500 years—to be part of a quantum leap forward.

CHAPTER 12

The Greater "Network" Revolution Ahead: Like the American Revolution in Democracy and Industrial Revolution 250 Years Ago

Final Thoughts from Harry Dent About Our Longer-Term Future and Options

If there is one clear trend in human evolution, it is toward greater freedom . . . and you could also add to that rising income and standards of living, as they both tend to evolve together. Freedom typically does not come easy, and it is critical to building rising incomes. It took hundreds of years of basic economic development and growth, then decades of rebellion and years of war for the US to transition from a third-world colony to a self-governing democracy and leading nation—and a model one at that! And there have been long periods of time when such freedom and standards of living have retrenched in the world, like the Dark Ages from 450 to 950 or the Great Depression of the 1930s. But such periods only tend to lead to the next expansions in human freedom and prosperity.

Most people were slaves even in the prosperity of Ancient Roman times, and much more so before that. Recall the scene from *Ben-Hur* of the men being whipped and pushed beyond human limits to row the warships for the Roman navy in battle. Most people were treated more like we treat animals today (or worse) hundreds and thousands of years ago. Most people today live in third-world countries that are largely that way because one leader or regime controls all of the resources and wealth, as in

Myanmar and Libya, and local warlords who have similar control region-
ally in Afghanistan and many countries in Sub-Saharan Africa, like Sudan
and the Democratic Republic of the Congo.

Even China has an almost mafia-like government today, despite its
massive economic progress. Though that government seems to get the
credit for pushing the Chinese growth model so effectively, the bubble
burst we will likely see in the coming decade would bring that model into
question for the world and for the Chinese people, who are likely to have
their own revolution ahead—if only they had a younger, educated population like Iran, such a revolution would be a near certainty as it is in Iran.
People need freedom to grow and to gain from their own efforts if their
incomes, wealth, and contributions are going to grow. But younger, large
generations, like the one in America in the mid- to late 1700s, create such
revolutions. In recent decades the massive baby boom has created a new
revolution: from the 1960s and 1970s when the young boomers first ques-
tioned the "system and authority," as their spending increased, into the
2000s, and now the 2010s as they have aged and gained more power. Such
possibilities for freedom have been the highest in countries like the US,
Canada, Australia, and New Zealand—and in small island nations such
as Hong Kong and Singapore in East Asia. These countries tend to have
the highest standard of living and freedom in the world, along with many
countries in North and West Europe.

In Chapter 3 of *The Great Depression Ahead*, we looked at some very
long-term cycles, including a 5,000-Year Civilization Cycle wherein we
make major transitions: from living in towns first in places like Jeri-
cho 10,000 years ago to forming cities and trading centers first in areas
like Uruk in Mesopotamia and Luxor in Egypt 5,000 years ago. Today
we are witnessing the mere beginning of the transition to a global economy dominated by megacities with 10 million-plus populations, which
allow ever greater specialization of labor and the productivity that has
stemmed from such specialization throughout history, driven by innovations in technology and the growth of population centers. We looked at a
very clear 500-year cycle around mega-innovations and major population
surges, as we saw with the printing press, tall sailing ships, and gunpowder
in the mid- to late 1400s, and as we have been witnessing with the information revolution, and the development of atomic bombs, jet airplanes,

Chart 12-1: 250-Year Revolutionary Cycle

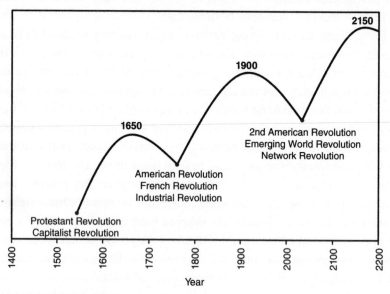

Data Source: **HS Dent Foundation**

computers, and TV almost exactly 500 years later—along with a massive baby boom generation and a powerful new, rising middle class around the world to leverage and adopt these new technologies.

The most prescient longer-term cycle that is hitting right now is the 250-Year Revolutionary Cycle that we show in **Chart 12-1.** This cycle couldn't be more obvious. We saw the Protestant Revolution in the early 1500s (leveraged by the new printing press), which liberated much of Europe from the iron rule and social laws of the Catholic Church, which had gained too much power. That revolution was followed by a very expansive period through the 1500s and early 1600s called the Elizabethan Golden Age, which was first adopted with the sanction of Henry VIII, Elizabeth's father, in England. Then we saw the American Revolution in the 1760s and 1770s, followed by the French Revolution. Economically, the very powerful Industrial Revolution that soon followed ultimately took root in the 1800s and 1900s in the growing nation state of America, which had vast land and resources to be exploited by railroads and myriad new technologies. America then led in innovation, especially in its deployment of electrical and assembly-like technologies, from the electricity and assembly-line revolution, from the early 1900s forward into the information revolution today.

From 2008 to 2023, as we have been forecasting for decades, another major political and social revolution is emerging. We have been calling it the Network Revolution. Paul Hawken in *Natural Capitalism* calls it the Second Industrial Revolution. It could be called the Asian Revolution, as Joel Kotkin first termed it, given that the two most populous countries with the most growth potential and most megacities in the world are China and India. China is starting to compete in leading-edge industries like alternative energy and biotech, and India in information technologies and movies. It could be called the Emerging World Revolution as this largest part of the world and population is just urbanizing and moving toward more capitalistic and democratic economic and political structures for the first time—some quickly, some slowly. But a revolution to overthrow past top-down government models and dictatorships will continue to be necessary and clearly is already occurring, as we also forecast many years ago.

The days for top-down, exploitative dictatorships in emerging countries is coming to an end. The same is true for top-down business and management models. Bottom-up, customer/citizen, and people-oriented models will be the key trend for decades to come—which simply means unleashing the freedom and power of more individuals to become more entrepreneurial and more focused on what they do best. The more obvious emergence of this trend will come from the global economic crisis between 2008 and 2023, as it takes a crisis to accelerate changes that should be occurring naturally. Old powers do not voluntarily give up their power. Britain did not give up its power over its colonies without a fight; the French monarchy did not give up its powers voluntarily; and Saddam Hussein and Muammar el-Qaddafi did not give up theirs.

We prefer the Network Revolution, as that title is more pervasive, and networks and the information technologies that enable them bring the ultimate in human freedom and user control—whether the users are voters in a developed country like the US, or citizens in a dictatorship like Libya or Sudan or Myanmar, or workers and customers for most companies. Companies commonly use advertising campaigns to associate their products with values you hold, even though that association has nothing to do with those products, simply to lure you in. Then of course there are the "fine print" clauses in their contracts that sting you when you least expect it. Do most companies actually have your best interests in mind? Economically, we are still slaves more than we would like to think. Here's the key point:

Portable computers, smart cell phones, and the internet allow information to be put directly into the hands of consumers, frontline workers, and voters, allowing them to make informed decisions and to see what is real and what is to their benefit, without as much top-down advertising, marketing, bureaucracy, management oversight, government, and controls as in the past. "Real-time, personalized service" and companies and governments that "revolve around their customers" become both possible and inevitable. We have always said, "Management is the problem, not the solution." Top-down systems are going to revert to bottom-up and customer/people-centric approaches ... much more than they were in the beginning stages in the recent boom.

Until recent decades, management was needed to coordinate scarce and expensive information and to hand down policies, rules, and orders to workers through a hierarchy of middle management and experts. Now management continues to exist largely because many people love having the power to boss people around and interfere in their lives, just like the affluent loved having slaves in the "good old days" and still moan privately about having to give that up. Power is a big ego trip.

Real power comes from leadership and influence, the ability to motivate people to a higher cause by giving them more freedom, incentives, information, and resources to accomplish their own goals within that greater cause. That is precisely why free-market capitalism has been more productive as a general rule vs. top-down and socialistic or communist-based governments that control and manipulate people more through fear and conformity than rewards, individual freedom, and aspiration.

Free-market capitalism has proven to be the best model since Adam Smith's "invisible hand" theory in the late 1700s, which also emerged with the last 250-Year Revolution. But there is a big caveat that has been learned slowly, albeit not by everyone as of yet:

Free markets need rules, just like any game. To unleash the power of the many, the greed and power of the few has to be curbed, and people

need to interact in a way that maximizes the benefits to the many, not just themselves or the few.

That is actually a spiritual law that the Indians call karma—actions that benefit others, and ultimately the most people, create the best karma (as you simply can't please all of the people all of the time with any decision or action). The "judgment" in classical Christian and Western spirituality ultimately revolves around "do unto others as you would have them do unto you," or as Jesus said more clearly: "Judge not, lest you be judged." Who would want other people pushing you into being who you are not and trying to get you to conform to the corporate or national standard of conduct and behavior? Or, in historical terms, who would want to be a slave or, in more modern terms, a mere subordinate employee? If you see other people as not being the way you want them to be or as having bad traits, then how could you not recognize the bad traits in yourself, or the "man in the mirror"?

How can we decide as presidents of countries, CEOs of companies, or department heads or team leaders how the people we oversee should be and how they should react and respond? There is a bell curve of capacities and qualities that seems already to be set by natural law. Everyone is different and everyone is a unique package, yet more people are more similar, i.e., "the middle class," today. Still, the greatest innovations and wealth are created by the 1% on one side, and the opposite 1% create the most crime and are in jail! Are you going to question that reality or solve that dilemma? Who are we to try to fit all of these different-shaped pegs into prescribed round holes? Who are we to question why it is that 1% of radical innovators and entrepreneurs most advance our standard of living, whereas similar people with similar aspirations fail and go bankrupt, and a seemingly equal number of others who question the status quo end up in jail? Do criminals not motivate us and prompt changes to society as much as successful entrepreneurs? Enterpreneurs and criminals both attack society and the status quo. Where is the good and bad in that? Copernicus and Galileo were seen as criminals. With their theories that the universe did not revolve around the earth, they were threats to the status quo in religion and the accepted values. They were forced to recant on threat of being burned at the stake, yet they were eventually recognized as the geniuses of their time, as was Darwin and others of keen insight.

The secret is to understand that people are different, that they are unique, but that they all tend to have the motive to "be someone." Everyone wants to have significance, to contribute and be recognized for who they are, which simply translates into "the pursuit of happiness," that was the foundation of the American Constitution almost 250 years ago. Which leads to the bigger secret: to motivate people, give them clear incentives to achieve their part in their own best way and have clear measurements of their results to reward them, or redirect them according to their results. As a mother, love people as they are, unconditionally; don't judge them and think they should be this or that way. But equally, as a father, hold them to growth, goals, and accountability for results—and reward them for that directly, not just for the overall results of the company or country, which are natural to a degree anyway. Who doesn't benefit from being involved in a company, culture, or country that is succeeding and growing?

As we commented in Chapter 10 and covered in depth in Part 3 of *The Roaring 2000s* (1998), business owners and managers should simply see and conceive of their companies as individuals and small frontline teams or "browsers." These people or teams should be focused on serving the unique needs of small groups of similar customers for greater customization and personalization of services—which adds the most value and benefits—and can respond in real time, not in days, weeks, or months. Then organize your product, service, and specialized experts into backline "servers" that respond in the same real-time framework to the needs of your frontline browsers, not your previous top-down hierarchy and bureaucracy that took forever to organize things into batches and worked on the principle that they would respond when they had time and felt like it.

Have rules for decisions, and incorporate fixed and variable costs of all frontline and backline teams into your software so that all can make decisions effectively and in real time. If possible, the profits of those decisions should get reflected in real time as well. In this way, each individual or team operates just like a small, highly motivated, and accountable business. Their survival and success depend on their customers and their profitability! Units that are profitable and are growing get increasing autonomy and capital resources to keep growing, making decisions, and serving the company's customers. The frontline browsers are the customers of the backline servers. Management's role, like in the already real-time stock exchanges that we give as an example, is to design the "network" rules, goals, measurements, and profit systems, and to make the mission, strategic direction, and focus of the company clear. What does the company do best, and where does it struggle? Where do we want to grow, focus, and dominate, depending on our core strengths? If some unit discovers, by mistake or brilliance, a very new and profitable direction, then the vision may get revised a bit or even radically. Management becomes a great enabler, but increasingly invisible. Hence, it is no longer "the problem" but the solution to more rewarding and profitable work, as well as lower cost and more customized products and services.

Management's goal should be to make every individual and/or frontline and backline team a real business with real customers, clear goals, and a measured bottom-line profit and loss. We as individuals should simultaneously strive to create and become our own business within our companies or outside of them . . . doing what we love and do best, being more in control of our own destinies, contributing the most we can, and being the most we can be.

In this context more of us can work, part time or full time, from our own homes and make use of those extra bedrooms and the McMansions that are now increasingly obsolete as our kids leave the nest. This saves commuting, auto and energy costs, extra real estate in office buildings, heating and air-conditioning costs, and on and on. There is always a better way to organize and do business. There are always ways that we as individuals can specialize and focus more on what we do best and delegate more tasks to others who do what they do best.

The history of growing human freedom and our rising standard of living can best be summarized as new technologies that allow us to reorganize production, business, and organization to create greater entrepreneurial activity and greater specialization of labor. That paradoxically creates rising inflation as we all earn more but delegate more tasks to others and pay more for increasingly efficient products and services.

That is why we have always viewed inflation as a sign of human progress, not as an evil to be fought. Inflation from waste, excessive artificial stimulus, and debt shorter term is another issue—but is the exception more than the rule in history. The real truth is that our human progress has been marked by both rising inflation and rising standards of living. Inflation just tends to lead by 10 to 30 years over history. The greatest inflationary period in modern history, the 1970s, was followed by the greatest boom in history, peaked in 2007, 27 years after the peak in inflation in 1980!

That brings us back to the argument of free markets vs. socialism and so on. Unfettered free markets with no rules end up with mafias in control both at the highest and at the local levels. We've just seen how the power of the few can wreck the largest and wealthiest and seemingly most free-market-oriented economy, as well as bring the world down with it. This occurred just when the few rules we had were largely abandoned as the system seemed to be working better than ever!

We have commented in our past books that free-market capitalism and democracy work well together precisely because they largely work on opposite principles. Capitalism rewards the fittest to survive and gives them the greatest rewards, like nature. But nature also rewards cooperation for survival, and that is often less noticed. Democracy gives everyone an equal vote, even if they don't have equal resources or economic power. That tends to force the system to curb the power of the most successful and creates systems that protect the rights of the individual, busting monopolies and giving way to innovations like Chapter 11 bankruptcy, which allows individuals who fail to reorganize their debts and not be banished to "the dungeons." Such a system will tend to punish and curb the powers of the major financial and government institutions, the very ones that allowed this unprecedented bubble in credit and real estate to be so "unprecedented."

Going back to Adam Smith's "invisible hand," the principle was that if you have freer markets and greater individual initiative, then the system works toward greater goals and progress from the bottom up, not by top-down design or something like "power to the people." Today's technology and economies have taken that to even higher levels. Consumers and workers not only have instant access to information and knowledge, but they have new information infrastructures like Amazon and eBay, where people can market products, services, and skills they have through a powerful distribution channel that is already set up and inexpensive to access. People can form and join like-minded lifestyle and interest groups with people almost anywhere in the world and have social and economic relationships with them without any big company structures—through blogging, Facebook, Twitter, and so on.

These same information technologies spread faster to emerging countries once they have developed here, albeit often in more basic forms. The Network Revolution brings more information through TV, the internet, PCs, and most often just basic cell phones to people in emerging countries who previously had little access to information and could more easily be controlled and manipulated by top-down governments, just like top-down management in organizations. It's not long before they see how much they are being held back by dictators like Qaddafi in Libya and then learn how much money he had stashed in the US and Switzerland, and how much better other people in other countries live. The next thing you know, they are rioting and protesting and leading a revolution. The same phenomenon occurred in the Soviet Union into the 1980s, when TV infiltrated that country, giving rise to its citizens' discontent with its top-down rule. We were predicting in Chapter 9 of *The Great Depression Ahead* that between 2008 and 2023 we would see many dictators and corrupt governments overthrown in emerging countries. In 2011 we already see riots and protests across the Middle East and North Africa, and a few dictators and powerful leaders have already stepped down.

It will take many years and even decades to truly see fruitful revolutions that result in more democratic political and capitalistic economic structures in more countries in the emerging world, and many will fail at first. This is very likely to be the biggest revolution that has ever hit the emerging world, where 5 billion people and all of the population growth for 5 decades now reside.

In Chapter 6 of *The Great Depression Ahead,* we show in depth why such emerging countries, including China, will not be nearly as rich as the US. The best, like Malaysia, achieve per capita GDP of only $10,000 as they urbanize more fully, but that is still far richer than many countries, like Kenya, that still have closer to $1,000 per capita GDP. An estimated 2 billion people in the emerging world live on less than $2 a day. With demographics growing slowly at best in most developed countries and, at worst, populations shrinking in some, almost all of the growth ahead is likely to come in the emerging world for many decades ahead.

Although China is the second largest economy in the world, it is still far behind the US, with total GDP in 2010 of $5.3 trillion vs. $14.6 trillion for the US, and roughly $3,900 GDP per capita vs. $47,400 in the US. When adjusted for purchasing power, China's GDP per capita is more like

$7,400. Either way, the US GDP per capita is 12.2 times China's in dollars, and 6.4 times in purchasing power—a huge gap. Note that in 1989 economists were predicting that Japan would overtake the US economy by 2010, but now it has slipped to the third largest economy in the world and has slowing growth in demographics, workforce, and population as far as the eye can see. Similar forecasts are made for China to overtake the US due to its massive 1.3 billion in population vs. the US with 300 million. But China's population will age faster than that of the US after 2015, with its workforce slowing after then and more so after 2035. China would have to achieve GDP per capita of $13,000 plus (3.3 times 2010 levels) in today's terms to achieve an economy the size of the US in the decades ahead. How is it going to do that with a contracting and aging workforce? Our projections for China at the highest urbanization remotely possible, 80% (vs. 45% today), would be $8,800 in today's values. Hence, the US will still be the largest economy in the world in our lifetimes, unless something we can't comprehend or project occurs.

On the other hand, China is now the biggest polluter. Less affluent countries typically can't afford the pollution controls that more affluent countries can, and frankly they don't tend to care as much, any more than we did 50 to 100 years ago. China also has the fastest-growing military and navy. Its growing power has its dangers, as China clearly doesn't see eye to eye with the developed-country leaders in North America and Europe, as it and Russia almost always tend to side with rogue dictators whenever the actions of these "crazy" leaders come to a head, largely because they fear their more dictatorial powers will be threatened by the greater economic and political power of the US and Europe. Was Saddam Hussein sane? Or his two kids? Does Qaddafi from Libya seem like he is a bit delusional, like most dictators? And did it make sense that he had $30 billion stashed in US banks? Did he have the best interests of his citizens in regard? Does China's unprecedented pollution, which impacts its own citizens and its environment most directly, and that spills into the rest of the world, make sense? What rights do their citizens have to fight this? What leverage does the rest of the world have to fight this? What rights do people in the emerging world have to fight the pollution that the much more energy-intensive developed countries have foisted on their environments and the world?

We need a more effective global government infrastructure to deal with the increasing number of global issues that cannot be resolved at national levels. We need a "new deal" between the more affluent developed countries and the less affluent but growing emerging countries. The developed countries are more concerned about pollution and environmental issues. So why not trade investments in infrastructure and green technologies, both for a share of the returns and the pollution savings that affect the global environment? Why not invest in building branch campuses of our more highly regarded educational universities in countries like India?

The almost total lack of decisive action on the growing and massive crisis in global pollution—and its most obvious symptom, global warming—shows that we simply do not have the global political infrastructures necessary for an increasingly global economy. We also have little ability to resolve major political violations by countries such as Iran, Iraq, or Sudan, or even China or Russia. Would we allow these countries' transgressions to occur within our own country? Sanctions rarely work, nor do military interventions like the US invasions of Iraq and Afghanistan. That unilateral policy has seemed to be more of a disaster without worldwide support. These actions would not even have been necessary if there were global institutions that had clear vision, sanction, and power to act. Such institutions are more likely to emerge in the global crisis ahead into 2023.

There is a continued debate globally and even within the US (but not as much within Europe) about whether global pollution is an important issue. Within the scientific community, it is a serious concern, and more a matter of how much, where, and when it will impact. We have been raping our oceans and the world's largest rain forests, which are CO_2-recycling machines, destroying the very species that we depend on for food, treating animals like we were treated as slaves in the past, polluting waterways, exhausting our soils, and, more basically, simply refusing to pay the simple and clear expense to recycle our waste. Our fast food and heavily processed meats and grains are making the wealthiest citizens in countries like the US fatter than in any time in history and far more prone to heart disease, diabetes, and cancer. Now these diseases are spreading even faster in emerging countries. Global warming is partly a natural cycle, but much more recently a human-created cycle as well—growing slowly since the acceleration of our Agricultural Revolution 5,000 years ago, and exponentially since our Industrial Revolution over 200 years ago. Scientists have identified very predictable long-term cycles in climate, and we are much warmer today than we should be on those cycles, which tends to prove the "global warming" argument despite some shorter-term cycles that are moving in that direction as well.

I had a response from a newsletter subscriber in which he decried the government's fight against rising CO_2 levels and global warming describing climate change as a "giant hoax." My only response was, "If you think exponentially growing CO_2 levels in the atmosphere are OK, then go suck on your car's tailpipes for a few minutes!" That may seem cruel, but it is similar to the reality we are trying to bring you about our economic, demographic, and overall future after the greatest bubble boom in history. People just naturally tend to get very delusional about the future. Our future is not so good, or bad, for that matter, just our delusions about it. Issues like pollution and global warming are also opportunities for new industries and technologies to address them.

In *Natural Capitalism*, the authors make a clear argument for how companies and their production and delivery systems could be redesigned to create massively less waste and pollution, and the savings from such wastes would make them even lower-cost and more competitive over time, if they had the vision and guts to make such investments. The principles are similar to those that drive the new "Network Corporation" that we discuss. But those principles are the opposite of what management has been used to doing in the last century or more. The new principles include producing directly to demand, not inventories; continuous flow processes with quality control handled by the production workers as they occur; sourcing more locally, not globally; targeting zero waste at all levels, and many others that we don't have time to address here.

Beyond all of these new opportunities to restructure our organizations and production processes for a cleaner and lower-cost world, we in countries like the US should literally kiss the ground and just be thankful we were even born here or immigrated here, legally or illegally. We should be thankful that we made the unprecedented progress we and other developed countries have made in the last three decades, the last 200 years, the 1,000 years before that, and so on. Even with this progress, we should always reevaluate and discern where it has been real and where we have cheated to get ahead.

The reality is that our progress in the last decade has been made more from debt and delusion than real progress, and increasingly at the expense of our environment for decades and centuries. Our environment and natural resources, which have developed over the ages, are like our natural capital that we take for granted but are immensely valuable. How could anyone argue against protecting and preserving such capital resources? Erasing the great bubble in debt and asset prices only means going back to the years 1996–2000 in home values or 1993–1995 values in stocks, not back to the 1930s or the Stone Age! But the revolution that occurs from such an extreme boom and this bust to follow will be the real reward for decades to come, as it was from the 1940s onward in the last 80-year economic cycle, and from the early 1800s forward in the last 250-Year Revolutionary Cycle.

From the broader and environmental point of view, we have made unprecedented gains in our standard of living and freedoms in the last 250 years, yet we aren't willing to make a small sacrifice in investments and costs near term to better recycle our wastes and to better sustain our food and natural support systems—we are throwing rotting trash in our own yards and getting used to the smell! The investments and costs required to deal with this would actually make us more productive longer term. It is very similar to our debt and credit bubble, where we tried to get more and more without paying the real price in savings for our future retirement. And we are willing to accumulate evermore private and government debt and obligations that doom our children and grandchildren—even as we decry our government's irresponsibility as the sole cause! We are often questioning the government's stimulus programs but quietly tolerating them and getting used to the smell of stubbornly high long-term unemployment and ever stagnating home prices and rising foreclosures.

We have all contributed to this unprecedented bubble in debt, real estate, and financial markets, as well as to the growing environmental crisis. I still like my "fast and fuel-inefficient car" even as I drive it less now that I work largely from my home. It is the classic "try to get something for nothing" principle that has always plagued human nature. Life is hard, progress is hard, attaining freedom is hard . . . and at some point you just want to believe that it can become easy. You can retire as an internet stock investor or a real estate flipper, and so on. That's why we get bubbles in the Fall Season, just when technology and economic progress are at their greatest, inflation and interest rates are falling, and it seems the boom will go on forever. As we commented in Chapter 2, such bubbles in the Fall Season actually have an important purpose and function. They maximize experimentation in new business models and the entrepreneurial spirit with easy access to credit and capital when new technologies are changing the potential for growth and our standard of living for many decades into the future.

The reality is that 90% or more of those new business models and new ventures from the Fall Season will fail. The Winter Season quickly lays low the weak competitors and then clears out those failing businesses, the debt that came with the bubble, and the banks and financial institutions that financed that debt. The best business models, businesses, banks, and institutions survive and get stronger in their market share and scale from the failure of their competitors, then bring the new technologies, products, and services to even greater mass affordability along with increasing the wages of the workers that produce them so they can afford them. Did this not happen in the last century with electricity, autos, phones, electrical appliances, the assembly-line revolution, worker wages and middle-class incomes, greater wealth and retirement benefits, and even greater freedoms? This progress was only more apparent in the top 10% of households in the Roaring '20s boom or Fall Season, and the rich benefited much more, as they have in this bubble boom from 1983 to 2007. But the middle-class household benefited more from the Winter Season that followed the boom, and then the Spring and Summer Seasons that came after. That will occur again, with the emerging world being the greatest beneficiaries from a global perspective.

The only problem was that we abused the natural bubble of the Fall Season to unprecedented degrees, and now we have to restructure the debt we incurred and get real about the benefits and entitlements that were promised to us. We have to restructure all of the debts in our country, and around the world, like a simple Chapter 11 process in business. This will in great part mean accepting that much of the retirement and health care benefits promised from all entities—from our companies, state and local governments, and the federal government—were simply unrealistic! Let's accept that, get over it, and move on like adults instead of children.

Now back to the dynamic between free-market capitalism and democracy. The same dynamics come from booms and busts. It is actually the busts that foster the next great innovations out of the achievements, failures, and excesses of the past boom. Then those innovations move mainstream and flower the most in the boom to follow. The same dynamic comes from males and females. Males are designed more to be focused on the future, achieve goals, conquer and, for most of their evolution, to hunt. Females are designed to be more laterally focused on relationships, to raise and nurture children, and to socialize and gather. They are more sensitive and balance the male tendency and vice versa.

We need to balance the massive debt and imbalances from this great bubble boom, both from the longer perspective of the last 250-Year Revolution since the late 1780s, as shown in **Chart 12-2,** repeated from Chapter 9, and from the extreme end of this long boom in the Roaring 2000s, from 2002 to 2007/2008, with the greatest real estate and credit bubble in

Chart 12-2: Stocks from 1700 to Present

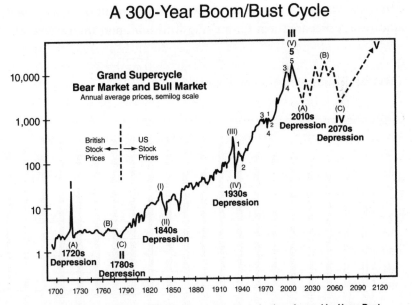

A 300-Year Boom/Bust Cycle

Data Source: Robert Prechter, *Conquer the Crash,* pg. 33, with projections forward by Harry Dent

modern history. It will take this next decade to do this, and it will happen more easily, or with more difficulty, depending on how we react at all levels.

We are facing two monumental challenges:

1. **Growing environmental pollution, which threatens the environment itself and also threatens our standard of living if it continues to deteriorate and ultimately fails, and**
2. **The slowing in population growth that is inevitable, given long-term trends in lower birthrates in an increasingly urban world that sees higher financial costs and the loss of more social opportunities from having and raising more children.**

Chart 12-3 shows the projected peak in world population around 2065, given clear demographic trends in birthrates and rising life expectancies. As we have grown more affluent and more urban, we have naturally had fewer children, as they are more expensive to raise in an urban world and they are less useful economically than they were on the farm. In addition, our social opportunities have grown, and too many children interfere with those. More of us want to have fewer children, allowing us to better educate and prepare them for a rising world of opportunity. This move

Chart 12-3: Projected Human Population, 2010–2100

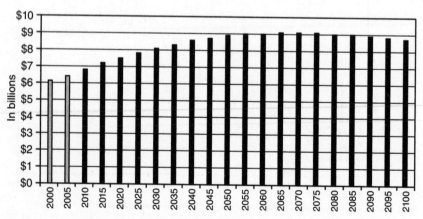

Data Source: Investor's Business Daily, 4/22/2004, Pg A16

to fewer children is slowing our growth, which slows innovation from younger people and growth in income and in spending capacity to follow as they mature.

Chart 12-4 shows the bubble in human population for thousands of years that has accelerated dramatically since the late 1700s and the last 250-Year Revolution in democracy and industry. If bubbles ultimately peak and correct, then this is very scary! This would say that the peak in human population projected for around 2065 could be a longer-term peak and be followed by a major drop sometime in the future. Could this be from a major environmental disaster created from our own technological success, near term or decades ahead? As a long-term student of cycles and bubbles, I would almost have to assume that to be the case at some point. At the same time, technology visionaries like Ray Kurzweil project that by the 2040s we will reach "the Singularity," where computer technologies exceed our human intelligence and our brains and body parts can be replaced and we live forever!

Chart 12-4: Exponential Population Growth Over the Past 10,000 Years

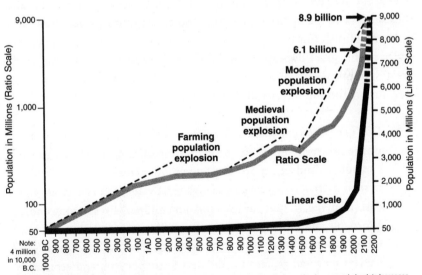

*Ratio scale shows constant percentage growth rate as a straight, upward-sloping line; linear scale shows equal absolute increases, so steady percentage growth rate; to curve up.
Source: *Forbes*, January 25, 1999, pp 58-59.
Research: Edwin S. Rubenstein, research director, Hudson Institute, Indianapolis.
Data: Colin McEvedy and Richard Jones, *Atlas of World Population History:* UN Secretariat, World Population Prospects: The 1998 Revision: Census Bureau.

So what is the future? All I know is that the reality of this inevitable economic downturn ahead will force decisions and structures for the better, as the greatest decisions and actions come in a real crisis when people at all levels are finally forced to face the truth and reality. There is no doubt we do have such a crisis ahead from 2012 into 2015, and longer into the early 2020s by our best calculations, which led us decades ago to see the unprecedented boom in the 1990s and 2000s.

We in the developed world may not be able to grow as fast as we have in the past few hundred years, but with greater innovation and longer work spans beyond the traditional retirement ages of 62 to 65 (which are already obsolete), we can make gains from greater productivity and new industries that address our needs for aging and the environmental and green revolution that will likely become even more obvious and urgent in the crisis ahead. But how many older people expect to grow as fast physically as they did from age 1 to 14, or emotionally from age 12 to 26, or financially from age 26 to 46, or in wealth from age 46 to 63? The biggest payoff in retirement is finally accepting who you are and what you really want to do in life now that your obligations for raising your kids are over, and you don't have to be so sexy anymore, etc. Many older people report having the best sex ever despite their declining capacity, simply because they don't have the need to "perform" and be someone they are not.

We will finish this book with the summary of the most important principles of this great depression and deflation ahead that will usher in the greatest political, social, and organizational revolution since the American Revolution and the Industrial Revolution:

1. **Don't see this very challenging time as a threat, but as an opportunity to preserve your assets and gains from this unprecedented boom and bubble, and an opportunity for you, your country, and the world to shed itself of costly debts and high asset values like real estate and costs of living, so that our lives and our children's lives become more affordable and prosperous again. You will be able to invest and buy things at much lower costs in the coming years and decade, if you harvest now and replant for the next Spring Season and economic cycle to come.**

2. **Don't be blind to the environmental crisis that has been building for centuries, especially in the last several decades. See it as the natural**

outcome of our unprecedented technological progress in the last 250 years and more. See it as an opportunity to learn from our excesses and develop whole new approaches to growth and progress that are more balanced, fair, and sustainable.

3. Don't see the growing political, ethnic, and even terrorist threats in the world as insurmountable problems. See them as a wake-up call for us to expand our consciousness and unlearn the cultural and religious biases we have accumulated, so we can create a greater global economy with new governmental structures that can make this a more win-win world in the future—both for the aging developed countries and the younger, emerging countries that will create more of the growth going forward.

4. See this time of challenge as an opportunity to accelerate our ever-growing pursuit of greater freedom, security, and higher standards of living. This very crisis will force us to shed old government, management, and work models faster than we did in the great boom that made us all more complacent in the past decades, despite very clear new models for growth emerging.

5. As business owners, managers, and entrepreneurs, understand the very clear principles of information technologies, network logic, and organization. These principles allow us to become freer, more entrepreneurial—and to create organizations and work environments that revolve around the end customer and from the bottom up, not the top down. They bring greater customization in products and personalization in service, and a greater sense of personal significance and contribution for the employees . . . what we all want!

6. Be more proactive in this crisis, not reactive. Don't merely blame others. See your own role in the bubble and the crisis . . . and "do unto others as you would have them do unto you; judge not, lest you be judged!" Don't focus only on your survival and prosperity in this crisis—help others to as well. And do it in your own personal mission and business that you create within your company or outside of it!

As a final parting insight: learn to appreciate the natural cycles and processes of life. Cycles are everything to my research and learning—from the smallest to the largest cycles. Our research has focused more on demographic trends and cycles of 40 and 80 years. But these cycles have become dominant only over the last century as technologies and organizational innovations have allowed everyday people to drive economic trends due to their mass affluence. Cycles and changes may seem to be fair or not fair at times. They may seem to be leading more to progress or not at all, at times. But our creator or the universe, or however you tend to see it, did not create such cycles and the "four seasons" that pervade everything we have studied about the largest and smallest cycles of life and evolution for no reason! There is a logic and design inherent in life that only creates higher evolution, greater freedom, standards of living, and consciousness—whether we understand that process fully or not. We can never understand this greater process fully, as much as many scientists, and our own researchers, are trying to.

Our research has evolved the most when we have failed and have had to reevaluate our most cherished principles and assumptions. You can't be the toenail and understand the entire human body. We can't be a small part of the universe and all of creation and fully understand the whole of it. We can only continue to grow and learn by succeeding and failing. But the ultimate truth seems to be that we learn the most when we fail, as that is when the paradox of learning from "unlearning" most comes.

This next decade is one of those unique times in human history when we can unlearn the very principles that have brought us such great and unprecedented success, just in time to reinvent ourselves and many of our principles and institutions so as to then experience the next "golden age" that we cannot yet conceive. Where we are in the cycle naturally dictates a more challenging time for us in the coming years and decades to reinspect everything before we move forward again.

Best of success to you in navigating the most challenging and most opportune Winter Season ahead, and the greater revolution in human freedom . . . the greatest since the American Revolution in democracy 250 years ago.

You can get free access to Harry's very popular webinar "Understanding the Economy and What Lies Ahead" by registering at http://www.hsdent.com/webinar.

FARMING'S CHANGING ROLE IN THE NATION'S ECONOMY
1900   41 percent of workforce employed in agriculture.
1930   21.5 percent of workforce employed in agriculture; agricultural GDP as a share of total GDP, 7.7 percent.
1945   16 percent of the total labor force employed in agriculture; agricultural GDP as a share of total GDP, 6.8 percent.
1970   4 percent of employed labor force worked in agriculture; agricultural GDP as a share of total GDP, 2.3 percent.
2000/02   1.9 percent of employed labor force worked in agriculture (2000); agricultural GDP as a share of total GDP (2002), 0.7 percent.

Source: Compiled by Economic Research Service, USDA. Share of workforce employed in agriculture, for 1900-1970, *Historical Statistics of the United States*; for 2000, calculated using data from Census of Population; agricultural GDP as part of total GDP, calculated using data from the Bureau of Economic Analysis.

Index

About the Authors

Harry S. Dent Jr. is the president of the HS Dent Foundation, whose mission is "Helping People Understand Change." He is the founder of HS Dent, which publishes the *HS Dent Forecast* and the *HS Dent Perspective.* He oversees the HS Dent Financial Advisors Network. He is the author of the *New York Times* bestseller *The Great Depression Ahead*, as well as of *The Great Boom Ahead*, in which he stood virtually alone in accurately forecasting the unanticipated "boom" of the 1990s. A Harvard MBA, Fortune 100 consultant, new venture investor, and noted speaker, Mr. Dent is a highly respected figure in his field.

Rodney Johnson is the president of HS Dent, an independent economic research and investment management firm. He oversees the Dent ETF and is a regular contributor to the *HS Dent Forecast* and the *HS Dent Perspective.* A graduate of Georgetown University and Southern Methodist University, Mr. Johnson is a frequent guest on radio and television programs to discuss economic changes in the United States and around the world.

Get More Information in the HS Dent Forecast Newsletter.

If you trust Harry Dent's enormous capacity to see, understand, interpret, and advise on our global economic future, then you won't want to be without his newsletter!

If what you read in this book got your attention, then you should stay informed through Harry Dent's monthly newsletter.

This will allow you to continually and accurately react to market conditions, such as the direction of mortgage rates, real estate prices, the prices of oil/gold/commodities, trends in the stock market, inflation, the federal budget, currencies, unemployment, and much more. Imagine having vital information to assist you in making the right choices, at the right time, throughout these dangerous economic times! Such a newsletter is not just valuable; it is invaluable!

"Thank you, Harry! With the information you provided in last month's (April 2011) report about sentiment readings on silver was invaluable. We managed to exit our entire client base using his idea of a trailing stop-loss on the precious metals holdings that you spoke about on the telephone conference calls (average exit was $45). This was a massive profit position for our clients and it would have not been possible without the help of you and your team. I still have the original charts where you forecasted silver would go from $12 to $30 plus per ounce. Harry, you were spot-on. Keep up the great work."—Alex Jamieson, Australia

"As an entrepreneur, I find the knowledge in HS Dent's Monthly Economic Forecast extremely helpful in targeting new business ventures. From upcoming technologies to understanding the right demographic for our targeted marketing or whether or not I should expand my business or take a step back, Dent's economic forecast has provided me with an excellent benchmark for making critical strategic decisions."—Steve H., Sequoia Unlimited, LLC

For only $397 per year (only $45 more for the Audio/MP3 version) as of this writing, you'll have ongoing access to Harry Dent's decades of experience and research. Few others possess his understanding of how the economy works, as well as the tools needed to accurately forecast what lies ahead. It is this body of knowledge and these forecasting tools that are shared with you each month in his newsletter. You can in turn use this information to make more informed life decisions regarding your finances, real estate, employment or your business, and even family affairs. In effect, Harry Dent becomes your own economic research team, your own economic think tank, from which you can gain insight.

Plus, You'll Get Free Updates, As Needed, Between Issues . . .

To thrive in this hostile environment, you'll need to know what important, even critical economic events are happening every day, and how Harry Dent suggests you react to these events on a moment's notice. Your newsletter subscription includes FREE e-mail updates. These updates will come as needed between newsletter issues. So as a newsletter subscriber, you'll miss nothing important. If something critical happens, and in the months and years ahead this could be often, you'll know about it and what to do about it *instantly!*

If you want this kind of high-level assistance, call now. You can choose a very affordable one—or two-year subscription. Plus, you can also get an audio version of the newsletter, so you can listen to it anywhere.

See What People Are Saying . . .

"Harry's latest update is excellent. Very well presented, with just the right balance of detail and overall concepts. It makes me feel confident in the depth of your team's analysis, and I appreciate the work that goes into that. Keep on doing great updates as we move into the coming economic transitions."
—L. W. Bardell

"I have found Harry Dent's newsletter absolutely invaluable. It helped me not only make a great deal of money, but to avert a financial disaster. I first became a subscriber around 2001, and through his newsletter I was not only able to make a great deal of money buying beachfront real estate as

investments before the real estate boom really got started. Then, thanks to his newsletter, I sold all my investment properties two months before the peak, and then put the profits into real estate in India, where I'm already up 150% to 200%."—A.J., Fort Lauderdale, FL

Purchase a subscription to the HS Dent Forecast Newsletter and get a 90-Day risk-free Trial! Visit: http://www.hsdent.com/newsletter

Special FREE Offer: Watch Harry S. Dent, Jr.'s Public Presentation in Webinar Format, FREE!

First of all, we want to thank you for reading *The Great Crash Ahead.* I hope you enjoyed it and . . . more important . . . I hope you will use Harry Dent's uncannily accurate, in-depth research to get the edge you need to make smart financial decisions from this day forward.

For over twenty years Harry has educated hundreds of audiences and consulted numerous well-known business leaders, key politicians, influential investors, and high-level CEOs about which direction the economy will turn in the months and years ahead.

Now, here's something you **don't** know . . .

Harry is compensated upwards of $50,000 by major corporations and conferences across the globe to share his research with their employees and shareholders; arming them with the very best economic education so they can make the best business and investment decisions possible. But you can watch an online version of Harry's presentation for FREE!

During this presentation you'll get a crystallized version of Harry's forecast of the long-term direction of the US and global economies. More importantly, you'll learn how you can prepare your business and/or investments for the imminent changes on the horizon. We have found through past experience that our readers get a clearer summary of the future from this presentation that focuses on the three major factors for the decade ahead: demographics, debt, and deflation.

On this webinar presentation Harry offers specific strategies on how to protect your current assets and business, how to prosper from the economy no matter what direction it goes, and provides details to back up his analysis.

When you watch the presentation you will learn:

- WHAT IS REALLY DRIVING THE ECONOMY TODAY: The real-world truth that will allows you to improve your trading and investing, protect your business, and keep your family's well-being safe and sound. Discover the biggest drivers in the current economy to leverage your success to the maximum.
- WHAT TO EXPECT ABOUT THE ECONOMY IN THE NEXT TWO TO TEN YEARS: To uncover new opportunities (and risks) so you're not making business and financial decisions in the dark.
- CURRENT U.S. ECONOMIC GROWTH FACTORS: How you can easily forecast booms and recessions in advance . . . and to exploit these extreme changes to your greatest benefit.
- WHY DEFLATION AND NOT INFLATION IS ON THE HORIZON: With deflation your business and investment moves are completely different than with inflation. Understand that difference and you will know which way to turn.
- THE TRUE "800-POUND GORILLA" IN TERMS OF THE ECONOMY: The so-called experts aren't talking about this . . . leaving you at maximum risk if you are not aware of the consequences.
- MAJOR TURNS IN THE STOCK MARKET AND OTHER INVESTMENT SECTORS: Now you can gain the supreme confidence to make the correct adjustments to your long-term retirement or 401(k) plans.
- And much more . . .

Now you can discover what Harry Dent has revealed to some of the world's most elite members of the financial and business landscape . . . and find out exactly how to use these insider forecasts and strategies to improve your own life to the fullest.

So don't you owe it to yourself, your company's competitive advantage, or even to your loved ones to provide the best life for them possible?

Take an hour or so from your busy schedule and sit in on Harry S. Dent Jr.'s provocative and informative webinar.

This is an easy decision.

Take advantage of this offer TODAY, and register on the webpage below to gain access to Harry S. Dent Jr.'s presentation: http://www.hsdent.com/webinar

---